D1761109

Richard Rorty

ACC. No: 02847759

For my beloved if . . .

Contents

So, when on one side you hoist in Locke's head, you go over that way; but now, on the other side, hoist in Kant's and you come back again; but in very poor plight. Thus, some minds for ever keep trimming boat. Oh, ye foolish! Throw all these thunder-heads overboard, and then you will float light and right.

Ishmael

Acknowledgements

Material from chapters 2, 3 and 6 has been presented at seminars at the Universities of Central Lancashire, Copenhagen, East Anglia, Granada, Keele, and Sussex, and I am grateful to those who took part for their comments. A draft of the first half of the book was written in 2005 while I was a visiting Senior Lecturer at the University of Auckland. I would like to thank John Bishop and Rosalind Hursthouse for hosting my visit; other members of the philosophy department for their kindness; and the students enrolled on my graduate class on Rorty for requiring me to give a clear shape to my thoughts. My visit would not have been possible without the support of colleagues at my former employer, Roehampton University, and in particular of the Dean of its School of Arts, Lyndie Brimstone.

I have learned a great deal about the subjects discussed in this book from conversations with friends and colleagues; pre-eminently, over the years, with Andrew Bowie and Tim Thornton. Others deserving of special mention are Rachel McEvilly, Julia Borossa, Richard Raatzsch, Jonathan Derbyshire, Jason Gaiger, and in particular Katerina Deligiorgi who gave me encouraging notes on an early draft. Comments from two anonymous readers at Polity also helped greatly in the production of this final version, as did those of my editor Emma Hutchinson. Needless to say, my greatest intellectual debt is to Rorty himself, who invited me out to the University of Virginia when I was a graduate student at Cambridge and showed me great kindness. I hope that in some small way this book will clarify the contribution he made to the subject to which he could never quite say 'farewell'.

Introduction: No Single Vision

1 Politics and the authority of philosophy

I am sometimes told, by critics from both ends of the political spectrum, that my views are so weird as to be merely frivolous. They suspect that I will say anything to get a gasp, that I am just amusing myself by contradicting everybody else. This hurts. So I have tried, in what follows, to say something about how I got into my present position – how I got into philosophy, and then found myself unable to use philosophy for the purpose I had originally in mind. Perhaps this bit of autobiography will make clear that, even if my views about the relation of philosophy and politics are odd, they were not adopted from frivolous reasons.

PSH: 5

This passage appears a little way into 'Trotsky and the Wild Orchids', an apologia for what many readers will regard as the hallmark of Richard Rorty's neo-pragmatism: the primacy of the political over the philosophical. The main theme of this book concerns how Rorty came to arrive at and defended such a view. Since this is not a biography, the theme will be elaborated in terms of changes that are internal to philosophical discourse. However, the fact that Rorty's attempt to exculpate himself of the charge of frivolity took the form of an *autobiographical*[1] reflection on how he came to view the political as pre-eminent is significant. After all, it is customarily taken to be part of the philosopher's remit that they strive to *transcend* the idiosyncratic and subjective in an attempt to arrive at objectively good reasons for the views they hold; reasons that, *as such*, can be used to convince others of the truth of their beliefs. The purpose of this introduction, then, is to explore both the content and use made of this stylistic device in order to present in outline the shape of Rorty's changing conception of philosophy's relation to political life; the detail will of course comprise the content of the subsequent chapters. Before turning to the autobiographical fragment, however, it will be helpful in situating it if we examine briefly what it is that for Rorty *unites* these otherwise antagonistic critics; namely, their conviction that philosophy retains a position of critical *authority* in relation to political discourse.

Rorty begins 'Trotsky . . .' by locating his political position:

> [the left] see [America] as what Foucault calls a 'disciplinary society', dominated by an odious ethos of 'liberal individualism', an ethos which produces racism, sexism, consumerism, and Republican presidents . . . I see America . . . as opening a prospect on illimitable democratic vistas. I think that our country . . . is a good example of the best kind of society so far invented. (p. 4)

While the right regard his pro-American stance as vitiated by the 'nihilism' of his 'relativistic, irrationalist, deconstructing, sneering' (ibid.), the left see it as little more than old-fashioned, cold war liberalism; the result of an invidious failure to follow through on the 'relativisitic' and 'deconstructive' critique of the philosophical tradition he purports to favour.[2] As Rorty observes, 'my philosophical views offend the right as much as my political preferences offend the left' (p. 5). The insinuation, then, is that the critical responses of leftist and rightist alike are shaped by a presupposition regarding the nature of the relationship between philosophy and politics. For rightist critics this is expressed in the belief that one's commitment to democracy and liberal values is genuine only if the latter are regarded as *objectively* good: expressive of a rational order that all right-thinking people will acknowledge once prejudice and parochialism are overcome. The American philosopher John Searle offers a pithy account of the central tenets of this traditional philosophical picture:

> Knowledge is typically of a mind-independent reality. It is expressed in a public language, it contains true propositions – these propositions are true because they *accurately represent that reality* – and *knowledge* is arrived at by applying, and is subject to, *constraints of rationality and logic*. (1992a: 69; emphases added)

As we'll come to see, one of Rorty's long-standing aims was to debunk this metaphysically realist or 'representationalist' view of the relationship between language (or mind) and the world. What Searle brings out nicely is the assumption that this philosophical thesis has a much wider import. Specifically, on this account of knowledge we have the idea of a 'mind-independent reality' being 'accurately represented' ('mirrored' as Rorty famously has it) by knowers *only* when subject to the 'constraints of rationality and logic'. Since these normative constraints are operative across *all* discourses, the clear implication is that philosophy, which takes them as its unique subject matter, has a natural *authority* over not just political discourse but all areas of action and inquiry.

It would appear, then, that the rightist's conviction that an authentically held liberalism requires a rigorous Realism about values presupposes this structure of authority. Turning once again to Searle, we find this conclusion given ingenuous expression:

> An immediate difficulty with denials of metaphysical realism is that they remove the rational constraints that are supposed to shape discourse, when that discourse aims at something beyond itself. To paraphrase Dostoevsky, without metaphysical realism, anything is permissible. (1992b: 112)[3]

At first blush it seems odd that a mere *denial* of a philosophical thesis could have so corrosive an effect on our norms. To adapt an example of Carnap's (1967), Idealist and Realist chess opponents have incompatible metaphysical beliefs, but they don't as a result disagree either on the norms (rules) of the game[4] or on its value. Since it seems improbable that even the majority of those who espouse liberal values would know what metaphysical realism *is*, Searle seems to be suggesting that they are either self-deceiving nihilists or unwitting Realists. Of course, we can reject this disjunction without denying that there are strong inferential connections in the minds of *some* between Realism and liberalism; even to the extent that they *appear* to them to be necessary. But this implies that what is being challenged when Realism is denied is not the validity of a *person's* beliefs or values but the *authority* of a certain discipline to identify the norms ('constraints of rationality and logic') that are 'supposed' to shape them: philosophy qua representational realism. Indeed, this helps explain why Searle's foreboding sounds so paradoxical. After all, if the contents of our beliefs are fixed by something as hard and

ultra-human as 'mind-independent reality', it's difficult to understand why the norms that constitute our methods of inquiry and
action should be so vulnerable. It's almost as if the greater the
degree of the world's mind-independence, the more fragile our
purchase on it and the more acutely felt the need for an authority to police our norms. This suspicion is reinforced when one
considers that amongst the consequences that Searle fears follow
from the 'rejection of the Western Rationalistic Tradition' and the
abandonment of the 'traditional standards of objectivity, truth
and rationality' is that it 'opens the way for an educational agenda
one of whose primary purposes is to achieve social and political
transformation' (1992a: 72). Once again, the implication is that
only a formal commitment to the central tenets of Realism will
sustain an otherwise fragile culture and keep the barbarians from
the door. The *authority* of philosophy is reinforced by the view
that it is only under its tutelage that the political values of liberalism are safe.

Turning now to those leftist critics, Searle's paraphrase of Dos-
toevsky reveals all they need to know about the quasi-religious
strivings and authoritarianism of Realism. But, although they mock
such pretensions, they believe that if you're serious about your rejection of the concepts of 'disinterested knowledge' and 'objective
truth' you must be willing to throw out the liberal baby with the
'Western Rationalist' bathwater. They see claims like those made by
Searle as the shadow-play of an overweening cultural arrogance, or
as expressions of the will to power; forces which, when unmasked
by theory, will expose 'liberal values' for what they really are and
bring about the 'social and political transformation' Searle fears.
Whereas for the right the sign of Rorty's 'frivolousness' is his disdain
for the rational foundations of the values he purports to cherish, for
the left it's his blatant disregard for the *political* implications of his
predilection for 'anti-Platonic, antiessentialist, historicizing, naturalizing writers' (*PSH*: 128).

From Rorty's perspective, then, critics from the left and right
share the same dogmatic belief that philosophy is privileged over
politics. For the rightist, philosophy is authorized to legitimate the
norms that shape political discourse; for the leftist, it is authorized
to unmask those selfsame norms. The task, then, is to decouple the
liberal values shared with Searle and others from the philosophical
views shared with those on the left by adumbrating an understanding of the source of the authority of norms that neither requires for

their legitimacy, nor is subject to the (ultimate) criticism of, a 'master' discourse like philosophy. This requires articulating or in some way defending the view that norms are embedded in contingent practices; though, crucially, not by conceiving of the standpoint from which that defence or articulation is made in the same way as those who aspire either to legitimate those norms or to subject them to a fundamental critique. With this in mind, let's look at how Rorty presents his own path to this insight, which constitutes both a defence against that 'hurtful' charge of 'frivolousness' and a continuation of the ongoing attempt to persuade his audience that they too could share it.

2   Actor and martyr

In the romantic fragment the then sixty-year-old narrator tells the story of how a 'clever, snotty, nerdy only child['s]' attempt to combine his adolescent passion for orchids with his inherited belief in social justice led to philosophy:

> I grew up knowing that all decent people were, if not Trotskyites, at least socialists . . . So, at 12, I knew that the point of being human was to spend one's life fighting social injustice.
>
> But I also had private, weird, incommunicable interests. In earlier years these had been in Tibet . . . A few years later . . . these switched to orchids . . . I was not quite sure why those orchids were so important, but I was convinced that they were . . . I was uneasily aware, however, that there was something a bit dubious about this esotericism – this interest in socially useless flowers . . . I was afraid that Trotsky . . . would not have approved of my interest in orchids.
>
> At 15 I escaped from the bullies who regularly beat me up . . . by going to the so-called Hutchens College of the University of Chicago . . . Insofar as I had any project in mind, it was to reconcile Trotsky and the orchids. I wanted to find some intellectual or aesthetic framework which would let me – in a thrilling phrase which I came across in Yeats – 'hold reality and justice in a single vision'. By *reality* I meant, more or less, the Wordsworthian moments in which, in the woods around Flatbookville . . . I had felt touched by something numinous, something of ineffable importance. By *justice* I meant what Norman Thomas and Trotsky both stood for, the liberation of the weak from the strong. I wanted a way to be both an intellectual and spiritual snob and a friend of humanity – a nerdy recluse and a fighter for justice. (*PSH*: 6–8).

In 1946 the University of Chicago was dominated by neo-Thomists, and refugees from Europe like Leo Strauss. They shared a disdain for the pragmatism of John Dewey, whose 'relativistic' rejection of absolute values and deflation of truth to what 'worked' seemed to leave no standpoint from which to justify one's moral rejection of the barbarism that had engulfed Europe. To his '15-year-old ears', the view that 'something deeper and weightier than Dewey' was needed to explain why 'it would be better to be dead than a Nazi' sounds 'pretty good' (*PSH:* 8). Talk of moral and philosophical absolutes recalls those orchidaceous *numina*; and since Dewey was a hero to his parents and their friends, scorning him is 'a convenient form of adolescent revolt' (p. 9). Lacking 'the humility which Christianity demanded', Platonism beckons as the most promising way in which to combine the contemplative life towards which the orchids gesture with the 'ability to convince bullies that they should not beat one up, the ability to convince rich capitalists that they must cede their power to a cooperative, egalitarian, commonwealth' (p. 10).

From age fifteen until twenty, then, the task is to elaborate on the Platonic-Socratic identification of virtue with knowledge. Unfortunately, the virtue-knowledge pairing proves inadequate to overcome the original dualism; for it can be constituted *either* by the public use of reason to convince others *or* by the private bliss one feels when one contemplates the eternal, but not both. At the same time, the journeyman philosopher finds himself confronting another, equally ancient, problem: it seems reasonable to ask of any two competing philosophical theories what justifies the choice of the fundamental principles of one over those of the other. Since they *are* fundamental, the question cannot be posed from a neutral (but inclusive) standpoint and so cannot be answered without begging the question in favour of one or the other (or a third, etc.). Of course, this sort of sceptical impasse is precisely the sort of thing liable to occur when one exercises one's public use of reason to convince others, and is thus apt to disturb one's pursuit of private, incommunicable and ultimately not terribly socially useful bliss.[5]

The failure to make good on the promise of Platonic realism constitutes an original disillusion with the discipline that accompanies him on to Yale, where he acquires his doctorate, and thence (after a spell teaching at Wellesley College) to Princeton.[6] The leitmotif of the ensuing forty years is a response to that original disenchantment: the search 'for a coherent and convincing way of formulating . . . worries about what, if anything, philosophy is good for' (p. 11). There is, however, a lesson learned from the earlier period; namely, that if the notion of philosophical *truth* can be given no purchase, the *activity* of philosophy can nevertheless be given some content as a power of *redescription*. Moreover, a discovered 'flair' for being able to respond to philosophical arguments by 'redescribing the nearby intellectual terrain in such a way that the terms used by one's opponent would seem irrelevant, or question-begging' (p. 10) takes on greater significance with the discovery of the *Phenomenology of Spirit*, and the first inkling of how one might construe a non-absolutist conception of philosophy. What Hegel offers does not rely on the Platonic promise of escaping appearances in order to get to the unchanging Reality held in abeyance. When the world is embraced in its finitude and contingency, the power of redescription – of *changing* concepts rather than merely aiming to *understand* them (cf. p. 25) – becomes a way of world-*making*: an opportunity to put philosophy in the service of freedom and justice (p. 11). 'About 20 years or so after I decided that the young Hegel's willingness to stop trying for eternity, and just be the child of his time, was the appropriate response to disillusionment with Plato, I found myself being led back to Dewey':

> Dewey now seemed to me a philosopher who had learned all that Hegel had to teach about how to eschew certainty and eternity, while immunizing himself against pantheism by taking Darwin seriously. This rediscovery of Dewey coincided with my first encounter with Derrida . . . Derrida led me back to Heidegger, and I was struck by the resemblances between Dewey's, Wittgenstein's and Heidegger's criticisms of Cartesianism. Suddenly things began to come together. I thought I saw a way to blend a criticism of the Cartesian tradition with the quasi-Hegelian historicism of Michel Foucault, Ian Hacking and Alasdair MacIntyre. I thought I could fit all these into a quasi-Heideggerian story about the tensions within Platonism. The result of this small epiphany was a book called *Philosophy and the Mirror of Nature*. (*PSH*: 11–12)

Despite its success 'among nonphilosophers', however, this comes to be regarded as something of a detour, for it does not address the very task that aroused his interest in philosophy. The apotheosis of the search for a 'single vision' comes with the realisation that 'the whole idea of holding reality and justice in a single vision had been a mistake – that the pursuit of such a vision had been precisely what led Plato astray' (p. 12); that the narrator's own 'hope of getting a single vision by becoming a philosopher had been a self-deceptive atheist's way out' (p. 13), a sort of sublimation of the religious desire for a 'surrogate parent who, unlike any real parent, embodied love, power and justice in equal measure' (p. 12).

The identification of philosophy's self-arrogated authority with that of a quasi-parental deity that transcends anything within the control of finite creatures like us – a trope ever present in Rorty's work from the late 1970s onwards – is a variant on a common theme;[7] as is the idea that metaphysical thinking is misleading or deceiving. If there is anything to Whitehead's apothegm that philosophy consist in 'a series of footnotes to Plato', then Plato's dream of a single vision is philosophy's defining goal, one that can only be pursued by a philosopher in the mode of self-deception. Of course, if a thinker wishes to expose that deception the temptation is to render it part of a grander narrative of how her *predecessors* were misled and how she liberated herself from it: a narrative exposing the sources of the deception within a *true* account of how things *really* stand philosophically, thus retaining for the discipline its traditional authority. One might of course simply turn one's back on philosophy; refuse to continue doing something that has betrayed one's intellectual ambitions. And perhaps there are those who have liberated themselves from the philosophical impulse and disdain the compulsion to communicate how they did it; or, rather, *feel* no such compulsion because that too is an expression *of* the philosophical urge. In this case one frees oneself from the authority philosophy had over one's own intellectual projects, but one does nothing to liberate others from it.

The narrator did not choose the latter path; perhaps because, although the tranquillity it would bring might recollect the orchidaceous, it would bring no peace to those feelings inspired by Norman Thomas, Carlo Tresca and his own parents: the unavailability of a 'single vision' does not dissipate its components. Of course, many people address these in their own lives without troubling themselves with philosophy. So evidently the narrator's conclusion that there is no single vision does not alone necessitate a wholly negative answer to the question 'is philosophy any good for anything?' It would seem that if he is to remain loyal to the animating desires of his youth he must free not only *himself* from the authority of metaphysics but also liberate others. Ultimately, then, what philosophy is good for is to help bring about its own demise in a way that frees others from the idea that there is an authority (philosophy, God) that transcends the merely human. The task is to unfetter the authority invested in something *other*, and make it available to renew the sense of our own control over our own (human) destiny; the sort of autonomy announced by Kant as the theme of Enlightenment thinking:

> Enlightenment is man's release from his self-incurred tutelage. Tutelage is man's inability to make use of his understanding without direction from another. Self-incurred is this tutelage when its cause lies not in lack of reason but in lack of resolution and courage to use it without direction from another. *Sapere aude!* (Dare to be wise) 'Have courage to use your own reason!' – that is the motto of enlightenment. (Kant 1784: 462)

It is in this sense that, as Habermas notes, Rorty 'attributes a culturally critical significance to his anti-Platonic turn, a significance that is supposed to extend far beyond his own person and his private switch of philosophical allegiance' (2000: 32). It is only on the assumption that Western culture is constrained by its 'self-incurred tutelage' in the form of an immature desire for a quasi-parental authority that Rorty's own rejection of such – in the form of Realism – could have greater significance. And it is only by simultaneously offering a diagnosis of that immaturity, and a vision of what human beings might be like without it, that the renewal of the Enlightenment's promise of freedom can be given shape as a task for us.

Rorty's account of his intellectual progress ends with the publication of *Contingency, Irony and Solidarity* in 1989. That work constitutes the most complete expression of how a dominant conception of philosophy's task is exhausted in and through the recognition that the Platonic desire for a single vision is deceptive, and aims to give intellectuals a narrative of self-understanding that is free of such deception. It is written from the perspective that the autobiographical fragment reveals as the one its author achieved at the point when the controlling deception was unmasked, which in turn allowed the 'narrative of maturation' (Habermas ibid.: 31) to be written. To share the viewpoint of the narrator is to see that in promoting philosophical *theory* over political *practice* both leftist and rightist critics are captivated still by the Siren-call of that 'single vision'; and that it is indeed possible both to reject it and, as 'a single person' (*CIS*: 198), combine *in one's life* the elements that comprise it.

3   Far, far away . . .

I have dwelt upon the link between Rorty's self-reported overcoming of his Platonic sickness and the diagnosis of philosophy's original sin in order to convey some sense of what he came to regard as his intellectual project and of the sort of considerations that attempts to overturn or 'overcome' philosophy's authority give rise to. This emphasis on Rorty's metaphilosophical concerns does no more than reflect his own preoccupations, however, and we will never be far from them in what follows. A further, related reason for having stressed this link appertains to how Rorty's work might usefully be approached. It is, for example, a familiar criticism that finding common ground upon which to engage critically with it is hard to find.[8] It is not difficult to sympathize with both sides here. The common ground for most intellectual disciplines at most periods is in part constituted by the existence of recognized problems with identifiable criteria for their resolution. This is not inconsistent with the thought that new theories, or new ways of looking at things, aim to determine the norms according to which they are evaluated; but such theories or world-views generally have sufficient overlap of substantive content or of human interest with their competitors to be regarded as (say) *physical* theories or *historiographical* approaches.

Like all putative 'revolutionaries', then, Rorty's aim in offering his revisionary alternative to the 'Platonic' view of human self-understanding is to set the standard by which it is to be judged. For many, however, the redescription he offers is not something recognizable from 'where we are'. Broadly sympathetic critics like Habermas, McDowell and Putnam share Rorty's disdain for the view that the world has an objective and unchanging, value-neutral structure which is accurately represented in the minds of the cognitively well-endowed. Nevertheless, although they regard *Philosophy and the Mirror of Nature* (1979) as a considerable achievement, even these are apt to regard the positions on truth and objectivity promulgated in *Contingency, Irony, and Solidarity* (1989) and related pieces as relativistic or idealist *inversions* of Realism, as constituting a view that could not even be construed as self-understanding.

Needless to say, most critics are not of the sympathetic variety. These are the 'fellow philosophy professors' who 'disliked' (*PSH:* 12) the earlier book's attempt to diagnose a restricted form of the Platonic 'self-deception' to which they had fallen prey, one which ramified to the analytic philosopher's pet inquiries into the nature of mind and meaning. Part of the reason for this antagonism brings us to an aspect of Rorty's story that he leaves out; namely, his 'successful career as a young analytic philosopher' (Habermas ibid.: 31) whom 'Carnap and others had persuaded . . . that philosophers should . . . try to become more "scientific" and "rigorous" ' (*PSH*: 177–8). He initially made his mark in the 1960s when he advanced a new materialist response to the traditional mind–body problem and edited an influential collection of papers under the title *The Linguistic Turn*. For the sympathetic critic, then, Rorty is a game-keeper turned poacher; for the non-sympathetic, an apostate whose abandonment of the Platonic project amounts to what Thomas Nagel calls 'a rebellion against the philosophical impulse itself,' part of 'a vain effort to grow up too early' (1986: 12).

With the foregoing in mind, the suggestion prompted by Rorty's autobiographical reflection is that a similar sort of narrative redescription might provide for his work a more critically amenable context. On behalf of the non-sympathetic critic, the aim is to show how a tension Rorty comes to diagnose in his early analytic work in the philosophy of mind leads to a 'turn' in his thinking and thence to the more flamboyantly 'postmodern' views with which he becomes associated latterly. This will in turn conduce to a better understanding of what is at stake in the conflict with the sympathetic critic, and of where to locate the burden of evidence in it.

To this end, chapters 2 and 3 focus on how Rorty's original contribution to the debate about the mind–body problem – his so-called *eliminative materialism* – is motivated by a metaphilosophical concern to understand the phenomenon of conceptual change. Of central importance here is the construal of normative authority in terms of a concept's *embeddedness* in a social practice, rather than through a purported ability to help 'represent' the world or because of its role in the 'logic' of ordinary language. The attack this implies on the authority of philosophy becomes increasingly radical, and in chapters 4 and 5 is expressed through the effort to articulate what a post-philosophical culture might be like. This involves a shift from the *eliminativism* of the early work to the more familiar account of concept change that constellates around metaphors of *redescription*. It culminates with the attempt made in *Contingency, Irony, and Solidarity* to redescribe the Enlightenment's promise of autonomy by proposing a new self-image for the liberal intellectual, one suited for a milieu in which the dream of a single vision is no longer the dream of reason.

What becomes apparent from chapter 3 onwards is the importance of Rorty's non-Realist conceptions of truth and objectivity. Chapter 6 examines the criticisms made of these on the part (largely) of sympathetic critics, while the conclusion evaluates their implications for the cogency of Rorty's neo-pragmatism. For the most part, chapter 1 fills in some of the philosophical background against which Rorty's eliminativist account of mental events appears and will be helpful for those unfamiliar with the work of the positivists, Ryle, Quine and Kuhn. However, it begins by attempting to alert the reader to what might be involved in eliminating concepts that play a central role in the way people make sense of their lives. To that end, it describes a place both far away and close to home . . .

1

Out of Mind

1 Our Rortian ancestors

Far, far away, lies an astronomical body much like our own precious Earth, populated by creatures much like us. On this planet – long ago named Rort by an amateur Terran astronomer who'd taken a few philosophy classes before becoming disillusioned – there are two distinct civilizations. The Nortians have a tribal society, with the title of chief passed along the male line and deriving its authority from the purported adventures of a distant ancestor Da-Ka, who had stopped to fish and pulled the world up on the end of his line. They have many strange beliefs, in turn peculiar and repulsive by our standards, amongst which their view of the aetiology of various maladies is noteworthy. For them, illness in general is caused by demons, with each distinct complaint caused by a specific fiend. The Nortian world-view is dominated by speculation about these demons, which were dragged up along with the world and whose fate is intimately linked with that of the chiefs and thus to the legitimacy of their rule. Interestingly, a certain priestly caste, after ritually consuming a particular kind of plant, purport to see the various demons that make people sick lingering by the bodies of the infirm. A bilious blue demon, for example, accompanies the epileptic, and a lewd fat red one pursues the asthmatic. These adepts have discovered a variety of naturally occurring substances, each of which drives a particular type of demon away when administered to the patient, thereby (indirectly) facilitating their recovery.

Turning to their neighbours, Sortians have evolved a liberal-democratic, welfarist, political system, based on principles of justice and the rule of law. Although technologically advanced and economically dynamic, there is little material inequality in Sortian society; but since most Sortians have rich intellectual and cultural lives, they express little concern with whether they have more or fewer material possessions than others. Sortian society is in many respects, then, much like our own ... There is, however, one big difference. A peculiarity of Sortian intellectual history is that it was the area of the brain sciences that emerged first and developed fastest. Neurological knowledge has been central to Sortian self-understanding for so long that it is not second- but first-nature for them to report on specific states of their brain and central nervous system. Young children are told that if they go too near to the fire their C-fibres will fire, and adults occasionally report that although neuronal bundle S-1101 is excited there is in fact no castle hovering in the air. Indeed, since their knowledge of physiology is such that any sentence in Sortian can be correlated with a specific neural state, it is rather a matter of personal style if a Sortian chooses to say 'I had X-10474 so I ducked my head' or 'I saw the ball come flying towards me so I ducked my head'.

Imagine now that an expedition from Earth finally arrives on Rort. What would they say about the Nortians, and in particular about the existence of demons? While the tender-minded anthropologists in the team might conclude that, since there is no *neutral* standpoint from which to evaluate a culture, from the only one that matters (the Nortian) demons clearly do exist, the tough-minded scientist would doubtless disdain such relativism. For these the operative contrast is not between competing world-views but between true and false beliefs; or, at the very least, between good theories and bad theories. With that contrast in mind it seems clear what to say to the Nortians: germs and bacteria cause sickness and disease, not demons. The so-called demon-perceptions of medical experts ('witch-doctors!') are hallucinations brought on by the ingestion of psychotropic chemicals found in the local flora, the manifest content of which is suggested by the culturally pervasive concern with demons and, in particular, its retrogressive relation to political authority.

Given the intimidating presence of Terran technology, demon-talk might be radically undermined by this confrontation with another race, and begin to loosen its hold on Nortian culture. But since no prediction that Nortian medical science makes is disconfirmed by Terran medicine it is entirely open to the sophisticated Nortian to reply that Terran science has shown merely that the presence of demons is constantly correlated with the microbiological entities of Terran medicine, and that eating certain plants can make some people see things that aren't there. It seems the only response available to the Terran is to emphasize the relative minimalism of his approach: eliminating demon-talk simplifies medical theory by reducing the number of entities it needs to pay heed to; especially those entities the existence of which suggests some rather perplexing questions. But now the complexity and embeddedness of demon-ontology in Nortian social and political life (in Nortian self-understanding) ensures that their medical practices are not as readily isolatable from such broader concerns as they are for the Terrans. The appeal of, and to, simplicity is not in itself neutral.

With that in mind, let's continue the expedition with a visit to the Sortians. While their culture will be of little interest to the anthropologists, their grasp of neurobiology will attract the delight rather than the disdain of the scientists. And yet despite this there seems to be something wrong here. One way of capturing this intuition is to remark that the Sortians *don't seem to know that they have minds*! Although they use intentional idioms to communicate, they do not think that this talk about beliefs, desires, feelings and so on refers to mental *as opposed to* physical states; rather, it refers to (in general) the same sorts of states as talk about 'sexual arousal' and 'standing up'. Now one can readily imagine a person not knowing that they are ill or in trouble, but not knowing that they have a mind seems altogether different. That difference seems to lie with the intuition that knowing that one has a mind is in some way *constitutive* of having a mind. This is why Terran thoughts about the mind are linked to the topic of consciousness: to have a mind is to have that special sort of awareness of, and unmediated access to, the 'inner space' that *is* the mind. If this is the case, then to be ignorant of the fact that one has a mind is not to lack some specific item of knowledge: it is to lack a mind, to lack consciousness. But without a mind how can one *know* anything at all, since knowledge is quite naturally thought of in terms of the mind's representation of the world 'outside' or 'beyond' it? And without a mind how *can* something be a moral agent, a person? An assemblage of brain-states following whatever neurological laws there are doesn't seem like the kind of thing that could be considered free, and therefore be judged in moral terms.

Such reflections lead to the conclusion that the Sortians don't have minds, are not persons, and don't know anything; they are just biological organisms interacting in complex ways, making meaningless noises that nevertheless have multifarious effects on other such organisms; like a colony of featherless bipedal ants. But how can this conclusion be squared with the active interest taken in these meaningless noises by the Terran scientists, economists and others who find the achievements of Sortian civilization fascinating? Pragmatically, at least, *they* are treating the Sortians as persons; so the question 'do the Sortians have minds or not?' is clearly neither one that interests them nor one they are qualified to answer. So who is so qualified, and how would they go about answering such a question? It seems natural to turn to philosophy for an answer, since philosophers have traditionally been concerned with identifying the nature or essences of things, and one clearly needs to know what the mind 'is' in order to determine whether an entity has one or not. But the very concepts the philosophers have at their disposal to describe what it is that they have and the Sortians lack are those for which the science of the latter can find no *use*. While tender-minded Sortian anthropologists might say that minds exist when one adopts a Terran world-view, the neurophysicists are likely to conclude that this is rather a matter of better and worse theories; that given the explanatory superiority of Sortian science over its Terran counterpart there is no compelling reason to believe that Terrans possess something the Sortians themselves either lack or are unaware of. Eliminate talk of minds, they tell the Terran philosophers, and not only will you be able to embrace fully the neurophysiology we can teach you, but you'll be spared all those tortuous philosophical problems that involve the relationship between the mind and the world, and be able to get on with the more productive business of improving the lives of less fortunate Terrans.

It is not clear how things will develop here; after all, the complexity and embeddedness of mind-ontology in Terran social and political life – and therefore in Terran self-understanding – ensures that brain sciences are not as readily isolatable from such broader concerns as they are for the Sortians. But at this point we might begin to feel a certain sense of resistance. The narrative tries to seduce us into seeing an analogy between the Nortians and the Sortians and make it seem that in respect of the concepts the Terrans use, those relating to the mental are no more determined by their essential nature or by the essential nature of the world or of language than the pre-scientific concept of a demon is. But, despite the distancing device of the thought-experiment, are we not Terrans? Is the concept of mind not of a wholly different order? Our intuition is not just that it would be *difficult* to abandon it – that it is central to how we *see* ourselves – but that it is essential to what we *are*. Allied to this is the suspicion that the insistence that scientific practices establish the appropriate linguistic norms is far more tendentious than the view that it's rather how things *feel* to us minded creatures. In this regard it seems that the unquestioned phenomenology of conscious experience is on the side of philosophy against science.

The case of what I have called the Nortians is freely adapted from an analogy offered in one of Rorty's earliest contributions to the debate about the nature of the mental;[1] the (similarly modified) example of the Sortians is the central thought-experiment in chapter II of *Philosophy and the Mirror of Nature (PMN)*.[2] Both texts focus on demonstrating the in-principle eliminability of the concept of mind, and tracing how Rorty's approach to this task develops in the intervening period will highlight its significance for our understanding of conceptual change, and of the relationship between language and the mind. More importantly, since the possession of a mind is connected to the capacity for rational reflection, and the latter naturally thought of as, in its highest form, constitutive of philosophical inquiry, Rorty's attempt to undermine the idea that having a mind is an intrinsic feature of creatures like us has obvious implications for one's understanding of the status and limits of such inquiry, in relation both to the natural sciences and to culture conceived of in the broadest sense.

Although this will be detailed in chapters 2 and 3, it can be related to the foregoing by reflecting briefly on the relevance of thought-experiments to philosophical inquiry. In general such imagined forms of life help us to see ourselves from a perspective other than the one we normally occupy. By allowing certain features of the world or of ourselves to vary, we hope to loosen the grip of customary thinking and investigate just how different things might (be thought to) be while remaining in some crucial sense possible. Another way of describing this process is that it allows us to explore the geography of our concepts, with regard both to their plasticity and their potential eliminability. This is pursued customarily as an armchair exercise, but such reflections are not immune to empirical change. Certain things that *we* can imagine as possible – indeed, many beliefs we hold true – could not only not have not been conceived as *possibilities* in the past; they could not have been *thought* at all. Likewise, it would be hubristic not to imagine that as yet unthinkable thoughts will be thought in the future, or are perhaps being thought right now on some distant planet.

For present purposes, then, thought-experiments can be regarded as heuristic devices that help us explore the possibilities of concept change in general; but there is a temptation in philosophy to think that, robustly analysed, they can help identity concepts that are *ineliminable*: irreducible features of our, or perhaps of any, conceptual terrain. This is one way in which philosophy aims to mark itself out as a distinct activity with a specific subject matter: one dealing with pure meanings or the logic or our language; standing icily aloof from the pressures of empirical change and whose cognitive authority requires that some sense can be made of such detachment. It is one of Rorty's principal claims in *PMN* that philosophy cannot arrogate to itself legitimately any such authority (p. 3 ff.) because such a disengaged standpoint cannot be rendered fully intelligible; which is to say it is of ill-defined *use*.

In the Anglo-American tradition, the attack on the authority of philosophy that Rorty develops – and in particular the authority philosophy claims as an enterprise wholly distinct from the empirical sciences, the former searching for conceptual truths, and the latter for mere empirical generalizations – emerged as part of an immanent critique within the philosophy of science, and is associated above all with Quine and Kuhn. In section 3 we'll look briefly at an account of the contribution these made to the naturalistic, historicist, anti-authoritarian turn in the philosophy of science, which will provide a basis from which to appreciate the broader significance of Rorty's neo-pragmatism. As we've already observed, however, this originally manifested itself as an intervention in the (then) ongoing debate about the mind–body problem. In order to better appreciate Rorty's contribution to that debate, it will be useful to have some account of what had occurred prior to the arrival of the 'Nortians' on the philosophical scene.

2 Materialism and the mind–body problem

The Kantian shift of religious concerns into the realm of faith helped consolidate the Enlightenment's project to undermine the intellectual appeal of theology, and in particular its claim to any cognitive authority over the fast-developing natural sciences. An increasingly secular culture emerged in the West in the nineteenth century, with discoveries such as Lyell's in geology, and this was given a huge boost with the publication of Darwin's *Origin of the Species* in 1859. The advances in physics associated with Bohr, Heisenberg and Einstein tempt us to think of the twentieth century as exemplifying an increasing confidence in the ability of the natural sciences to explain phenomena that had hitherto eluded the nomological net. Notwithstanding the enormous cultural shift expressed in this more naturalistic conception of the world, one area in particular seems recalcitrant to such a view, and that the most fundamental to our self-understanding: the mind. Attempts to view the mind or the mental as on a par ontologically with the material world go back in the modern tradition at least as far as Hobbes, but successive versions of 'materialism' have failed to unsettle the intuition that even if the mind doesn't comprise some non-material 'stuff', as Descartes supposed, mental states nevertheless have properties like intentionality and phenomenal ('raw') feel that resist reduction to the properties of any physical or material entities or processes. In addition, there is the familiar conviction that the possession of a mind is linked to the capacity to recognize the norms of rationality and through that to the capacities for cognition and agency. This leaves us with something of a split conception of ourselves and of the world: we look to science to explain the latter, and regard ourselves as but one more set of objects in that world subject to the same fundamental laws. And yet, as possessors or instantiations of minds (and thus as *knowers*), we seem not only set apart from the world, but *necessarily* so in order *that* the world becomes an object of such scientific knowledge in the first place. But how can we finite creatures of blood and bone, having evolved on this planet as a result of innumerable contingencies, not *be* a part of that knowable world? One name for this paradox – of how to find a place for the mind or the mental in nature and thus achieve a unified conception of ourselves – is the mind–body problem.

In the first half of the twentieth century it had come to seem obvious that, if the mind–body problem did not merely evoke the Cartesian distinction between *res cogitans* and *res extensa*, then it must take its form from a distinction found within language. That is to say, the mind–body distinction came to be regarded in terms of the contrast between sentences that deploy mentalistic or psychological terms (M-sentences) and those that do not. This is one expression of what was, according to Bergmann's immortalizing phrase, philosophy's 'linguistic turn' away from a speculative concern with the constitution of what there *is*, for which no clear criteria of success had been forthcoming, and towards how we *mean*, how we come to speak with objective purport. Accordingly, semantic analysis can provide the necessary criteria of success; and, since our prima facie evidence for the presence of a mind is the behaviour of the organism in question, one suggestion was that M-sentences could be analysed into sentences that contain only terms that refer to the behaviour of bodies and to their dispositions to behave (and not to mental entities). This led European philosophy in two, oftentimes antagonistic, directions depending on how this linguistic-behaviourist intuition was interpreted. According to the tradition deriving from the Vienna School, which was later to flourish in the United States, the analysis is in terms of an *ideal* language, which derives its semantic authority from its conditions of empirical verification. The competing tradition took its naturalistic inspiration not from the natural sciences but from language as purportedly used in the *ordinary* contexts of everyday life. We'll take Hempel's as an example of the ideal-language attempt to eliminate the referring use of mental terms, and Ryle's as an example of the ordinary-language attempt to do likewise.

'Analytic' or 'logical behaviourism' is associated with the work of Carnap and Hempel in the 1930s and 1940s. In 'The Logical Analysis of Psychology' Hempel opens with a question that will recur in later chapters: 'Is psychology a natural science [*Naturwissenschaften*], or is it one of the sciences of the mind and culture [*Geisteswissenschaften*]?' (1935: 373). Hempel acknowledges that the concepts (mass, field, intensity, etc.) and methods (causal explanation) of physics[3] appear remote from those of psychology, which 'has for its subject-matter notions which are, in a broad sense, mental' (p. 374). He identifies this with 'the fact that the objects investigated by psychology – in contradistinction to physics – possess an intrinsic meaningfulness' (ibid.) and consequently require not explanation, but understanding.[4] The following dramatizes the image of an unbridgeable divide:

> Take . . . the case of a man who speaks. Within the framework of physics, this process is considered to be completely explained once one has traced the movements which make up the utterance to their causes, that is to say, to certain physiological processes in the organism, and, in particular, to the central nervous system. But, it is said,

this does not even broach the psychological problem. The latter begins with an understanding of what was said, and proceeds to integrate it into a wider context of meaning. (1935: 374–5)

For Hempel, what motivates the linguistic reconstruction of the mind–body problem is the threat of a fundamental metaphysical cleavage that places human beings astride an ontological and epistemological gap between the objects referred to in one discourse and those referred to in another. As such, it is a standing challenge to the unity both of human understanding – of 'science' broadly construed – and of the creatures so understood.

In response Hempel remarks that, although Watson's attempt to restrict psychology to talk of 'bodily behaviour' is on the right track, it is nevertheless not within the gift of psychology to announce itself a science.[5] That is to say, Hempel assumes that only philosophy, through the epistemological insights of the Vienna School, can legislate with respect to the cognitive status of a putative scientific discipline. At this point, he offers a quick summary of the most important of those insights; namely, that we know the 'content' or the meaning of a proposition 'when, and only when, we know under what conditions we would characterise it as true, and under what conditions we would characterise it as false' (p. 376). Consider the following:

Today at time t in place x the temperature was 31°C

What it is to *know what this sentence means* is to know that it is true when at the time and in the place specified, the upper extent of a line of mercury, inside a tube of a certain kind, coincides with a mark on a scale numbered '31'.[6] The important points are:

1 A target sentence can be *translated*, 'without change of meaning' (p. 376), into a (longer) sentence that makes no use of a term, the *referring* use of which might be thought to imply the existence of some problematic entity.
2 'That *the meaning of a proposition is established by the conditions of its verification*' and thus two propositions have the same meaning or content 'when, and only when, they are both true or are both false in the same conditions' (p. 377).
3 A proposition that has no verification conditions has no content or meaning: it is 'a sequence of words correctly constructed from the point of view of grammar' but not a real proposition.

In (2) and (3) attention is drawn to how the verificationist criterion of meaning allows the logical positivists to give a semantic (neo-Kantian) twist to the legacy of Locke et al. Rather than complex ideas being relations of simple ideas, whose aetiology is to be traced back to the simple impressions that cause (*and justify*) them, the positivist argues that talk about a particular object X is meaningful only if it is possible to analyse (reduce) it into reports by a cognizing subject of what is 'given' to her in elementary experiences. This in turn offers an apparent solution to the standing problem of the status of necessary, analytic, a priori truths. When we undertake the semantic analysis of certain claims, their truth turns out to rest entirely with the meanings of the concepts used. The truth of 'a dolphin is a mammal,' for example, follows from the meaning of 'dolphin': if you know what a dolphin is (that is to say, the conditions under which it is correct to use the term), you know that a dolphin is a mammal. So it turns out that all truths are either verifiable or satisfy the principle of contradiction (are so-called 'conceptual truths': true in virtue of the meanings of the words used, rather than because of the way the world is). The relationship between the analytic–synthetic distinction and the translation thesis of (1) is important, but for the time being let's return to Hempel.

At this juncture the line Hempel takes should be clear. Recall that unless we are willing to dismiss an overwhelming number of utterances as meaningless, thereby depriving psychology of any subject matter, we must acknowledge that they have truth-values; and, indeed, that many if not most are true. But the meaningfulness of a sentence seems to commit us to the existence of the entity to which it refers. Russell had shown that grammatical form could mislead us with respect to what entities must or must not exist if a sentence is to be meaningful. For example, the sentence 'I met nobody today' seems to function in the same way as 'I met Tim today'. Since the latter can only have a truth-value if Tim exists, one might be led to suppose that 'nobody' names an entity. Of course, we know that the sentence 'I met nobody today' should be *translated* into something like 'It's not the case that I met any people today', which does not include the term with the problematic referring use. Given the analysis of the theoretic term 'temperature' and the desire for the unification of science, Hempel's view is that sentences with mentalist/psychological terms are to be treated likewise: translated into physical test sentences that specify – or, rather, constitute – their meaning or content through the use of 'only the concepts of physics' (p. 378). So in the sentence:

The Terran is in pain,

the translation will eliminate the referring use of 'pain' in the way the referring use of 'temperature' was eliminated, thus allowing that such statements have truth-values while retaining ontological parsimony.

Hempel recognizes, in one form, an objection that will take on many others: that 'physical test sentences . . . are absolutely incapable of formulating the *intrinsic nature* of a mental process' (p. 379; emphasis added). For the verificationist this is only so much hand-waving, of course. No one can ascribe a mental state to another without *some* behavioural clues, which are describable using sentences that make no use of mentalist terms. But those clues aren't just the physical evidence for the mental state, they are *what it means* to ascribe the state, just as the height of the mercury column lining up with the number 31 isn't a tip-off to the temperature, but *constitutes* what it means to be 31°C. If 'intrinsic nature' is meant to indicate the possession of a property that cannot in principle be expressed using a 'concept of physics', then any sentence deploying it is devoid of content. It follows swiftly from this that since there are no contentful sentences deploying mental terms that cannot be translated without loss into the physical test sentences that constitute their meaning, there is no standpoint from which one could even *state* the mind–body problem: it is a pseudo-problem (p. 380). More importantly, since all meaningful sentences are so by virtue of their conditions of verification, there is no body of sentences – those pertaining to the *Geisteswissenschaften* – that require their own method of scientific investigation. In Hempel's view, *'all the branches of science are in principle of one and the same nature; they are branches of the unitary science, physics'* (p. 382).

Hempel's piece has the virtue of presenting a vision of epistemology as philosophy of science when it was at its most confident, and the latter half of the twentieth century saw that confidence fade as the image fragmented. For present purposes it's worth noting the core problems confronting Hempel's view. Firstly, regarding the specific problem of translating psychological talk, note that the only way to verify a sentence like 'Tim believes that drinking is bad for his health' is through observation of his behaviour. But it is not obvious what the link is between the confirming behaviour that one might look for in Tim, and the requirement that this involve 'only the concepts of physics'. The way in which ordinary folk verify what they take to be Tim's belief (or what Tim himself says) seems to

require employment of the very psychological concepts that are to
be avoided. Following Carnap, Hempel offers a sort-of intermediate
vocabulary for verifying such sentences; namely, in terms of 'the
states, processes and behaviour of groups of individuals . . . and
their responses to one another and to their environment' (quoted
p. 382). But although the 'states and processes' may be amenable to
translation, they are unlikely to be seen as verifying Tim's behaviour; for that is customarily specified in terms of the *intentional
actions of agents*, and therefore to presuppose the very vocabulary
the analysis is intended to eliminate. That is to say, if 'verification'
has any meaning in this context, it is to be understood in a much
looser, more holistic way.[7]

The notion that verification is holistic is a theme we will encounter in Rorty's work. A preliminary hint in that direction is suggested
by the most telling rebuttal of the project of Hempel et al., which
relates to the principle of verifiability itself. Not only was no one
able to formulate a criterion that even vaguely corresponded to our
intuitive classification of real sentences (including the theoretical
sentences of science that were intended as a paradigm), but the
principle is of course in stark violation of its own criterion: the
vague statement 'the meaning of a proposition is established by
the conditions of its verification' is neither analytic nor can it be
associated with any such conditions. And yet it is this legislative
semantic principle that does all the work. Without it there is no
reason to suppose that the price of semantic respectability for mentalistic talk is its in-principle translation into sentences of physics,
and no consequent motivation to reject the mind–body problem as
unreal. The subject matter of the *Geisteswissenschaften* does not
appear reducible to that of the natural sciences.

Despite these (and other) shortcomings, it's important to remember that the logical empiricist project was resolutely metaphilosophical. Its aim was to rid us of the sense that there are any real
metaphysical problems. Moreover, the key to this project of *elimination* was the contention that philosophical problems are in essence
problems of language. As that most exuberant of positivists Moritz
Schlick wrote, since all 'real problems are scientific questions', all
(so-called) philosophical problems will either be 'shown to be mistakes and misunderstandings of our language' or 'found to be ordinary scientific questions in disguise' (1932: 51).[8] For Schlick and his
confrères, the 'troublesome problems ar[i]se only from an inadequate
description of the world by means of a faulty language' (1936: 170),
and are to be remedied by invoking an 'ideal' language, which

carries the imprimatur of the verification principle. As we'll see in chapter 4, the sense that can be given to this 'ideal language' and the 'adequacy of description' once one has rejected the verification principle will be important for understanding Rorty's developing metaphilosophy. But as noted above, one's naturalistic urges can be satisfied equally by appealing to ordinary language, and not to a promissory note issued in the name of some future physics. This is the sort of approach associated with Wittgenstein, but his contemporary Ryle is easier to summarize.

In *The Concept of Mind*, Ryle sets himself the task of 'rectify[ing] the logical geography of the knowledge [about minds] that we already possess' (1966: 10). His method is to 'reveal the logic of the propositions in which . . . concepts of mental powers and operations . . . are wielded, that is to say, to show with what other propositions they are consistent and inconsistent, what propositions follow from them and from what propositions they follow' (ibid.). According to this approach, philosophical confusion arises because concepts apt for deployment in one logical space (appropriate to their 'logical type' or 'category') are mistakenly employed in another. To take a famous example,

> A foreigner visiting Oxford or Cambridge for the first time is shown a number of colleges, libraries, playing fields, museums . . . [&c.] He then asks 'But where is the University?' . . . He was mistakenly allocating the University to the same category as that to which the other institutions belong. (1966: 17–18)

The visitor does 'not know how to wield the concept *University*' (p. 19): he is ignorant of (at least some of) the ways in which 'it is logically legitimate to operate with it' (p. 10). Likewise, Ryle approaches the mind–body problem by observing that, since mind-talk and body-talk operate in distinct logical spaces, the very idea of confronting one with the other in order to generate a problem is a ('category') mistake. Just as no one could reasonably be asked to respond to the questions, 'just how heavy *is* the colour brown?' or 'exactly which building *is* the University?' there is no common logical space in (no standpoint from) which such a confrontation might be staged.

Unlike with Hempel, then, there is no Rylean *translation* of mental-into (ideal) physical-talk. Indeed, the notion violates the account of what constitutes the understanding of the relevant concepts; namely, knowing what inferences are and are not permissible. But note that

for Hempel it is the standing *possibility* of such a translation – analysing away the referring use of mental terms and sanctioned by
the verification principle – that redeems psychology qua mental-
talk for (unified) scientific inquiry. For Ryle, however, there is no
such threat to the existence of the mental once it is recognized that
' "existence" is not a generic word' (1966: 24) but one whose sense
is tied to the logical space in question.[9]

We have a clear idea of what characterizes existence claims in the
logical space of physical-object talk. If I insist I can see an object
that no one else can (in principle) see and which I claim occupies
no specific spatio-temporal location, then I violate the norms of the
relevant logical space and am not entitled to have my claim taken
seriously. Likewise, we've noted that for Ryle the logical space of
physical-object talk is categorically distinct from that constituted by
mental-concept talk. Since logical spaces are *normative* spaces –
spaces of *meaning* – this raises the question of what gives mental
talk its specific norms, including when existence claims are true and
false. This is in turn one aspect of a more general question; to wit,
how should differences in logical spaces be conceived? If it is maintained that the logic of our concepts rules in certain discursive
moves ('brown is dark') and rules out others ('brown is heavy'), it
seems natural to ask whether or not this logic is fixed in all cases?
If it is, then what is it that determines the norms of meaning in such
a way? If it isn't, the implication is that all barriers between such
'logical spaces' are permeable and that no proposition is such that
it might not come to be (held) true. One might then ask what forces
shape our linguistic practices and give rise to changes in our norms
of meaning? As we'll come to see, these sorts of general considerations are at the heart of Rorty's metaphilosophy, and derive directly
from his response to the specific question; namely, what is distinctive about the normative space of mental discourse? What is the
criterion or hallmark of the mental? For the time being it will be
helpful to keep the question in focus and follow Ryle's response
to it.

At this point it would be tempting to classify Ryle as a behaviourist. But Ryle does not think one can analyse psychological talk
in reductively behaviourist terms.[10] Indeed, when he offers an
analysis of:

A.   He boasted from vanity,

it is of the form

B. He boasted on meeting the stranger and his doing so satisfies the law-like proposition that whenever he finds a chance of securing the admiration and envy of others, he does whatever he thinks will produce this admiration and envy (1966: 87),

an analysans that veritably *revels* in mentalist terms. Likewise, unlike Hempel, Ryle is alert to the danger of metaphysical inflation deriving from the temptation to contrast the 'physical world' with something else – such an epithet is, he says, 'philosophically pointless'. He remarks that to 'talk of a person's mind . . . is to talk of the person's abilities, liabilities and inclinations to do and undergo certain sorts of things, and of the doing and undergoing of these things in the ordinary world' (1966: 190); but despite the 'is', this observation takes its meaning in the main from a critique of what it would be to think *otherwise*: to think, for example, as Hempel does.

As (B) suggests, however, there is an important continuity with the positivist tradition. To see this, note that the analysis of (A) Ryle favours (B) over is:

C. 'He boasted and the cause of his boasting was the occurrence in him of a particular feeling or impulse of vanity' (1966: 87).

Like Hempel, then, Ryle is primarily motivated by the desire to demonstrate that terms like 'vanity' have no referring use. Exhibiting the logical geography of our mental-talk is intended to demonstrate that it gives rise to philosophical perplexity only when the 'sense' of the existence of intentional items – their mode of being – is illegitimately assimilated to that of physical objects. What (B) offers is an example of how a term that appears to suggest the existence of a pseudo-object – a *feeling* – can be treated as signifying an ontically neutral disposition. Likewise, talk involving terms like '"know", "believe", "aspire", "clever" and "humorous" . . . signify abilities, tendencies or pronenesses to do' things, but it is a mistake to think that 'there must be corresponding acts of knowing or apprehending and states of believing' (p. 114). These dispositions are no more occult powers lurking in agents than the solubility of sugar haunts the products of Tate and Lyle.

So whence derives their normativity? Imagine that it is discovered that a particular bacterium causes a specific illness, and we formulate a law accordingly. We do not think that the 'causal connection' we have discovered is a new entity: a supernatural umbilicus linking cause to effect (though a Nortian witch-doctor might disagree). Rather, the formulation of the law provides us with an 'inference-ticket' (p. 119) that, amongst other things, licenses us to infer from disease to bacterium. Likewise, the normativity of disposition-talk derives from the fact that when we use such terms we suppose the existence of law-like propositions, such as the one mentioned in (B), that warrant those who know them to make certain moves in the logical space of mental-talk. Just as knowledge of the rules of chess authorizes participation in the game and licenses players to offer explanations of the moves they make, these 'inference-tickets' permit us to draw certain conclusions from given facts and to offer particular explanations of those facts. And, just as there is no entity named by the 'causal connection' between bacterium and illness, there is no entity named by a disposition term.

This brief account can hardly do justice to Ryle's text, and in particular to its influential critique of the view that sees us divided up between a publicly accessible 'external' physical world, and a private, 'internal' mental world to which each individual has privileged access. Indeed, his irreferentialism about the mental seems at its most compelling when the states ascribed to agents are complex beliefs, desires, intentions, moods and so on. Here it does seem that mentalist ascriptions are most productively viewed as Rorty also sees them: 'merely ways of talking about organisms, their parts, and the actual and possible movements of their parts' (*PMN*: 18). This might be because the more complex the mental state the less inclined we are to judge that the putative 'owner' of that state can claim the privileges accruing to privacy. If, despite all the behavioural evidence to the contrary, Tracy denies that (she *believes* that) her boss is out to get her (or asserts that she doesn't *feel* depressed), one would not be violating those privileges if, with one's 'inference-tickets' in hand, one concluded that the converse is true.

There is, however, a problem here, which takes us back to Ryle's insistence that the relevant areas of discourse are *logically* distinct, and illustrates how intimately this issue relates to the problem of avoiding the referring use of mental terms. Consider, then, not Tracy's denial that she is depressed but her avowal that she is in pain. The 'simpler' the state, the less disposition-like a mental term appears and the less likely we are to question the privilege – and therefore the *authority* – of first-person reports. And the more we attribute authority to the subject of the mental state in question, the more we are inclined towards the view that the explanation for that authority is that the meaning of mental terms – whence they get their normativity, their 'inference-tickets', the criterion that distinguishes them from physical terms – derives from the special, 'private' mode of access each subject has to the mental states, processes, or objects to which the terms refer, and not from the law-like propositions they exemplify. The demons return!

It is for such reasons that, post-Ryle, attention turned away increasingly from complex mental features, which are susceptible to treatment as dispositions *as long as this is not undertaken reductively* (as an attempt to reduce dispositions to non-dispositions), to the investigation of short-term mental states, and in particular to sensations. These came to be seen as the greatest impediment to irreferentialist approaches and the key to identifying the criterion of the mental. As Cornman notes:

> whatever optimism about the future unification of sciences is justified, there are now, as there have been for centuries, difficult problems confronting the materialist. Perhaps the crucial problem concerns the status of sensations, a problem clearly evident as far back as Hobbes. (1971: 1)

The reason sensations are regarded as 'the most difficult to handle' is because they 'seem to have directly presented phenomenal properties, properties we seem to experience clearly and indubitably' (ibid.: 2). What could more clearly constitute what it is to 'possess' a stream of consciousness – to have a mind – than to undergo unmediated experiences like that associated with the *raw feel* of pain? How can *that* – the painfulness of pain – be likened to the solubility of sugar?(!) Questions like these arise from a host of mutually supporting intuitions, the most evident of which link the form of a subject's experience (clear, indubitable, private) of a certain sort of property (painfulness) to the existence of a state that has that property (being in pain). It is this experience, and its link to the existence of a state, that motivates realism about these particular mental items, with the idea that (unlike demons) they exist. This gives us a taxonomy like the one shown in table 1.1.

As hinted above, there are other reasons for thinking that irreferentialism about mental states is not satisfactory, especially in relation to occurrent thoughts and sensations. Unlike the 'causal connections' Ryle disparages, these latter states have a role to play

Table 1.1   All in the mind

Mental tokens with phenomenal properties (items directly before the mind)	Mental tokens without phenomenal properties (items that are not directly before the mind)
'Mental events . . . paradigm cases of the nonphysical' (Rorty 1970a, 420): Occurent thoughts, mental images, raw feels (sensations) – resistant to Rylean analysis	'Mental features' (Rorty 1970a): Beliefs, moods, desires, and intentions – susceptible in principle to Rylean analysis

in the explanation of action. We ascribe states like 'the pain in Jones's left leg' and are sufficiently realist about them to allow not only that they help us to explain what people do, but also that it is part of such explanations that people are able to report authoritatively on them. Relatedly, it seems not accidental that to have a mind one must have a functioning brain and central nervous system (in humans at least), and thus that physical states play some role in the explanation of behaviour. In the late 1950s and early 1960s this led a number of philosophers to a bold conclusion: mental terms *do* refer to actual states, those states *do* play a role in the explanation of behaviour, and they *are* states that people can make reports on. But these states aren't mysterious because the mind *is* the brain; mental states *are* physical states. Here's a classic statement of what is known as the Identity Thesis:[11]

> in so far as 'after-image' or 'ache' is a report of a process, it is a report of a process that *happens to be* a brain process. It follows that the thesis does not claim that sensation statements can be *translated* into statements about brain processes. Nor does it claim that the logic of a sensation statement is the same as that of a brain-process statement. All it claims is that in so far as a sensation is a report of something, that something is in fact a brain process. Sensations are nothing over and above brain processes. (Smart 1962: 56)

Smart's emphases announce that although the identity of a sensation with a brain-process is 'strict' (ibid.: 57) it is nevertheless contingent. One can no more analyse the *meaning* of 'sensation of pain' in order to arrive at 'C-fibres firing' than one can analyse the meaning of 'lightning' or 'water' in order to arrive at the 'happens to be' identities 'lightning is an electrical discharge' and 'water is H_2O'. In all these cases we have the empirical discovery that terms that *mean* different things nevertheless *refer* to the same thing, as when you discover that the person who satisfies the description 'The bloke who always beats me at squash' is none other than the legendary cousin who ran away to sea at the age of fifteen. The virtues of this account are worthy of enumeration:

1   In line with our linguistic intuitions, both other-ascriptions and a subject's reports are referring expressions: mental states exist.
2   There is no mystery about how mental states can figure in explanations of action because, qua states of the brain, they give rise to other brain-processes, bodily movements and so on.
3   The privileged status of a subject's reports is to be expected since it is, after all, a state of the subject's brain that is being reported on.

There is, of course, a problem. Recall that the identity of mental state and brain-process is 'strict'; that is to say, it conforms to Leibniz's principle, according to which if two objects are identical then any property possessed by one is possessed by the other. That is to say:

$$(x)(y)[(x = y) \supset (F)(Fx \equiv Fy)]^{12}$$

In order to discover the strict (but contingent) identity at least two conditions must be satisfied:

a.   There have to be discrete (non-synonymous) ways of picking out the (common) reference.
b.   Any and all properties ascribed to the object under one description must be ascribable to it under the other description.

Consider the example above:

A(i)   The chap who always beats Neil at squash.
A(ii)   Neil's cousin who ran away to sea at the age of fifteen.

One side of the identity is pinned down through (let's call him) John's property of being unbeatable at squash; the other side through his property of being a seafaring relative. No philosophical confusion is sown when John is identified as the common subject of these properties because running off to sea and being good at racket-games are not properties we ascribe to radically different sorts of objects. Now consider:

B(i)   Sensation of pain.
B(ii)   C-fibres firing.

We identify B(i) through a first-person, non-inferential *report*[13] on the presence of the property of being painful, and B(ii) through a third-person (inferential) *explanation* in terms of neuronal properties. That is to say, to pin down the mental side of the identity requires the existence of an individuating mental property, without which we would not be able to give content to the assertion that we are identifying a *mental* state with a physical state; and recall that it is regarded as a virtue of this approach that mental states are not 'translated away'. But now we seem to have shifted the original translation problem up a notch: we have properties that cannot be accounted for by the materialist because they are not material properties. But if we *can* translate this mental-property talk into physical-property talk then it seems that there are no distinctively *mental* properties and so no way of picking out mental (as opposed to just more physical) states.

When we try to make sense of condition (a), then, we generate something of a paradox; namely, that some kind of mental feature is needed if one is to individuate mental events and yet these features are not physical. So a condition of possibility of the identity theory appears to be the existence of properties that make it unintelligible! This is reinforced when we consider (b), because the form of the identity statement requires not only 'that mental events have physical properties . . . it also seems to imply that some physical events have nonphysical features' (Feyerabend 1963: 172):

> if the Identity Theory is correct, it seems that we should sometimes be able to say truthfully that physical processes such as brain processes are dim or fading or nagging or false, and that mental phenomena such as after-images are publicly observable or physical or spatially located or swift . . . we can say that [these] expressions are meaningless in the [Rylean] sense that they commit a category mistake; i.e., in forming them we have predicated predicates, appropriate to one logical category, of expressions that belong to a different logical category. This is surely a conceptual mistake. (Cornman 1962: 77)

The identity theorist cannot duck this problem by denying the existence of first-person reports, which would suggest a lapse into behaviourism. Smart's preferred solution is to suggest a way in which the mental side of the identity could be pinned down in a self-report without reliance on an irreducible mental property, and therefore without making conceptual mistakes. Taking an 'after-image' as a paradigmatic occurrent mental state, then:

> When a person says, 'I see a yellowish-orange after-image,' he is saying something like this: '*There is something going on which is like what is going on when* . . . I really see an orange'. (Smart 1962: 61)

This makes no reference to any particular sort of property since it merely refers to a 'going on' that is like another 'going on' in some unspecified way: it is 'topic-neutral'. The thought is that the 'goings on' *will* be empirically discovered to be certain brain-processes – and the hitherto unspecified properties physical properties – and that that is what someone has been reporting on all along. Unfortunately, this says too much and too little. On the one hand, what we seem to have are definitions of occurrent mental states as associations or products of certain stimulus conditions, or as reports that bring such conditions to mind; and this comes close to inviting the problems the behaviourist confronted. On the other hand, the topic-neutral descriptions do not seem to be plausible translations of mentalistic sentences, because the former underdetermine the latter: there's a sense in which more or less *any* experience can be likened to another. Sensations of red, orange, pink, green, etc., are all like what goes on when one sees a red object, but since they are mutually exclusive the latter can't be a translation of any of the former.[14] Indeed, the only way to constrain the candidate translations would be in terms of the very properties one was attempting to avoid. So one could say a sensation of red can't be like what goes on when one sees a green object because the phenomenal property of greenness is distinct from that of redness!

These variations on what is sometimes referred to as the 'property problem' are generally regarded as 'decisive against' (Rosenthal 2000: 10) a materialist version of the identity theory like Smart's. And yet the suspicion lingers that it expresses some basic truth about the nature of the mental. But if that truth is to be articulated it has to avoid the conceptual confusions to which it seems doomed. At this point it would be salutary to recall the shape of the developments outlined above. Both 'ideal' and 'ordinary' language theorists redeem the use of mental terms, whilst seeking to obviate the improper metaphysical speculation into which a realistic construal of them tempts us. For Hempel, Schlick, Carnap et al. this means that their meaning is exhausted through their conditions of verification, which are specified in the translation into physicalistic statements. In other words, 'the act of verification . . . is always the same sort: it is the occurrence of a definite fact that is confirmed by observation, by means of immediate experience' (Schlick 1936: 56–7). Crucially, then, not only is the mental modelled on the scientific, but also the *meaning* of scientific statements is stipulated in terms of the verification principle; and both scientific method and the idea of progress in the sciences are understood in like manner.[15] So, we have a great curiosity: a view that science is the measure of all things based on a decidedly non-scientific criterion of what is and is not science, and of how science does and does not progress. Although the positivist wishes to stand alongside the scientist in the traditional garb of the under-labourer, it seems that he can nevertheless retain his lofty philosophical standpoint.

The identity theorist seeks to address the problem that derives from attaching ontological significance to the distinction between incommensurable ways of talking – areas of discourse (the mental and physical) with their own discrete norms. He does so by denying that the lack of suitable translations (of synonymy relations) necessitates rejecting the idea that sensation terms refer to entities. Although this seems permissive, unlike Ryle the identity theorist does not accept that criteria of existence are intra-discursive; rather, the referential status of these terms is redeemed because they stand for entities identifiable by the discourse of the natural sciences. What the property problem highlights is the fact that unless one has an *antecedent* argument to the effect that materialism is true, and that as a consequence the criteria of existence are determined by the discourse of the physical sciences, there is no reason to believe that the *same* entity is being 'talked about' when one talks about sensations and brain-processes. One cannot avoid the conceptual mismatch between mental- and physical-talk by purporting to occupy a standpoint that is ontologically neutral with respect to their respective existence-claims when that standpoint clearly favours a specific area of discourse. The identity theorist's view about criteria of existence is as metaphysical as the positivist's about meaning.

This suggests that the problems confronting the logical positivist and the identity theorist arise from adopting a standpoint that derives its authority from proclaiming the superiority of one discourse (that of the natural sciences) over others. Although both aim to undermine the traditional privilege philosophy held over science, they do so by assuming a non-scientific standpoint on science. It is the context of how an understanding of the relationship between philosophy and science bears on questions relating to concept change that Rorty's original contribution to the debate about the mind–body problem is to be understood; and it is in terms of his developing understanding of what this involves that his subsequent thought will be elucidated. Before discussing this we need to examine some major changes that took place in the understanding of the relationship between science and philosophy in the 1950s and early 1960s, and how a new appreciation of the problem of conceptual change affected thinking about the mind.

3   Dogmas of empiricism

In 1951 Quine published 'Two Dogmas of Empiricism'. Its opening statement makes evident its relevance:

> Modern empiricism has been conditioned in large part by two dogmas. One is a belief in some fundamental cleavage between truths which are *analytic*, or grounded in meanings independently of matters of fact, and truths which are synthetic, or grounded in fact. The other dogma is reductionism: the belief that each meaningful statement is equivalent to some logical construct upon terms which refer to immediate experience. Both dogmas, I shall argue, are ill founded. One effect of abandoning them is, as we shall see, a blurring of the supposed boundary between speculative metaphysics and natural science. Another effect is a shift toward pragmatism.
> (1980: 20)

For the positivist the meaning of a mental term is constituted by the physical test sentences into which it can be *translated*. The test sentences themselves require no interpretative work: they wear (as it were) their meanings on their sleeves by being directly correlated with observational experiences. It follows from the verification theory of meaning, then, that in general a *translation* of A into B has been effected (that A and B are shown to be synonymous) when it is established that A and B are 'alike in point of method of empirical confirmation or infirmation' (1980: 37). Consequently, it is central to the project of translation that a sentence has, with regard to its content or meaning, an individuating set of such methodological tests. This is Quine's 'dogma of reduction'. Notwithstanding the discredit heaped on the verification principle, which would appear to undermine the very basis of such a programme for translation, Quine has remarkably little to say *directly* in opposition to this dogma other than to state his holistic alternative; namely that 'our statements about the external world face the tribunal of experience not individually but only as a corporate body' (p. 41). Nevertheless, he does note that it is 'intimately connected with the other dogma . . . [they] are, indeed, at root identical' (p. 41). What *the* dogma amounts to, then, is a philosophically tendentious interpretation of a *truism*:

(Q) 'truth in general depends on both language and extra-linguistic fact' (p. 36).

As it stands, (Q) just means that the truth-value of the statement 'demons exist' covaries with both the worldly facts *and* the meaning of the terms. If 'demon' means 'supernatural being' and there are no such things then the statement is false; if it means 'bad person' it is probably true. What the dogma supposes is that the linguistic component and the worldly contribution (the 'range of confirmatory experiences' (p. 41)) can, in any particular case, be analysed out. And it is as the limiting expression of that dualism that the analytic–synthetic distinction should be regarded, with analytic statements being those for which 'the factual component should be null . . . where the linguistic component is all that matters' (pp. 36, 41). It is in these terms that Quine's attack on the analytic–synthetic distinction should be seen. Although Quine occasionally suggests that no sense can be given to the distinction, it has as much of one as any distinction with a use, and it clearly has a use (students quite quickly learn to deploy it).[16] The real probative force of Quine's attack is that the distinction cannot carry the weight the philosopher wishes to load onto it. That is to say, in the case of empiricism it cannot intelligibly pin down either side of an untenable dualism (fact versus language; the conceptual versus the empirical) forced upon us when (Q) is subjected to the demands of a metaphysical account of meaning (verificationism). As construed, 'there are no analytic sentences, and there are no synthetic ones' (Dummett 1978: 375).

Ultimately, then, the failure of verificationism leads to the conclusion that if meaning is to be associated with the 'range of confirmatory experiences' then 'the unit of empirical significance is the whole of science' (Quine 1980: 42) and not something that can be apportioned sentence by sentence. This in turn leads to Quine's 'web of belief' analogy: if no sentence has its *distinct* fund of confirmatory experiences – no determinate meaning qua empirical content – and the class of sentences immune from all confrontation with experience is empty, then there are no sentences that cannot in principle have their truth-values revised. The appearance of a demon may cause me (or, if widespread enough, 'science') to assign the value true to the sentence 'demons exist'; but the demands of consistency would mean that the truth-values distributed across many other (related) sentences would have to change. It may therefore be more expedient to keep a 'demons don't exist' belief and accommodate the apparition by an alternative distribution of truth-values. The point is that given the inter-connectedness of beliefs it is impossible to *know* in advance exactly what the outcome will be. For Quine, 'the conceptual scheme of science' (p. 44) is a tool for predicting the course of experience, so any entities posited by science in pursuit of that generic goal are on *the same epistemological footing*, be they demons or germs. Likewise, since 'ontological questions . . . are on a par with questions of natural science' (p. 45), we can't escape from the web in order to work out either *what* to believe or what to believe *in* – the considerations that guide us are 'where rational, pragmatic' (p. 46).

Quine develops the implications of his attack on the dogma of empiricism in *Word and Object*. The crucial thought-experiment occurs in chapter 2 when he offers a more concrete version of the 'web' analogy. Rather than a 'web of belief', fringed at its limits by experience, Quine asks us to consider to what extent our conceptual scheme is determined by the world, impacting on our senses ('stimulus conditions'), and how much is 'empirically unconditioned variation' (1960: 26). The thesis to be defended is that 'manuals for translating one language into another can be set up in divergent ways, all compatible with the totality of speech dispositions, yet incompatible with one another' (ibid.: 27). To dramatize this he imagines the process of *radical* translation: the attempt to make sense of language where no assumptions can be made about the host culture. The classic example comes when a native, confronted by a scurrying rabbit, utters the word 'Gavagai', to which the field-linguist responds by writing down the tentative translation '"Rabbit" (or "Lo, a rabbit")' (p. 29). Quine's thought is that nothing in the environment – no variation in the stimulus conditions – prevents it from being the case that 'Gavagai' applies, not to rabbits, but to 'brief temporal segments' or 'undetached parts' of rabbits (pp. 51, 52). Different choices like these on the part of different translators would give rise to 'incompatible' manuals of translation but, *ex hypothesi*, each translator would have dealt with all the available behavioural evidence – hence the indeterminacy of translation. However sacred the concept, nothing *in principle* stops Sortians taking up Nortian-talk, or Terrans taking up either.

As we'll see (3.3), Quine's notion of 'incompatible' conceptual schemes dealing with the same sensory input is problematic. However, the figure of the radical interpreter suggests a way of thinking about the philosophers' standpoint that does not require a position 'outside' the web (or 'language'). The analytic–synthetic distinction is of no use to the philosopher-as-field-linguist because the meanings of sentences cannot be determined by their confirming instances; the distinction between necessary and contingent truths is of no use because there are no 'pure' meanings divorced from empirical considerations. For Quine, then, the rejection of the possibility for the philosopher 'of a vantage point outside the conceptual scheme that he takes charge in' – the denial that there is 'such cosmic exile' (1960: 275) – means that philosophy is *continuous* with both science and common sense.

Another way of putting this is to note that the field-linguist's inability to make sense of the distinction between questions of language and question of fact in the determination of the truth-values of sentences (in the alien tongue) undermines the traditional sources of the authority of norms. If the way in which we view the world is determined neither by the logic of our language, because conceptual truths are just those we can least imagine changing, nor by the way the world is, because it does not determine the truth-values of sentences in isolation; that is to say, if truth has become partly decoupled from meaning; then the authority that philosophy arrogates to itself from its former standpoint dissolves along with the sources of that authority.

If all the field-linguist has to go on is the extent to which people are or are not willing to give up their beliefs, and in what circumstances, then there is a wholesale migration of epistemic authority into the realm of linguistic practices, and a consequent shift in attention towards the sociological evaluation of the institutions and activities relating to belief change. And since what people can get away with saying – can be regarded as rational believing – cannot be referred to any other authority, the implication is that norms are to be regarded in the light of what 'moves' in a linguistic game are admissible by the standards of one's peers. For Quine, the foregoing relates to 'the conceptual scheme of science and common sense'; but if philosophy is on a level with science it seems reasonable to require an account of wherefrom derive the norms of science that *doesn't* derive its authority from a purported place of 'cosmic exile' outside that scheme. At this point we see the emergence of a conception of scientific inquiry that is consonant with this new emphasis on the importance of human practices and institutions; namely, in the work of Thomas Kuhn.

In their introduction to a classic collection of writings in the philosophy of science, May Brodbeck and Herbert Feigl give us a feel for the pre-Kuhnian era. The 'function of the Philosophy of Science,' writes Brodbeck, is:

> to produce an understanding of the structure and meaning of science itself . . . to exhibit the links in the chain . . . from abstract, technical words to concrete ordinary language. In particular, it is the philosopher of science who formulates the *principle* by which the chain is formed, that is, the logic of scientific concept formation . . . [to] clarify the basic ideas and methods of the sciences. (1953: 4–5)[17]

For most of these philosophers the sorts of considerations we have already encountered underwrite the normative status of their inquiry; namely, that meaning derives from confirmatory experience. It is for this reason that Feigl can, without hesitation, suppose that the question 'What, then, are the basic characteristics of the scientific method?' (1949: 8) has an answer, and that that answer is to be given by the philosopher. Adherence to the semantic programme *des jours* was not required for this proprietorial attitude, however. Popper (1986), for example, noted that although science seems to progress on the basis of inductive reasoning, whereby a prediction, made by a theory, lends credence to that theory if confirmed, the logic of such reasoning involved a basic fallacy. Instead, he argued, the *Logic of Scientific Discovery* required the formulation of bold theoretical conjectures, the derived predictions from which could be tested to falsify the theory but never to prove it true.

Although motivated by historical study, what Kuhn did was offer an alternative understanding of 'the logic of scientific concept formation' and thus of how and why conceptual change ('scientific progress') takes place, one that does not discern an underlying rational method from a standpoint outside of scientific activity itself. In brief, he periodizes science into three stages of development. In the first, immature phase, one finds what one might call scientific interests expressed in the travails of various inquirers, but these are pursued rather haphazardly, and in the absence of shared goals or methods. As with alchemists, then, since there is no agreed upon method of transmutation, each may systematically pursue his own experiments in the light of his own metaphysical prejudices regarding the nature of the cosmos. The passage to the next stage – 'normal science' – comes about when inquirers agree upon a model of what constitutes appropriate scientific practice. In other words, what characterizes 'normal science' is the adoption of a 'paradigm'. Kuhn's use of this term has come in for much scrutiny and it has, as a result of his work, been adopted across the humanities and social sciences. In a postscript to *Structure* he offers the following definitions:

> On the one hand, it stands for the entire constellation of beliefs, values, techniques and so on shared by the members of a given community. On the other, it denotes one sort of element in that constellation, the concrete puzzle-solutions which, employed as models or examples, can replace explicit rules as a basis for the solution of the remaining puzzles of normal science.

'Philosophically, at least,' he goes on to add, 'the second sense . . . is the deeper of the two' (1970b: 275). The significance of the 'deeper sense' will become evident as we proceed. In its maturity, then, science is 'normal' and it is at this stage that scientists can confidently work through the implications of their paradigm. During the course of the activity of normal science, however, various problems arise which cannot be dealt with by the existing methods. Since there is an entire field of force supporting the current paradigm, taking in the education of scientists, their career prospects, etc., these anomalies can for a while be sidelined or ignored; but eventually enough build up to present a challenge to the paradigm. At this point a *crisis* occurs, and the paradigm can no longer be looked to as a source of normative authority, of ways of correctly going on. What is required is a new paradigm, the adoption of which constitutes a *scientific revolution*. But note that because norms derive their authority from a mature paradigm, with all its institutional, methodological and social practices in place – because, that is to say, those practices *constitute* the norms of scientific rationality – the adoption of a new paradigm cannot be rationally explicated in terms either of the old or of the promissory new paradigm. That is to say, when the new paradigm is mature it will seem retrospectively that the revolution was rational because the new paradigm determines what counts *as* rational; but that evaluation is not available at the time, *and there is no trans-paradigmatic standpoint from which such an evaluation could be made*. It is in this ('deeper') sense that successive paradigms (qua 'disciplinary matrices') are said to be *incommensurable*.

Commonalities between Quine's critique of empiricism, and Kuhn's of empiricist philosophy of science should be clear, as should the extent to which these involve undermining the idea of any superior standpoint that can be taken on our practices, one that has privileged access to the putative sources of their normativity. In concluding this chapter, there is one final point to make in relation to this. As we've seen, for Quine translation is *in*determinate because it is in part[18] *under*determined by the conditions in which speakers assent to sentences (their 'stimulus meaning'). However, the articulation of such a thesis requires the supposition that there is theoretically neutral access to those conditions. For Kuhn, however, the very idea that we have access to 'a neutral sub-linguistic means of reporting' (1970b: 268) is wrong-headed because the *world-as-experienced* is paradigm-constituted.[19] In this sense, Quine is another field-linguist whose translation embodies a theory that determines what counts as an observation.[20] But note that Kuhn too finds himself required to take up a standpoint outside that of his own revisionary description of scientific activity, because although 'with a change of paradigm, the scientist after works in a different world . . . the world does not change' (1970a: 121). As with Kant, on the traditional 'two-world' interpretation,[21] the vertiginous relativism induced by the idea that 'there is . . . no theory-independent way to reconstruct phrases like "really there"' (ibid.: 206) is ameliorated by the idea that there is a (largely) unknowable world acting as a transcendental guarantor to hold everything in place.

2

What is Eliminative Materialism?

1 Introduction

No philosophical distinction elicits more conflicting intuitions than that between the mental and the physical. The desire to identify what is distinctive about human beings seems to require some account of mental states, features or processes. And yet this very aspiration runs counter to the naturalizing thrust of late Enlightenment thought, threatening a form of ontological recidivism. One of a constellation of dilemmas these intuitions generate is brought out in the following argument:

The Realist Argument (for pains)

R(1)   'There are Xs' is true just in case 'X' is a referring term.
R(2)   'There are sensations of pain' is true.
R(3)   'Sensation of pain' is a referring term.
R(4)   Sensations of pain exist.

If one accepts that people make true statements of the form 'I am in pain' one is required to acknowledge that pains exist. But since pains don't seem at all like the sort of existents that fit into the world as understood from a physical or material point of view, this appears to warrant the conclusion that sensations of pain and other mental items belong to a different ontological realm. On the other hand, to *deny* something like R(2) implies that cognitively we're all more or less on a par with those who believe in demons or unicorns.

In chapter 1 we examined several attempts to find a place for mind in the world that avoids this dilemma, the most influential of which is the materialist's attempt to *reduce* mental states to brain states. Accordingly, mental-talk is legitimate not because it refers to a distinct realm of existents but because it refers to material entities. This in-principle reduction of the mental to the physical has a dual ontological significance:

(i)   It functions *negatively* by eliminating the need to advert to mental existents.

(ii)   It functions *positively* by favouring one particular vocabulary for providing the criteria of existence.

What unifies these two functions is the assumption of what I'll call a *Realist Attitude*. One aspect of this is an adherence to the following apparently uncontentious principle:

(P)   'X' is a referring term just in case Xs exist.

Formally speaking, this is required to complete the Realist Argument. Underpinning it is something rather more interesting:

(RA)   There is a standpoint (a privileged vocabulary) available to the philosopher from which the criteria of real existence can be determined.

(RA) does not imply that the criteria are philosophical of course; indeed, the materialist assumption is that they are dictated by the best available science of the day. Rather, the point is that the chosen vocabulary has to be *legitimated*: there must be *philosophical* reasons for conferring its privileged status. It is the adoption of the Realist Attitude, then, that makes the Realist Argument seem compelling.

Despite its initial promise, the so-called identity theory of mind turned out to confront at least one major conceptual problem; namely, that the attempt to distinguish the mental from the physical in order to assert their (contingent) identity involves a commitment to the existence of properties that render it at best convicted of that most heinous of 1960s thought-crimes, a category mistake.[1] The attempt to ameliorate this conceptual confusion through a topic-neutral *translation* of self-reported states seemed doomed to fail, thereby vitiating the promise of a fully naturalistic account of mental events.² This is in part the context for a series of papers that first brought Rorty to prominence in analytic philosophical circles, beginning with the publication in 1965 of 'Mind–Body Identity, Privacy, and Categories' (MBIPC). In this piece, Rorty acknowledges that if one takes it that the identity of sensation and brain-process claimed by the identity theorist is one of *strict identity*, the identity theorist cannot escape the need for topic-neutral translations. Despite his sympathy with Cornman's criticisms, however, Rorty maintains that this leaves the materialist's withers unwrung because there is another version of the identity theory available that 'preserves the full-force of the traditional materialist position' (MBIPC: 178) while circumventing the need for such translations. Rorty calls his alternative to the *translation* form of the identity theory the *disappearance* form, but it is always referred to as *eliminative materialism*.³

According to Brandom, Rorty's materialism was 'the first genuinely new response to the traditional mind–body problem that anyone had seen for a long time,' and the 'rich and original line of thought' that the argument for eliminativism represents is 'important for understanding the subsequent course of Rorty's intellectual development' (2000b: 157, 158). For Brandom, the crucial insight is that a change in the norms determining what can and cannot be said about something constitutes not so much a shift in the angle of inquiry that reveals some new feature of an object or concept that was previously hidden as a change to the thing talked about. Objects or experience, then, do not dictate these norms; rather, they originate in what is authorized by social practices. As we saw in 1.2, Ryle holds that criteria of existence are not 'generic' but relative to the logical space in which they take place. Rorty in effect takes up such a view, with the proviso that, given Quine's attack on the analytic–synthetic distinction, 'logical space' connotes no more than a social practice so entrenched one can't easily imagine giving it up. The important point here is that no matter how deeply embedded in a form of life it is, a social practice remains contingent.

Following Brandom's hint, then, the task of this and subsequent chapters is to demonstrate how the sorts of considerations Rorty brings to bear in evaluating the status of mental-talk come to exemplify a general view on the phenomenon of conceptual change, and the implications this has for our understanding of the nature and limits of philosophical inquiry: an elucidation of *the metaphilosophical significance of eliminativism*. The key to this is the apparent conflict between the foregoing characterization of Rorty's 'crucial insight' and the fact that it initially emerges as part of a defence of what Rorty construes as 'traditional materialism'. After all, it would seem that while a social-practice construal of normativity takes up the *negative* project of deflating the possible ontological pretensions of mental-talk, materialism implies the sort of *positive* view about the nature of things associated with the Realist Attitude. Our initial concern will therefore be to show how Rorty's self-diagnosis of the conflicting elements in his early attempt to 'defend' materialism leads him to isolate and reject the controlling influence of something like this attitude on his early position. This constitutes what I will call Rorty's *Kehre*, or 'turn'. Amongst other things it leads him to disdain the idea that the (bare) possibility of conceptual change in the form of reduction or elimination has any ontological significance and is *therefore* of any philosophical interest; or, with a different emphasis, that a distinction between different ways of talking – like, for example, between mental-talk and physical-talk – is of philosophical interest *only if* what it is to be of philosophical interest is that a distinction reveals how things *must be* with the world.

The question of whether or not a reduction or distinction *can* be of philosophical interest without presupposing the Realist Attitude will be taken up at the end of this book. What does seem clear is that the enticement to take a view of conceptual change as having positive ontological significance issues from the notion that philosophy can take up some sort of privileged external standpoint on human activities, and as we saw in chapter 1 that is a temptation that even Kuhn found hard to foreswear. Nevertheless, the idea that such change can be understood in terms of successive paradigms displacing each other, and in doing so determining their own normative standards, seems in principle to require no adversion to the idea of a world standing even as transcendental guarantor of human strivings towards objectivity. As Rorty observes, 'reading [Kuhn's] *The Structure of Scientific Revolutions* (1962) had given [him] the sense of scales falling from [his] eyes' (*PSH*: 175), and there is no doubting the influence of Kuhn's work for Rorty's developing sense of the 'metaphilosophical implications' (ibid., 178) of the 'paradigm' paradigm. Nevertheless, it is Quine not Kuhn whose work casts the longer shadow over Rorty's original contribution to the debate about the intelligibility of the identity theory. Indeed, although Cornman describes Rorty's as a 'subtle kind of eliminative materialism' (1968b: 17), distinct from Quine's, Rorty demurs:

all my new line amounts to is the suggestion that the reporting role of sensation-discourse could be taken over by a neurological vocabulary. (1970b: 227, fn. 13)

This suggestion returns us to the question to which we were led in chapter 1: what distinguishes the mental from the physical; what is the criterion of the mental? We'll take that up in section 4, after outlining Rorty's approach to eliminativism in section 3. Before doing so, it will be useful to return to Quine and link this debate in the philosophy of mind in with some of the topics already touched upon. This will in turn give us a better appreciation of the extent and limits of Quine's influence on Rorty's early work, and hence is of primary importance for understanding the latter's 'turn'.

As noted in 1.1, Rorty's early eliminativism is indebted to Quine's work. Significantly, Quine's pragmatism emerges as part of an attempt to position himself as a critic of both the 'ideal' and 'ordinary' language traditions; a critic, that is to say, of the two dominant 'European' schools of philosophy and of their traditional sources of authority (experience; language). What these schools share for Quine is a questionable commitment to the *philosophical significance* of the analytic–synthetic distinction, upon which this assumed authority depends. As well as informing his view of the relationship between science and philosophy, Quine's development of this idea underpins his approach to the mind–body problem. Although Quine's case differs from the positivist's, he ultimately rejects the intelligibility of the mind–body problem on the basis of a similar prejudice concerning the relative status of the natural sciences.

2 Analysis, explication and elimination

Quine ends *Word and Object* (1960) with some metaphilosophical reflections on the nature of philosophical analysis. These derive from considerations underlying the attack on the analytic–synthetic distinction and demonstrate its relevance to Quine's other foe, the ordinary language philosopher. Moreover, he goes on to link these specifically to the problem of conceptual revision as it features in the articulation of the identity theory. Recall that according to 'the paradox of analysis', the 'systematic pursuit of the problem of meaning by means of logical analysis of language' (Feigl 1943: 6) is uninformative, since the only criterion we have for a correct analysis is the understanding of the term we had prior to the analysis. Since the 'meanings' the analysis aims to uncover may be 'hidden' in some way from the speaker, there may be some 'therapeutic' gain from being 'reminded' of them, but the requirement for a criterion of success of analysis necessitates that it is 'descriptive' and not speculatively 'revisionary'.[4] So, the (descriptive) analysis of the concept of mind could never constitute a genuine empirical *discovery*: it must be in terms that at some level are always-already understood by speakers of so-called 'ordinary language'.[5] For Quine, however, the force of the charge embodied in the 'paradox' is parasitic on an account of analysis – or what he calls, following Carnap, 'explication' – that is founded on the relation of synonymy: it presupposes that one grasps *that* the explication is the *correct* one because one understands that the terms it equates have the same meaning (Quine 1960: 259).

For the radical translator meaning is of course indeterminate; so whatever explication is, it is not founded on synonymy; and neither does synonymy provide the criterion of correctness. So what is it, and what does? The examples Quine uses to introduce explication are rather technical,[6] but the point is clear enough:

> explication is elimination. We have, to begin with, an expression or form of expression that is somehow troublesome. It behaves partly like a term but not enough so, or it is vague in ways that bother us, or it puts kinks in a theory or encourages one or another confusion. But it also serves certain purposes that are not to be abandoned. Then we find a way of accomplishing those same purposes through other channels, using other and less troublesome forms of expression. The old perplexities are resolved. (Quine 1960: 260)

On this account the paradigmatic example of explication – Russell's analysis of proper names – is an example of elimination. When we *analyse* the function of a putatively referring term like 'nobody' in 'I met nobody today' in terms of quantification, we do not offer an explication such that the explicandum means the same as the explicans; rather, we make a *discovery* about logical form and in doing so *eliminate* the referring use of the problematic term while ensuring that whatever purposes it served are still satisfied. Quine suggests cheekily that since this means that any problem deriving from that discredited usage – like asking what strange manner of existent 'nobody' refers to – is shown to be 'unreal . . . in the sense of proceeding only from needless usages,' it resonates with an important thesis of Wittgenstein's to the effect that the task of philosophy 'is not to solve problems but to dissolve them by showing that there were really none there' (ibid.). That in turn leads him to denounce, as apostates, 'those philosophers most influenced by Wittgenstein' (p. 261), who insist explications qua eliminations are 'revisionary' deviations from ordinary usage.

From Quine's perspective it is the recalcitrant attachment to the analytic–synthetic distinction (and to the synonymy relation) that underpins 'the Oxford philosophers' (p. 259) commitment to 'ordinary usage' as the source of normative authority: it is what blinds them to the alternative; namely, that explication qua elimination shows us how to 'circumvent the problematic parts of ordinary usage' (p. 261). The distinction (and the synonymy relation) is of no philosophical interest because it is of no pragmatic use to the field-linguist. In the above terms, the assumption that the analytic–synthetic distinction *has* a philosophical use underwrites the ('Oxford') philosophers' privileged standpoint with respect to linguistic usage by investing normative authority in something called 'ordinary language' to which it has privileged access, demonstrable through the provision of analyses for which there is a criterion of success (synonymy of meaning). But if this standpoint and its attendant criterion are rejected, then so is the authority to *disdain* a putative explicans on the grounds that it constitutes a violation of 'our' conceptual norms. From the field-linguist's point of view there is no *criterion* that would allow us to draw a clear line between the empirical (the *facts*, what people *believe*) and the conceptual (what people *mean*, the *norms* they obey) and warrant the claim that a purported explication is not in fact an empirical discovery that brought about a change in the concepts we use to explain phenomena.

From this the following question arises: 'If the criterion of *success* of an analysis that is an explication isn't in terms of a prior grasp of meaning founded on the relation of synonymy, what is it?' After all – officially at least – the question of an *ideal* language of experience is no more on offer than the idea of getting ordinary language right. The first thing to note is that although all explication is elimination, not all elimination is explication: there must be some 'striking if partial parallelism of function' between the old and new forms of expression (1960: 261) if the elimination is to be an explication. Recalling the above quote, if we assume that by 'other channels' Quine means 'other theories' or 'alternative conceptual resources' or 'other forms of description' (or 'redescriptions') then we have something like:

V(1) A descriptive vocabulary {D_1}, in which X-talk figures and fulfils certain (description independent) purposes, is replaced by another {D_2}, in which Y-talk figures that fulfils (some of) the same purposes.

V(2) The functional role of Y-talk in {D_2} 'parallels strikingly' the functional role of X-talk in {D_1}.

An explication satisfies V(1) and V(2); an elimination *simpliciter* V(1) alone. From this we can derive the following:

Q(i)   The more narrowly one characterizes {D_1} and {D_2} (the more one can specify the relevant purposes of X-talk), the easier it will be to satisfy V(1).

Q(ii) The stronger the association between a term's functional role (in a descriptive vocabulary) and the purposes it serves, the easier it will be to satisfy V(2).

Q(iii) If objects are involved, an explication will lead to the identification of Ys with Xs. Explication is reduction.

Q(iv) If objects are involved, an elimination *simpliciter* will lead to a denial of the existence of Xs.

Q(v)   There are no strict criteria for distinguishing between elimination and explication/reduction.

Returning to our question, it should be evident that there is not going to be any *general* answer. In some instances of conceptual change the continuing 'purposes' may be relatively self-evident, and the precise nature of the 'trouble' to be eliminated clearly defined; but this is likely to be the exception rather than the rule. To put a name to this *lack* of a criterion, the considerations will be pragmatic. Understood this way, 'explications' are the post-verificationist version of the positivists' 'ideal language' idea, recommendations for linguistic change tailored to avoid 'problematic parts of ordinary language' and thus facilitating the job of inquiry. This is important for understanding Rorty's approach to concept change; but what does Quine make of it in regard to talk of the mind? His version of eliminativism comes fast and dirty:

> If there is a case for mental events and mental states, it must be just that the positing of them, like the positing of molecules, has some indirect systematic efficacy in the development of theory. But if a certain organization of theory is achieved by thus positing distinctive mental states and events behind physical behavior, surely as

much organization could be achieved by positing merely certain correlative physiological states and events instead ... the bodily states exist anyway; why add the others? Thus introspection may be seen as a witnessing to one's own bodily condition, as in introspecting an acid stomach, even though the introspector be vague on the medical details. (1960: 264)

How does Quine understand this 'brief for physicalism': as an elimination (satisfying V(1)) or an explication/reduction (satisfying V(1) and V(2))? For the philosophically behaviouristic field-linguist there are no criteria for 'real' existence that transcend the pragmatic demands of theorizing observable behaviour: to be is to be (theoretically) postulated in the vocabulary of natural science.[7] Nothing motivates the requirement that one come up with mental items/ events to explain even first-person (introspective) reports, so there is no need to make a distinction *in kind* between the mental and the physical. There is no 'unbridgeable gap', no 'philosophically interesting' distinction. Since the metaphysical (mental–physical) distinction is unmotivated, no sense can be given to the choice between:

(I)   an eliminative physicalism that would 'repudiate the mental state of pain in favor of its physical concomitant' (there are no Xs; Q(iv))

and,

(II)   an explicative/reductive physicalism that would 'identify the mental state with a state of the physical organism' (p. 265) (Xs = Ys; Q(iii))

Like that between the (notionally) rival claims 'there are no tables because everything is just clouds of molecules', and 'tables are clouds of molecules', the choice between (I) and (II) is 'unreal', in the sense of 'proceeding only from needless usages'.

We can summarize Quine's contribution as follows. Firstly, there is no a priori reason to think that change involving even our most fundamental concepts is impossible: there can be no insistence on evaluating alternatives on the basis of *current* (linguistic) practices. Secondly, pragmatic considerations govern decisions about whether we've rid ourselves of troublesome entities or have identified them with something more amenable to the new conceptual framework. Now, given that Quine *rejects* the idea that one can make sense of the distinction between eliminative and reductive physicalism, it may seem odd to characterize Quine's position as 'eliminativist'; but that would be to confuse the metaphilosophical point with the second order distinction between two rival brands of materialism. The aim is to *eliminate* the mental by articulating a standpoint from which the explanatory requirement to postulate mental terms does not arise.[8] However, insofar as the philosophical behaviourism of the field-linguist amounts merely to the *rejection* of metaphysical standpoint as Quine claims (1960: 260, fn. 5), it functions only to make a *negative* ontological point about mental existents. To eliminate them by showing they needn't be posited presupposes:

(a)   that mental-talk (like other talk) must be regarded as entity-positing; and
(b)   that physical theory is the privileged vocabulary in which the relevant terms are presented.

(b) is a version of (RA), the characteristic commitment of the Realist Attitude; and there is no (neutral) reason to conclude that from her standpoint the field-linguist need take such a view. The fact that Quine does indicates that, despite the rejection of the analytic–synthetic distinction, the positivists' conception of the 'ideal language' persists in his thinking. Moreover, the reason why we cannot make sense of the distinction between eliminative and reductive physicalism on this account is that the mental–physical distinction is unmotivated. The price paid to avoid the ontological embarrassment of an 'unbridgeable gap' is that the distinction disappears, and along with it goes the notion that anyone now or in the past was talking truthfully when they used mental terms, including those philosophers who assumed that there was a *real* distinction.

   With this in mind, recall that, according to Leibniz's principle, the strict identity invoked by the reductive materialist requires that any property ascribable to a mental-state must be ascribable to a brain-state. We can now see that the idea of topic-neutral translations of sensation-talk presupposes the very notion of synonymy of meaning that Quine attacks. To assume that all properties (R) ascribable to an entity posited by one scientific theory (call it $\{D_{mental}\}$) are attributable to an entity in a new theory (call it $\{D_{physical}\}$) would suggest a neutral schema of (say) experience that could be used to make the translations between the two (show they are synonymous). And, as we've seen, Kuhn's account of the incommensurability between scientific paradigms reinforces the problematic nature of assuming the availability of any standpoint from which such a translation could be effected. The Quinean solution is to avoid the property problem by consigning {D$_{mental}$} terms to the ontological slum. However, that leaves us with another version of our materialist dilemma: on the one hand, the translation form redeems our sensation-talk by identifying sensations with brain-states, but confronts the problem of casting those reports in terms that aren't mysterious; on the other hand, the eliminative form rids us of the need for topic-neutral translations at the cost of implying that most of us have empirically false beliefs because the existence of sensations (like unicorns and demons) is posited unnecessarily. Imagine a Quinean Sortian, informing a Terran intent on winning him over to mental-talk, that since Sortians have the requisite 'organization of theory' positing only 'physiological states and events' they have no need to 'add the others'. Sortians have no mental states to either eliminate or to identify with physical states; they merely refuse to accept that a theoretical (let alone metaphysical) distinction is required. From the Quinean Sortian's perspective, then, Terrans have empirically false beliefs because their mentalistic vocabulary is surplus to (theoretic) requirements. And if Terrans were to resile from indulging in mental-talk and adopt the Sortian standpoint their vocabulary would no longer *be* Terran. As a consequence they would no longer be able to make sense of mental-talk other than as something belonging to their embarrassing past.

One reason for questioning this is that Quine's elimination of the mental requires both (a) and (b), and (a) might be false. For Cornman, 'sensations cannot be eliminated' because a first-person report is a report of some*thing* that 'we directly experience' (1968b: 17), and so it cannot turn out at some future date to be a no*thing*, a posited item no longer required by theory. According to Cornman, what makes Rorty's eliminativism subtler is that he 'does not construe sensations as postulated' (ibid.). That is to say, he aims to preserve the reporting function of sensation terms – allow that someone who says that 'I am in pain' is saying something true – while nevertheless denying that this is inconsistent with the claim that there might turn out to be no sensations, thus validating the materialist position which in its negative mode denies that there are non-physical properties. In these terms, Rorty's suggestion is that the fact that we might in the future talk Sortian does not warrant the conclusion that right now we Terrans have empirically false beliefs. The possibility of coming to adopt the latter standpoint does not wholly infect the legitimacy of Terran mental-talk; which is to say that Rorty, unlike Quine, is obliged to retain some version of the mental–physical distinction without allowing it to either inflate metaphysically or degenerate into a version of reductionism. As we will see in section 4, this relates to the need to give some account of what we are to say of those Quinean 'witnessings' to bodily conditions that we have hitherto been inclined to call 'mental'. Before that, let's look at Rorty's version of eliminativism.

3   Eliminative materialism

To see Rorty's alternative consider the following:

(A)   Zeus's thunderbolts are discharges of static electricity.
(B)   Demoniacal possession is a form of hallucinatory psychosis.

Assertions of (A) and (B) appear to involve some sort of identity claim, though not the relation of *strict* identity. Taking his lead from Quine, Rorty suggests that:

> the sort of relation which obtains between . . . existent entities and non-existent entities when reference to the latter once served (some of) the purposes presently served by some of the former. (MBIPC: 176)

The suggestion is that (A) and (B) are elliptical for something like the following:

(A′)   What people used to call 'Zeus's thunderbolts' are discharges of static electricity.
(B′)   What people used to call 'demoniacal possession' is a form of hallucinatory psychosis.

In this case (A′) and (B′) do involve strict identity (ibid.: 177). The immediate advantage of this analysis is that the *relata* of the strict identities can belong to different 'discursive categories' without generating 'ontological' problems that require a topic-neutral dis/ solution. This approach makes explicit what is obscured in the *translation* form of the identity theory; namely, that the identity asserted is between a first-person report and a third-person explanation. Instead of

(C)   The sensation of pain = the firing of C-fibres,

we have a variation on semantic ascent:

(C′)   What people used to call 'the sensation of pain' = the firing of C-fibres.

It should be clear that if Rorty is to pull off this trick he cannot allow full flight to Cornman's intuition that (for example) a report of a sensation of pain is a report of some*thing* 'directly experienced'. The explication in (C′) is intended to achieve this by demonstrating that the *reporting* function of sensation-talk is replaced by a term amenable to some future science, like a state of one's brain.

To illustrate this, Rorty introduces the analogy between demons and sensations (the Nortians). For the Nortian priestly caste, demon-talk has both an explanatory function (to do with the aetiology of diseases) and a reporting function (to do with the type of demon they see). From the Terran perspective, it is germs that cause diseases, and the Nortian priests are having hallucinations. The Terrans cannot *demonstrate* the Nortians' error, since (by hypothesis) all their empirical predictions about the development of diseases match up with the Terrans'. Instead they suggest to the Nortian priests that they stop talking about demons and start talking about germs. Asked what they were reporting if not a demon, the Terrans tell them it was the content of an hallucination.

To see how the analogy works, recall that what the Sortian wants to say to the Terran is something like:

*   What (you) Terrans call 'the sensation of pain' = the firing of C-fibres.

That is to say, when they inform the Terrans that there are no sensations and that what the Terrans are reporting when they say things like 'I have a sensation of pain' is the occurrence of a particular brain-state, they are not suggesting that we have any necessarily false beliefs (because we use the empty concept *sensation of pain*) but rather that our true beliefs are not about what we take them to be about (because 'sensation of pain' refers to firings of C-fibres). Now there is an apparent disanalogy here. One way of putting it is that while Terrans are happy concluding that there are no demons, they would be resistant to concluding that there are no sensations. As Rorty sees it, the disanalogy is eliminated once we see that this is because the reporting function of 'demon' is distinct from its explanatory function. The former is to be explicated as 'content of hallucination'; the latter as 'cause of disease'. As a result, with

What (you) Nortians call 'demons' = _____,

there is nothing to fill in the blank, and so we conclude that 'there are no demons'. Nevertheless, for Rorty there is no difference in kind between the two proposed reductions:

> [both] can equally well be paraphrased as 'Elimination of the referring use of the expression in question ("demon," "sensation") from our language would leave our ability to describe and predict undiminished'. (MBIPC: 180–1)

There are two claims here. The first is that we do no violence to our understanding of persons if we cease to think of them and of ourselves as having sensations, as thinking that 'sensation' refers to some *mental* item: sensation-talk is not essential to our conceptual scheme. The second claim is that getting rid of mental-talk would not disadvantage us with respect to describing and predicting the world. Although these claims are separable, for Rorty the second claim determines the first.

This is a conclusion in sympathy with Quine's metaphilosophical stance. Although disease-talk (Y-talk) fulfils some of the purposes of demon-talk (X-talk), and thus satisfies V(1), the bifurcation of the reporting and explanatory functions in the new descriptive vocabulary mean that V(2) is not satisfied. In the second case, however, brain-process talk fulfils both the explanatory and reporting functions of sensation-talk, and so we get an explication-reduction proper. But here Rorty makes clear what is obscure in Quine: losses of reporting and of explanatory functions are losses of *referring* uses. *Sensations* are eliminated rather than reduced to brain-states because 'sensation' can no longer be thought of as referring to a specifically *mental* item. Of course, that conclusion can only be reached because the referring uses of 'sensation' are taken up by other terms. These determine the criteria of identity of reference and are not thought to engender ontological problems because they refer only to physical states and processes.

Before returning to this, let's look how Rorty defends the view that sensations are on a par with demons when it comes to their in-principle elimination. Consider the following:

(D')   What people call 'unicorn horns' = narwhal horns.
(E')   What people call 'tables' = clouds of molecules.

Of (D') Rorty says that '"This is a unicorn horn" commits one to the existence of unicorns, and there are, it turns out, no unicorns' (p. 181). So,

(I*)   What people call 'Xs' = Ys,

goes through *because*

(P)   'X' is a referring term just in case Xs exist,

and there are no Xs. In Quinean terms (D') is a case of elimination without explication. The purposes served by unicorn-horn talk are taken over by narwhal-horn talk, which allows for the circumvention of problematic questions ('So where *are* all these unicorns?'), but there is no 'striking' parallelism of function between the two. 'Unicorn horn' turns out not to have a referring function, and any unicorn-horn beliefs are empirically false.

Of (E'), Rorty wants to say that 'this is a table' does *not* commit one to an empirically false belief, that the identity 'does not suggest, or require as a ground, that people who say "This is a table" hold false beliefs' (p. 181). In this case (I*) goes through *despite the fact* that (P), and there *are* Xs in this case. So 'table' retains its 'referring' function: 'we are suggesting that something *more* has been found out about the sort of situation reported by "This is a table"' (pp. 181–2).

Returning to (C'), if we assimilate it to (D') we must conclude that 'people who have reported sensations in the past have (necessarily) . . . empirically disconfirmed beliefs' (p. 182); whereas if we assimilate it to (E') we seem to be stuck with the referring use of the term 'sensation', and a 'defender of [this form of the] Identity Theory *does* want to impugn the existence of sensations' (ibid.).

Note that, however great the difference between (D') and (E'), it can only be a matter of degree. An elimination of an X would only count *in favour of* a Y if there were *some* continuity of purpose between X-talk and Y-talk. For Rorty, then, (A') to (E') are *all* cases of elimination: the point of offering explications along these lines is to flag an *in principle* elimination of X-talk in favour of Y-talk that would 'leave our ability to describe and predict undiminished' (p. 182). So the reason we preserve the referring use of the respective term in (E'), whereas in (B') and (D') we eliminate it, 'is that nobody would dream of suggesting that we stop reporting our experiences in table-talk . . . it would be monstrously inconvenient to do so (pp. 183, 182).

A natural response to this is to ask 'experiences of what?' The answer 'tables' cannot be correct, however, for the injunction that we stop reporting our experience of *tables* in *table*-talk is nonsensical. So the assumption must be that there's a table-neutral (unicorn horn-, sensation-, demon-, etc., neutral) account of experience in play, which evokes the neutral framework of experience presupposed by Quine's radical interpreter. Neglecting this, the desideratum is to show how, given that from an ontological point of view tables are on a par with sensations, demons and unicorns in terms of their in-principle elimination, on pragmatic grounds sensation-talk can be assimilated to unicorn- and demon-talk when it comes to the elimination of the referring use of the term, but to table-talk when it comes to the truth of the beliefs expressed using it.

To this end, Rorty offers a general theory outlining how 'a term may cease to have a referring use without those who made such a use being convicted of having held false beliefs' (p. 183). Taking (C'), the crucial transition is from:

C'(2)   Sensations = brain-processes.
C'(6)   There are no sensations.

Recall that the *negative* ontological aim is to oppose a certain understanding of what sensations are: *immaterial* items that we cannot in principle cease to talk of because, being minded creatures, they cannot be eliminated from our ontology. In 'preserving the full force of the traditional materialist position', Rorty is opposing the idea that metaphysically speaking sensation-talk is ineliminable. Since there is no *in-principle* impediment to achieving C'(6), when the referring use of 'sensation' disappears, the existence of *sensations* – that is to say, of *mental* items – is impugned and immaterialism shown to be false. Of course, to reject the existence of (immaterial) *sensations*, while affirming that statements including sensation terms are not *necessarily* false, requires something for sensation-talk to be about; and the non-immaterialist option is brain-states. So in this case (I*) goes through *despite* (P) and the fact that there are no Xs, *because* X does refer to an existent; namely, to a brain-state.

But how, one might ask, if 'sensation' has lost its referring function in the year 2525, can one not conclude that when people *now* talk of their sensations they are not having false beliefs? In 2525 people think about sensations in the way we presently think about unicorn horns and demons, and we're not inclined to associate either with an existent. At this point, recall that for Quine the difference between C'(2) and C'(6) is as unreal as that between:

E'(2) Tables = clouds of molecules; and
E'(6) There are no tables.

These versions of Q(iii) and Q(iv) are 'unreal' because they 'proceed from needless usages'. However, by introducing a temporal dimension to the process of concept change Rorty provides a context in which certain usages can become needful for pragmatic reasons. For these reasons 'we' are stuck at C'(2) (and E'(2)) and, consequently, 'sensation' continues to have a referring use (to refer to the relevant brain-process). So Rorty's defence of the materialist's position is that construed as a prediction about the future elimination of the referring use of terms like 'sensation', it 'is almost certainly wrong.'

The only way to understand 'inconvenience' here is in terms of the number of belief-switches that would be required to effect linguistic reform: presumably eliminating demons and unicorns didn't require many; getting rid of tables and sensations would require a great number. What C'(2) allows, then, is that most of our statements about sensations continue to be true on the understanding that our beliefs are not about what we think they're about.

There's something vertiginous about contemplating Rorty's view about this sort of concept change: one is being asked to judge one's present practices both on the basis of where one stands now and where one might stand at some point in the future. It is, however, that point in the future that is privileged. In 2.5 we'll examine criticisms of this, which resulted in Rorty abandoning eliminative materialism. Firstly, recall that in 2.2 we observed that Quine's refusal to countenance the mental–physical distinction requires that false beliefs be attributed to those who engage in sensation-talk, and restricts what can be said about it. In 2.1 we quoted Rorty to the effect that his version of eliminative materialism added to Quine's only an account of how brain-talk might come to replace sensation-talk by taking over its reporting function. Rorty's innovation here is to naturalize the mental by construing the normativity of the reporting of sensations in terms of social practices. By offering up a criterion of the mental (for the *usage* of mental terms) that does not invite a charge of ontological dubiety, it allows the philosophical problematic to be redescribed in such a way that, although it could *come to be seen* as issuing from (as Quine might put it) 'needless linguistic usages', it is not to be regarded as *eo ipso* 'senseless'. However, the idea that sensation-talk can be so redescribed seems to support a certain sceptical (*negative*) attitude towards ontology, which is prima facie in tension with the idea that the analysis lends overall support to materialism. I associated that tension with the Realist Attitude. To get a better feel for it, and for how Rorty aims to address it, let's evaluate his attempt to identify an ontologically non-committal criterion of the mental.

4 Incorrigibility

One apparent impediment to the six-step programme for the (in principle) elimination of the referring use of 'sensation' is that the non-inferential reporting of a sensation has to be taken over by a report of a brain-process. In this respect, recall that for Cornman sensation-talk is ineliminable because it involves non-inferential reports of things that 'we directly experience'. And, since people who know nothing about the brain are able to report that they have a sensation of pain, it seems odd to maintain we directly experience the former. Our intuition is that people are in a position of epistemic privilege regarding *what it is* they are reporting on in a 'direct' experience.

Kripke (1980) makes clear how this intuition links in with the so-called property problem. Consider the sort of (contingently established) identity that excited the reductive materialist:

- Water is H_2O;
- Lightning is the discharge of static electricity.

None of the properties associated with water seem essential to identifying it as such. But what makes pain the mental state it *is*, is that a subject picks it out non-inferentially by immediate apprehension ('direct experience') of its intrinsic feel, its essential phenomenal property of painfulness. The intuition behind Cornman's translation objection is that our language will not accommodate the required translation because nothing 'topic-neutral' can explicate these intrinsic properties. For Rorty, the key presupposition here is that subjects have a pre-linguistic awareness of things *as* particular things. To give a brief example, one way of thinking about language is as a set of public signs to coordinate our essentially private experiences. So, for example, as an infant I have a number of sensations of pain and learn to correlate what I abstract from them (the concept or general idea) with the word 'pain'. On the view that originates from Kant's critique of empiricism, but is associated with Wittgenstein primarily, it is implausible to suggest that one can only be taught the word 'pain' if one is aware, before learning the word, of what 'pain' correctly names.[9] As Sellars notes:

> all awareness of sorts, resemblances, facts, etc., in short all awareness of abstract entities – indeed, all awareness even of particulars – is a linguistic affair . . . not even the awareness . . . as pertains to so-called immediate experience is presupposed by the process of learning of a language. (1997: 63)

Sellars's *psychological nominalism* is set against a critique of what he calls the Myth of the Given: the idea that there is sort of pre-linguistic awareness that constitutes the identity of being-in and knowing-that-one-is-in a particular state (like pain).[10] Wedding this Sellarsian view to Quine's, Rorty suggests there is no a priori reason why a brain-process should not be the subject of a non-inferential report.

As Cornman and Kripke imply, however, the main impediment to eliminating sensation reports is that one's relation to one's sensations is epistemically privileged. One cannot be wrong about being in pain because to be in pain is to *know* that one is in pain, and to have that sort of knowledge is to 'directly experience' something in a way that no one else can experience it. I can directly experience my pain, but only you can directly experience yours. And that particular quality of one's own sensations seems to rule out the possibility that they might be brain-processes. While you might learn to report non-inferentially on my brain-processes you can still be wrong, so we cannot eliminate that about which it is *impossible* to be wrong and which cannot therefore *be* a brain-process. The challenge, then, is to construe the epistemological authority that devolves to speakers when discussing their sensations in such a way that the in-principle elimination of their referring use is not blocked.

In different terms, the challenge is to dissolve the property objection to the identity theory by explicating a criterion of the mental that suffices to pin down one side of the identity without undermining the materialist position it seeks to advance. This requirement is evident even for the eliminative materialist. Just as we have to make sense of unicorn-horn- and demon-talk to effect their elimination, we can and do make sense of sensation-talk. Indeed, without a grasp of the mental–physical contrast the philosophical problem would not have arisen in the first place. Moreover, although the mental appears an affront to materialism, and the aim is to show that no conceptual confusion is involved in *establishing that* the mental is physical, there can be no a priori argument for materialism. For Rorty, any analysis of the mental in terms of physical entities would 'deprive the notion of "the physical" of sense by stripping it of its contrast with another realm of entities having properties incompatible with physicality' (1970a: 406). To 'make sense of materialism' we must 'explicate' (ibid.) the mental as it is understood from the perspective of common sense. This is 'irredeemably Cartesian' (ibid.: fn. 11) in holding that the mental 'must contain properties incompatible with properties of physical entities' (p. 406). So the mental–physical distinction must be construed both as a real distinction operating on Terran thinking, and in such a way that only pragmatic concerns ensure that it cannot disappear (and along with it the referring use of sensation terms).

In MBIPC, Rorty restricts himself largely to advancing various Wittgensteinian arguments to the effect that the so-called *privacy* of sensations cannot be a criterion for the epistemic privilege that attaches to reports of sensations. It is in the later 'Incorrigibility as the Mark of the Mental' that Rorty advances a more sustained account of what distinguishes the mental from the physical. As we noted in chapter 1, and have assumed since, the paradigmatic class of mental-states is taken to be 'mental events' and not mental features. Indeed, it is a consistent feature of Rorty's work in the period up to and beyond *PMN* that:

> we could make no sense of the notion of 'mental entities' as a distinct ontological genus without invoking the notion of phenomenal entities whose being was exhausted by the single property of, for example, painfulness. (*PMN*: 68)[11]

The task, then, is to identify the 'mark' of the mental. After canvassing various options (introspectibility, non-spatiality, privacy), Rorty concludes that only the latter does not presuppose the very criterion we're looking for. 'Privacy' itself has, of course, many uses,[12] but only one captures the intuitions of (Cartesian) common sense, *incorrigibility*:

> Mental events are unlike any other events in that certain knowledge claims about them cannot be overridden. We have no criteria for setting aside as mistaken first-person contemporaneous reports of thoughts and sensations, whereas we do have criteria for setting aside all reports about everything else. (Rorty 1970a: 413)

To see how mental-states could be regarded as having intrinsic features (criteria) that do not render them ineliminable, we need to return to Sellars. Notwithstanding his nominalistic hostility to the idea of a pre-linguistic awareness of the 'given', Sellars does not regard mental-talk as nonsensical. In the latter sections of *Empiricism and the Philosophy of Mind*, he offers an alternative to the 'Myth of the Given', the 'Myth of Jones'. In Jones's world, speakers are restricted to what Sellars calls 'a Rylean language, a language of which the fundamental descriptive vocabulary speaks of public properties of public objects located in Space and Time' (1997: 91), but which is 'enriched with the fundamental resources of semantical discourse' (p. 92), thus allowing Ryleans to talk of the meanings and truth-values of the verbal productions of their fellow Ryleans. According to the Myth, then, what the Ryleans don't have is any talk of mental features or states; until, that is, Jones comes along.

First off, Jones postulates certain theoretical entities to explain the overt behaviour of his fellow Ryleans. Since he models these on overt speech, these entities, although 'inside' speakers, share the semantical features of sentence-types, and he decides to call them *thoughts*. On this account, when a Rylean says 'Lo! An edible object' and proceeds to eat it, the *cause* of his eating it is the 'inner utterance' of the sentence, which Jones calls 'the *thought* that the object beheld is edible' (p. 103). Now, when someone makes a *report* to the effect that (say) the table is green, Jones can now suggest an associated perceptual *thought*: a *seeing that* the table is green. To explain these sorts of thoughts, an emboldened Jones goes on to postulate another set of theoretical entities, which he calls *impressions*. So the thought that there is a dagger in front of one (when there is not) is to be explained by the appropriate impression. These impressions thus have intrinsic features like being 'of-green' and 'of-a-dagger' where 'of' is not relational but is used to ascribe correlated features to impressions. Nevertheless, these correlations do not give analyses of meanings: although a dagger will give rise to an impression that is 'of-a-dagger' in standard conditions, 'impression of-a-dagger' does not simply *mean* 'impression such as is caused by a dagger in standard conditions (p. 111)). Most importantly, these entities are '*states* of the perceiving subject, *not a class of particulars*' (p. 110), and 'are not introduced as physiological states' (p. 113). It is therefore a mistake to identify/reduce these intrinsic mental concepts with/to physical properties, unless one expands one's account of the physical to include whatever is required to account for the observable behaviour of objects with physical properties – which is, after all, why Jones introduces them.

So far, then, on Jones's theory *thoughts* and *impressions* are theoretical entities, not immediate experiences, and are not the objects of non-inferential introspective reports. But now Jones submits his audience to a rigorous training regime in which they come to use Jones's theoretical apparatus to make reliable self-descriptions without recurring to the behavioural evidence used by others. In so doing they begin to use terms initially introduced in a theoretical context to make non-inferential reports of their own 'inner states' without it ever being supposed that there is something mysterious about such states, or that such states existed in pre-Jonesian times and went unnoticed until Jones came along to name them.

> The myth helps us to understand that concepts pertaining to certain inner episodes . . . can be primarily and essentially *intersubjective*, without being resolvable into overt behavioural symptoms, and that the reporting role of these concepts, their role in introspection, that fact that each of us has a privileged access to his impressions, constitutes a dimension of these concepts which is *built on* and *presupposes* their role in intersubjective discourse. It also makes clear why the 'privacy' of these episodes is not the 'absolute privacy' of the traditional puzzles . . . [because] the fact that overt behaviour is evidence for these episodes is built into the very logic of these concepts. (Sellars 1997: 115–16)

Although Sellars's myth offers a way of thinking about how theoretical terms might take on a non-inferential reporting role, he does not offer a criterion of the mental. Rorty takes it that Jones might just as easily have made a brain-process the bearer of the intrinsic property 'of-a-dagger' and that this would be no more non-physical than 'the spin of an electron' (1970a: 412). In other words, like Quine and unlike Sellars, Rorty is happy with the idea that one might 'expand one's account of the physical to include whatever is required to account for observable behaviour of objects with physical properties' and that once one does that the idea that there are any contrasting non-physical (mental) properties (that there is a criterion of the mental) disappears. So where does this leave us in relation to Sellars? Well, if we acknowledge that the terms referring to inner entities – entities that could *become* mental – don't give us the 'mental', we can see that the vital step is the last one: the training to make non-inferential responses that don't depend on self-observation and which issues in the epistemological privileging of the reporter. The curiosity here is that since 'the only thing that can make either an entity or a property mental is that certain reports of its existence or occurrence have the special status . . . of incorrigibility' (ibid.: 414), if brain-process talk had given rise to the same linguistic practices we would have had physical states with mental properties.

The preliminary conclusion, then, is that incorrigibility is the mark of the mental; but what exactly is incorrigibility? One common suggestion is that P is incorrigibly known by S if it is logically impossible that S believe that P and P be false. But this raises an obvious problem: before the Ryleans are trained to make non-inferential reports, impression- or sensation-reports are as defeasible as any other theoretical claim. So *either* the meaning of 'impression' when originally introduced changes when the relevant practices of self-reporting are established, *or* 'impressions' are not incorrigible in this sense. As we've seen, from the perspective of the radical translator there is no criterion one can apply to distinguish between a change of belief and a change of meaning,[13] but merely pragmatic considerations relating to simplicity, etc. Rorty nevertheless claims that for Putnamian (1963) reasons he opts for a change of belief rather than meaning. The official reason is that this allows us to avoid the conclusion that the norms relevant to the determination of incorrigibility are built into the logic of our language, and instead construe them naturalistically in terms of the linguistic practices adopted by Jones's audience as a result of his training regime. What he might have added is that this revisionary suggestion as to how to regard the authority of such norms forms the basis for a common-sense concept of the mental that will show how to avoid the philosophical problems otherwise generated.[14] We'll return to this point below.

To appreciate the sort of practices imagined, consider how, as the Ryleans become better and better at self-reporting 'inner' states, it may come about that conflicts emerge between the states ascribed to them by others, on the basis of the behavioural evidence, and the states they self-ascribe. As it turns out, a more rationally coherent explanation of a Rylean's behaviour is in fact achieved if, in these instances, one accords their self-reports more credibility. As a result, the assumption that a self-ascription can be rejected on the grounds that it conflicts with the available behavioural evidence becomes increasingly difficult to make, and eventually the need to rationalize behaviour around these authoritative self-reports becomes a normative constraint on the explanations of Rylean behaviour. At this point, then, incorrigibility is defined not in terms of the norms 'built into' the (modal) logic of language, but in terms of 'the procedures for resolving doubts accepted at a given era':

S believes incorrigibly that P at *t* if and only if:

(i)   S believes that P at *t*;
(ii) There are no accepted procedures by applying which it would be rational to come to believe that not-P, given S's belief that P at time *t*.

So the normative authority of incorrigible reports is contingent upon the linguistic practices a community has established. Any new procedure that would allow for a challenge to S's self-ascribed belief that P would undermine that authority and (potentially) lead to a reversal of the beliefs people have about thoughts (and sensations); namely, that they are incorrigibly known. The significance of this account for Rorty's overall view of normativity becomes evident when one appreciates that it applies to a priori knowledge and *seems*-statements as well as to statements reporting mental events: the authority of linguistic norms has wholly migrated into the realm of linguistic practices. Of course, in order to discern the 'mark' of the mental we need to be able to distinguish between a priori knowledge, *seems*-statements and mental events. Neglecting a priori knowledge, it's important to note that Rorty doesn't want to assimilate *seems*-statements to mental-talk because he believes pre-Jonesian Ryleans would have them. Before the introduction of mental entities, a statement of the form 'X seems to be a table' would be an *expression* of hesitation to say 'it is a table' and not a *report* of a hesitation. Given this proviso, we have our definition of a mental event:

If there is some person who can have an incorrigible belief in
some statement P which is a report on X, then X is a mental event.
(1970a: 419)

On this account mental features are not mental events, though since
we are nearly incorrigible about them there's a family resemblance.
The required contrast between mental and physical is conceived as
being between that about which we are incorrigible and that about
which we are not, where both are to be thought of in terms of the
linguistic practices of the community. What, then, is the materialist
supposed to conclude from this? Rorty offers two possibilities:

(a) He simply concludes that 'it might turn out that there are no
     entities about which we are incorrigible'. If methods develop
     that allow our sincere reports of our mental-states to be over-
     ridden through the use of cerebroscopes, etc., then mental-
     states will lose their status as *mental*. That is to say, we might
     continue using sensation-talk, but no normative authority
     would devolve to the reporters of such states.
(b) He claims that it might come to pass that we are able to explain
     behaviour 'at least as well' without reference to mental-states/
     features, in which case the latter might disappear from the
     language altogether and brain-process talk be used instead
     (1970a: 421).

Both (a) and (b) would involve changes in our linguistic practices,
but Rorty draws the following conclusion:

(EC) 'Either of these changes would give the "eliminative"
      materialist the right to say that it had been discovered that
      there were no mental entities.' (1970a: 422)

Now this might appear a little odd. If to *be* a mental event is to be
something reported on incorrigibly at t_1, and nothing at t_2 is reported
on in that way, then it seems reasonable to conclude that there *are*
no mental entities at t_2. That, of course, would be to view things
from where we are now – at t_1. But the 'right' of which Rorty talks
is something *acquired* at t_2, the thought being that at t_1 what were
thought to be incorrigible reports weren't in fact incorrigible, because
had the relevant technology been available they would have been
over-ridden. Again, this seems slightly disorientating: if a mental

event is defined not in terms of its in-principle incorrigibility but in term of its in-practice incorrigibility, then the intuition is that at t_1 there *are* mental-states. But the whole point of the explication is to impugn the existence of sensations – as the putative referent of the term 'sensation' – in the way that demon-talk was impugned, not (like a tender-minded anthropologist) to relativize existence to the linguistic practices of a tribe. So how is it to be understood?

Recall that Rorty aims to establish that what people at t_1 call *sensations* might be discovered to be brain-processes. As a result, the referring use of the term 'sensation' *would* (b) or *could* (a) disappear at t_2, thus 'impugning' the existence of sensations as the entities to which the word 'sensation' was supposed to have referred. So the bare notion of such a discovery involves no conceptual confusion if the incorrigibility of mental-states is explicated in terms of their normative standing amongst other linguistic practices. The suggestion, then, is that the specified changes in such practices would constitute (or at least accompany) the discovery that, say, when S said 'I have a sensation of pain' she was reporting on her C-fibres firing because the specifically *mental* content of sensation-talk only ever amounted to a contingent linguistic practice, and that practice has disappeared; and along with it the idea that S was referring to anything other than a brain-process. In other words, what has disappeared is a way of picking out the referent that sowed philosophical confusion because it implied the mental was radically other. To return to the question, then, the way in which it must be understood is that what is referred to at t_1 and t_2 is fixed across the imagined elimination, so that the belief at t_1 about a fixed referent (a brain-state) – *that* it is known incorrigibly – turns out to be false. So t_2 denotes the privileged standpoint from which that fixed referent is established because the relevant purposes are scientific; which is to say that, as with Quine and Sellars, science and not normative linguistic practice is the measure of all things.

5 Troubles with eliminativism

By the time *PMN* appears, Rorty has concluded that (EC) was an 'overdramatized' attempt 'to establish more of a difference between eliminative and reductive materialism than there really is' (*PMN*: 120, fn. 24):

only a philosopher with a lot invested in the notion of 'ontological status' would need to worry about whether a corrigibly reportable pain [see (a) above] was 'really' a pain or rather a stimulated C-fibre. (pp. 120–1)

Only such a philosopher would think there was an answer to the question asked in 1.1: 'Do the Sortians have minds?' The implication is that Rorty came to view his earlier self as having invested unwisely in such ontological stock. In 2.1 I associated this self-diagnosis with a 'turn' in his thinking resulting from having identified the controlling influence of the Realist Attitude. That turn was in part a response to criticisms of Rorty's attempt to distinguish his own brand of materialism from the reductive version. As we'll now see, these criticisms focused on the issues of reference and of the privileging of scientific discourse over other forms of description.

Objections to the in-principle eliminability of the mental tend to fall into two broad categories: the *transcendental*, and the *explanatory*. The *transcendental* objection derives from the Kantian thought that certain concepts are not just central to our world-view; such that their elimination would be inconvenient; but actually constitute in part what would count *as* a world-view. The consequent aim is to demonstrate that a condition of possibility of some concept the eliminativist accepts (like experience or personhood) is one that they doubt (like physical object or mental-state). Accordingly, the eliminativist's sceptical or 'revisionary' suggestions 'amount to a rejection of the whole conceptual scheme within which alone such doubts make sense' (Strawson 1959: 35).[15]

We can neglect responding to this objection here for two reasons. Firstly, MBIPC (p. 175) aspires to lend support to the Quinean claim that since no clear line can be drawn between the empirical and the conceptual, present usage does not insulate our concepts against the influence of future discoveries. Secondly, Rorty contributed a number of articles to the evaluation of transcendental demonstrations (1971, 1979), which we'll discuss in 3.3. Turning to the *explanatory* objection, this has two aspects; one of which is in effect the property problem tailored to suit Rorty's version of materialism. According to Cornman (1968a, 1968b) and Bernstein (1968), the problem is that Rorty subscribes to the following principle:

(W)   The elimination of the referring use of sensation terms in favour of neuro-physiological ones would 'leave our ability to describe and predict undiminished' (MPIBC: 181).

We cannot use neurophysiological sentences to make true descriptions like '*S*'s pain is intense and throbbing'. If, however, *we are in a position* to say that '*S*'s C-fibres are very stimulated' plays the same descriptive role as the sentence that deploys the mentalistic terms 'intense' and 'throbbing', then the physical description has changed its meaning to take on this role. The dilemma is that the elimination of mental-talk *either* leaves us with an impoverished vocabulary *or* alters the physicalistic terms in such a way that '*S*'s C-fibres are very stimulated' now means '*S*'s pain is intense and throbbing'.

Rorty's response to this aspect of the *explanatory* objection relates to the transcendental version. Where the latter claims that we are answerable to the concepts that comprise the inescapable core of any world-view that qualifies *as such*, the charge is that the former makes sense only on the assumption that our language is descriptively answerable to some ineliminable feature of human experience. So Cornman and Bernstein assume the existence of some pre-linguistic given (the intense, throbbing, painfulness of pain) which is what it is independently of our linguistic practices, and to which all possible language games are answerable. From Rorty's Sellarsian perspective, if (like the Sortians) we were trained up to use the neurological correlates of 'intense', 'throbbing', 'pain' and so on, then our experiences would be of things that have *those* properties; they would *not* stand proxy for the inescapable intense, throbbing painfulness of pain.

Cornman (1971: ch. 2) and Bernstein (1968: 206) acknowledge the devastating effect of Sellars's attack on the pre-linguistically given. The real force of their criticism emerges from the second aspect of the explanatory objection and derives from the imputation that, for Rorty, ' "ultimately" *the* legitimate form[s] of description is scientific description' (Bernstein 1968: 220). So, where Rorty sees them as committed to some pre-linguistic given, they take their task as demonstrating that sensation-talk is not an inchoate scientific theory that *could* be replaced by one with greater explanatory power. From this perspective, there is no need to presuppose any experiential given; one merely has to show that Rorty's revisionary suggestion privileges scientific discourse over other vocabularies. Does it? As Bernstein notes (p. 219), while Rorty's adherence to (W) implies the availability of inter-theoretic criteria, at other times he seems to suppose that when one vocabulary displaces another it does so in such a way that the entire descriptive resources of the first go as well. But since this leaves no criteria for inter-theoretic evaluation, it leaves no standpoint from which to assert (W).

Table 2.1 Varieties of materialism

		R(2). Is sensation-talk cognitively respectable? Are sentences of the form 'there are sensations' true?	
		Yes	No
R(4). Do sensations exist?	Yes	Reductive/translation form of Materialism (Smart, Armstrong, Feigl, et al.) (RM)	
	No	Rorty's Weak Eliminative Materialism (WEM)	Quine's/Feyerabend's (1963) Strong Eliminative Materialism (SEM)

This problem is clarified by turning to the criticism that led Rorty to conclude that his materialism didn't differ in kind from the reductionist's. Recall that he holds the following:

(i)   that people have true beliefs (or at least not necessarily false) beliefs when they talk of their sensations; and
(ii) that it might nevertheless turn out that sensations don't exist.

In 'What is Eliminative Materialism?,' Lycan and Pappas argue that Rorty's theory (what they refer to as 'Weak Eliminative Materialism') is inconsistent (see table 2.1). Consider the following:[16]

1   'There are Xs' is true just in case 'X' is a referring term.
2   'Sensations' refers to brain-processes (RM; WEM).
3   Brain-processes exist.
4   'There are sensations' is true (1, 2, 3).
5   'There are sensations' is true just in case sensations exist.
6   Sensations exist (RM; denied by WEM) (4, 5).

While Rorty accepts (4), he wishes to impugn the existence of sensations and deny (6). But (6) is implied by (4) and (5), and (5) seems to follow from (4) and (1) given the familiar truism:

(P)   'X' is a referring term just in case Xs exist.

According to Lycan and Pappas, then, Weak Eliminative Material-ism collapses into Reductive Materialism (RM), and Rorty is left with the need to offer topic-neutral translations.

The *negative* ontological aim of (ii) is to demonstrate that it is *inessential* to suppose that sensation-talk requires *immaterial* refer-ents because *it makes sense* to argue that those referents are brain-states. Moreover, understood aright this is consistent with the intuition that incorrigibility is the criterion of the mental (2.4). To establish the cognitive respectability of sensation-talk, then, Rorty presupposes that there must be some existents that such talk picks out, even if subjects are ignorant of their nature. So it appears that Rorty presupposes a *Realist* conception of reference. Now, in order for one's theory to be an *identity* theory, one must have some crite-rion of identity of reference. As Rorty remarks, 'entities referred to by expressions in one Rylean category may also be referred to by expressions in another . . . [and] expressions in the first category may drop out of the language [be eliminated] once this identity of reference is realized' (MBIPC: 197).

In this light, (W) indicates that the identity of reference is estab-lished in relation to a narrowly circumscribed range of *interests*; principally those relating to our ability to describe and predict, for which the candidate vocabulary is physico-neurological. Of course, if an identity theory is to be a version of *materialism* it is not surpris-ing that this turns out to be the privileged vocabulary: what is materialism if not a commitment to the kind of items that *ought* to be admitted into our ontology? In this respect, what Lycan and Pappas inadvertently reveal is that if one supposes that the identity of reference is fixed by means of a vocabulary that constitutes an ontologically privileged standpoint, then it is natural to suppose that when one refers to something by making true statements that mention it, the thing referred to *exists*. Since (5) is implied by (4) and (1), then insofar as he is a *materialist* Rorty is committed to (6): sen-sations are reduced to brain-states rather than eliminated.

As Bush (1974) shows, the fact that Rorty's materialism is in fact indistinguishable from Smart's does not have the consequences feared, because one obvious way to understand 'What people used to call "the sensation of pain" is the firing of C-fibres' is that it serves to characterize sensations in a topic-neutral way without the need for problematic translations. Consequently, it was open to Rorty to embrace the Realist conception of reference and to assert that what 'sensation' refers to just is what science discovers when it discovers that there aren't any sensations qua *mental* items. Instead he took

Lycan and Pappas's argument as something of a *reductio* of his earlier Realist Attitude, concluding rather that 'the notion of "mind–body" identity . . . should be abandoned' (*PMN*: 119). Bernstein offers a nice summary of the implications of this attitude and its relation to reference:

> in the discussion of scientific materialism . . . most of the attention has been focussed on the issue of reference with an attempt to show how we might plausibly identify the referents of such expressions as 'sensations' and 'certain brain processes,' or to show how expressions that we may think refer to irreducible mental events do not necessarily refer to such events. The motivation behind this approach is the belief that the theory of reference is the key for telling us what there is, or . . . for telling us what are the ontic commitments of a given conceptual scheme. But focussing on the theory of reference can blind us to the important differences in our modes of description and predication, and the significance of these differences for ontology. (1968: 221)

This comes very close to diagnosing the problem as Rorty comes to see it. On the one hand, he wishes to (*negatively*) deflate the philosophical (ontological) significance of our divers linguistic practices, and of proposed changes to them. But to that end he embraces a view of reference that suggests that linguistic reform does have (*positive*) ontological significance; namely, to justify materialism. The moral of Bernstein's (and Cornman's) criticism, then, is that one can establish identity of reference only if one has a prior sense of the lay of the ontological land: the conviction, for example, that materialism is true. Only then would one know what general criteria to apply when asserting identities.[17] But to operate with such a conviction is to blind oneself to the significance of 'modes of description and predication' that fall outside the materialist's domain of interest. Rorty's recognition of this point is central to the 'turn' in his thinking, but there is a further aspect that must be noted: whereas Bernstein takes the significance of differential modes of description (like 'mental' versus 'physical' say) to be ontological, Rorty comes to regard that extra step as egregious. Although he acknowledges that different 'vocabularies' express nonassimilable interests, he takes it that only a continuing commitment to the idea that philosophy nominates the privileged vocabulary – materialist or otherwise – would lead one to conclude that such differences had ontological significance and hence were of philosophical interest.

6   Far, far away, lies . . .

We began chapter 1 with a thought-experiment that combined examples taken from two distinct periods. The aim was to dramatize the change in Rorty's thinking by showing how the analogy drawn between the elimination of demons and sensations requires, in effect, that we simultaneously take up the standpoint of the Terrans when it comes to evaluating demon-talk but of the Sortians when it comes to conceiving of the eliminability of (our; Terran) sensations. This transition between standpoints is eased by assuming that the interests relevant to the evaluation of (Nortian) demon-talk are the same as those relevant to the evaluation of (Terran) sensation-talk: those identified with a physicalist or materialist (Sortian) vocabulary. One obvious response to this is that just as the Nortians might refuse to acknowledge this narrow characterization of demon-talk – insisting on its centrality to Nortian self-understanding, politics, etc. – the Terrans might have similar qualms about such a narrowing of the purposes of sensation-talk. And, in particular, they might have reservations about the supposition that the significance of all such talk is to be understood from the perspective of the concepts required to explain observable behaviour. For the analogy to work then, the materialist vocabulary, expressive of a narrow range of interests, has to be privileged, philosophically, from the outset.

In *PMN* Rorty describes such a view as predicated on the idea that 'philosophy should provide a permanent matrix of categories into which every possible empirical discovery and cultural development can be fitted without strain' (p. 123). From this metaphilosophical perspective, materialism is just an attempt to privilege the set of interests (prediction; control) constitutive of a certain vocabulary (the natural sciences). He does not, however, take that opportunity to reject materialism outright. Indeed, one of the reasons commentators have frequently found the Antipodean chapter (the inspiration for our Sortians) perplexing if not contradictory is the fact that, while acknowledging that whatever sense materialism or physicalism has depends entirely on sharing Terran philosophical prejudices (ibid.), he nevertheless claims that 'the proper reaction to the Antipodean story is to adopt . . . materialism' (ibid.: 119). So how is one to regard *this* materialism?

To approach this question let's take a step backwards and look at how the (eliminativist's) possibility that we might come to speak materialese was thought to constitute a victory for *materialism*. In 2.3 we identified the following key steps:

C'(2)   Sensations = brain-processes.
C'(6)   There are no sensations.

On this account, the stable point C'(2) turns out to be an expression of the *translation* version of the identity theory, one whose need for topic-neutral translations Rorty was aiming to obviate. That is to say, Smart, Armstrong et al. are giving philosophical expression to what are in fact constraints on belief-change: they are, as it were, capturing their thought pragmatically in time. Of course, the time of their thought, the time in which we speak truly of sensations qua brain-states, is not the time from which the grander narrative is constructed. Rorty's account of conceptual change is written from the perspective of the in-principle end of inquiry when it comes to be seen that (for example) 'sensation' does *not* refer. Now the force of the claim that eliminativism supports materialism seems to derive entirely from the supposition that it is from the standpoint of those future practices that the criteria relevant to determining when behaviour is predicted and explained 'at least as well' are to be identified. The thought, presumably, is that if the mental did disappear, then the mental–physical distinction that gave rise to the philosophical controversies involving dualism would also disappear, and materialism would emerge as the victor. But since in 1965 materialism gets its sense from the opposition with dualism, in 2525 materialism would no longer have its contrastive content. So it could only be considered a victory *for* materialism if one exported to that proposed future the present meaning of the word, one that would make no sense at that point in the future. On this synthesis of Quine and Hegel, the privileged materialist standpoint from which we will come to be regarded is a presupposition of the story of conceptual change on offer.

We've lingered sufficiently over the criticisms of Rorty's early materialism. However, in order to appreciate the angle of his response it's important to see how they link up with the tension between what he inherited from Quine (the variation on explication) and what was meant to 'merely' supplement Quine, namely, the analysis of incorrigibility. To summarize briefly, Ryle relativizes the criteria of existence to the relevant stretch of discourse. In order to assert the identity of mental- and physical-states the identity theorist rejects this division by investing the discourse of natural science with ontological privileges. Since this reinstates the difference between ontological categories at the level of properties (requiring topic neutral translations), Rorty's solution was to accept Ryle's division between discourses but, following Quine, deny that it has any grounding in the logic of our language. Instead, taking the lead from Kuhn, the different stretches of discourse (Terran; Sortian) could be lain out along an historico-conceptual (rather than 'logical') axis, and the 'boundaries' between them recast in terms of pragmatic constraints. While this allows that people could say truthfully that they were in pain, the only way to impugn sensations is to ultimately privilege not just a successor 'paradigm' (allowing us to judge the past, but live in fear that we might later be judged likewise) but a single vocabulary furnishing criteria of existence. But if those criteria were always applicable, then although it is *understandable* why people talked of sensations (just as it is *understandable* why people once talked of demons, unicorns and final causes), they nevertheless spoke falsely when they did so.

Turning to Rorty's account of incorrigibility, we see that the analysis of epistemic authority in terms of social practices helps undermine the idea that such authority is built into the logic of our language. As such it supports the idea that people are justified when they speak of sensations. Of course, one can discriminate between speaking justifiably and speaking truthfully (about an existent) if one has at one's disposal a criterion of real existence. But now the migration of epistemic authority into the realm of social practices cuts the other way, because from that perspective the natural way to understand speaking materialese is not as the one true description of things but as moves in a linguistic game, answerable to the same source of normative authority as sensation-talk. For materialism to be 'true', then, it simply has to be the case that one can get away amongst one's peers with speaking materialese; or, to put it another way, with speaking Sortian. And if one speaks materialese then it is (trivially) the case that there aren't and weren't any sensations, just as there aren't and never were any unicorns.

The metaphilosophical significance of eliminativism, then, is that redescription operates at all levels. Crudely put, it is this view that defines Rorty's work after the 'turn'. Once one rejects the idea of a privileged vocabulary in terms of which canonical interests (in 'what there really is', etc.) are expressed, what Quine (and the early

Rorty) thought of as 'explication' – which I associated with the positivists' 'ideal language' – undergoes a radical change. To give it a slogan, 'explication is redescription'. As with explication, explication-redescribed linguistic revisions are advanced on the basis of interests identified from 'where one is', but those interests are no longer expressive of a philosophically privileged vocabulary. They are recommendations for ways of talking, the promise of which is that they will conduce better to those interests than present ways of talking. On this basis, then, the materialism advocated in *PMN* and elsewhere[18] can be thought of as a redescription to suit the narrow purposes or interests that the materialist (qua metaphysician) took to be exhaustive (and therefore the tip-off to ontological privilege).

Now, a relatively quiescent materialism like this is adopted on the basis that no philosophical victory has been marked; which is to say that no metaphysical struggle is undergone. And yet the debate about sensations is supposed to stand proxy for something of considerable philosophical importance. Just as, in our fleshed-out version of the Nortian example, demon-talk was taken to be deeply culturally embedded, and not a mere place-holder for some neuro-scientific concept, Terran sensation-talk is meant to reveal something profound about the nature of consciousness, about what it is to be human. For Rorty, then, the quiet adoption of this 'local' materialism requires that our view of sensations be detached from a philosophical picture that holds us (all of us,[19] not just philosophers) captive; a picture according to which consciousness is linked to reason and personhood through the concept of mind as the great mirror of nature.

That greater task is the purpose of *PMN*. What recommends it as a redescription is that it promises to free 'our' interests from the restrictions placed upon them by an historically constituted and overweening concept of mind. We'll examine that redescription and to whom it is addressed in chapter 4, when we take up the general question of how 'interests' intersect with the general sweep of Rorty's thoughts about the nature and purpose of philosophy. There is, however, a preliminary task. The reason *we* cannot answer the question 'Do the Sortians have minds?' is because to do so either:

(i) presupposes the appropriate philosophical picture according to which Sortians have minds (because they make incorrigible reports); or

(ii) involves adopting another philosophical picture according to which the question makes no sense.

The choice here proceeds from 'needless usages' because the philosophical picture itself is not neutrally identifiable: it too comprises a set of linguistic practices authorizing certain moves in the game. To recommend a standpoint from which the mirror of nature imagery no longer holds us captive requires an alternative philosophical view. Whether or not this is rightly called 'materialism' or 'physicalism',[20] for Rorty, post-*Kehre*, it involves a (radical) redescription of the concepts that characterize the Realist Attitude. As we'll see in the next chapter, this articulation of what Rorty regards as pragmatism begins with a redescription of reference, and naturally extends itself to a redescription of the concept of truth.

3

Rorty's Kehre

1 Introduction

By the time *PMN* appears Rorty has abandoned the idea that the possibility of linguistic reform of the sort envisaged by eliminativism lends *positive* metaphysical support to the doctrine of materialism. As he comes to see, ontologically speaking the point of the exercise is primarily *negative*: both versions of the identity theory presuppose a certain 'picture' of the nature of concept change that needs to be excavated and 'eliminated':

> the reductive and eliminative versions of the identity theory are both merely awkward attempts to throw into current philosophical jargon our natural reaction to an encounter with the [Sortians] . . . they should both be abandoned, and with them the notion of the mind–body identity. (*PMN*: 119)

The picture elaborated in the 'current philosophical jargon' is the central target of *PMN* and is associated primarily with the assumption that some philosophical reassurance is needed that our thoughts or language make contact with the world. This diagnosis is not entirely absent from Rorty's early work: in MBIPC the view that we have infallible knowledge of the contents of our own minds is traced to the intuition that some items must present an absolute epistemological authority if we are to combat the sceptic.[1] However, the significance of his retreat from materialism concerns the extent to which this epistemologically fixated 'picture' comes to be seen as all-pervasive in its effects on both philosophical thinking and Western culture. Insofar as this fear of the 'loss' of the world can be associated with one philosophical idea it is with the scheme–content dualism diagnosed by Davidson as the 'third' dogma of empiricism, and redescriptions of Davidson's work figure centrally in Rorty's reformulation of the philosophical 'basis' of pragmatism.

We will discuss this in 3.3, but first another aspect of this idea of a 'picture' holding a thinker captive needs remarking; namely, the extent (implicit in the quote above) that Rorty's defence of materialism was itself caught up in the 'current philosophical jargon'. In 2.1 I suggested that the change in Rorty's thinking during the early 1970s constitutes something of a *Kehre*,[2] wherein the self-diagnosis of conflicting elements in his early attempt to 'defend' materialism leads him to isolate and reject the controlling influence of this 'jargon' on his articulation of the identity theory. Not unusually, this self-critique of what I called the Realist Attitude took the form of a critique of others, and focused initially on the use made of one particular item of philosophical jargon, the concept of *reference*. Rorty's redescriptive efforts on this topic are important for understanding both his interest in Davidson and his views on truth and on the utility of philosophical inquiry. The task of this chapter, then, is to show how Rorty's pragmatism relates to his attempt to offer revisionary accounts of the concepts that constitute the philosophical jargon and thereby undermine the appeal of that seductive 'picture'.

2   Realism and reference

As we saw in 2.5, Lycan and Pappas inadvertently demonstrate that if one adopts something like the Realist Attitude and assume that reference is fixed from the standpoint of a privileged vocabulary, the intuition is that one can refer only to existents. That is to say, Rorty appears to be committed to the following principle:

(P)   'X' is a referring term just in case Xs exist.

Adopting (P), however, undermines the purported uniqueness of the *eliminativist* version of the identity theory.

In a paradigm of what becomes his philosophical method, Rorty's response is distinguish between three different uses of reference (Rorty 1976). Reference$_1$ captures the 'casual' usage of the word, in which to refer to something is to 'talk about' it. In this sense, Nortian reference$_1$ to demons is on a par with our reference$_1$ to molecules, Mr Jarndyce, sensations and justice. In each case, *what* is referred$_1$ to depends on what speakers intend by their words, so the best way of finding out what they are talking about is to ask them. Opposing this is reference$_3$, according to which one can only refer$_3$ to what *exists*. Finally, there is reference$_2$, which can be glossed as 'really talking about' (*PMN*: 290 ff.), and which is used heuristically to comment on conceptual change. The principal difference is that, since one can refer$_1$ to items that are (uncontroversially) non-existent as well as to items that are (equally uncontroversially) existent, what one is 'talking about' is determined by what most of one's justified beliefs are about. Regarding reference$_3$, then, the order of existence (the World, as it were) determines the truth-values of our beliefs or sentences; in the case of reference$_1$ the world just is 'whatever most of our beliefs are true of' (*PMN*: 289).

To highlight the difference between reference$_2$ and reference$_3$, recall Lycan and Pappas's argument from chapter 2.

1   'There are Xs' is true just in case 'X' is a referring term.
2   'Sensations' refers to brain-processes (RM; WEM).
3   Brain-processes exist.
4   'There are sensations' is true.
5   'There are sensations' is true just in case sensations exist.
6   Sensations exist (RM; denied by WEM).

Given Rorty's rubric, premise (2) can be given two interpretations:

2'   'Sensations' refers$_2$ to brain-processes.
2"   'Sensations' refers$_3$ to brain-processes.

The gloss on (2") is that since one can refer$_3$ only to what *exists*, the existent picked out by the word 'sensation' is a brain-process, and as a consequence any truths involving the latter are 'exportable' to the former. If the brain-process possesses a property φ ('brain-process α is φ' is true), then, one can deduce the truth of 'sensation β is φ'. The gloss on (2') is that even though one is *really* talking about brain-processes, truths about these are not 'exportable' to sensation-talk. So, from the fact that a brain-process α possesses a property φ, one *cannot* deduce the truth of 'sensation β is φ'. Crucially, then, when people are talking about (referring$_1$ to) sensations, the truth or falsity of their statements is not evaluable in terms of what they are discovered subsequently to have been 'really talking about'.[3]

Now, if we cannot make truth-evaluations on the grounds of what someone is 'really talking about' then there can be no assertion of *strict* identity. Reference$_2$ is heuristic in the sense that (2′) amounts to the suggestion that a group of people stop using sensation-talk and use brain-process talk instead. That is to say, where the use of reference$_3$ presupposes the availability of strict criteria for determining a *philosophically significant* mode of existence, reference$_2$ does not. From this it follows that Lycan and Pappas presuppose that the only use of reference available is reference$_3$. The reason WEM collapses into RM is because (2″) is based on (P), which necessitates the conclusion that sensations *exist*. Rorty's suggestion, then, is that when we reject reference$_3$ we reject the idea that sensation-talk is justified in the light of the independently specifiable existence of *sensations*, and see that the *only* criterion for common-sense existence is that there is *justified* sensation-talk. Of course, justification here is construed along the lines of the analysis of incorrigibility, where the governing norms are understood in terms of pragmatically constrained social practices. To suggest that what people call 'sensations' might turn out to be brain-processes does not imply that 'sensation' fails to refer$_3$; rather, since common-sense existence is determined by justified usage, the dropping of sensation-talk (in favour of brain-process talk) *just is* the elimination of sensations. In mildly Kuhnian terms, any displacement of the (Terran) 'sensation paradigm' with the (Sortian) 'neural paradigm' would connote, not the ontological victory of the latter but (merely) its pragmatic advantage.

It is part of Rorty's diagnostic project that the *fear* of epistemological scepticism – of losing our grip on the world – motivates the *philosophical* use of reference. The 'redescription' of the term is intended to demonstrate that reference$_1$ and reference$_2$ can be used to say any of the *non*-metaphysical things we want to say, thus avoiding both Realism and scepticism. Having remarked how reference$_2$ is supposed to explicate conceptual change – and the temptation to go beyond it to reference$_3$ – let's turn briefly to one of the reasons philosophers have thought that reference$_3$ was needed to supplement reference$_1$, instead of adverting to reference$_2$. On the 'casual' account one's beliefs determine what one refers$_1$ to. So, for example, if someone thinks that Hillary Clinton is the wife of the former President, Senator for New York, the mother of Chelsea and a qualified lawyer (that is to say, that is what she *intends* by 'Hillary

Clinton'), then when she uses the name 'Hillary Clinton' she's refer-
ring$_1$ to the person of whom (most of) those things are true, and if
you want to know who she's talking about when she says 'Hillary
Clinton' the best strategy is to find out what those beliefs are. The
problem is that in *certain* cases it turns out that the speaker is not
in fact the best person to ask if you want to find out what she's
talking about (referring$_1$ to). If Rachel says she met Hillary Clinton
at a party the previous evening and you have good reasons for
thinking that unlikely, you might conclude that the person she was
really talking about was not Hillary Clinton but Hillary Plinton,
someone you know to have been at the party.

The gloss that some philosophers[4] have put on this sort of analysis is that Rachel was in fact referring$_3$ to Ms Plinton when she
thought she was referring$_3$ to Ms Clinton. That is to say, her statement to the effect that 'Hillary Clinton has luxuriant black hair'
expresses a *true* belief about Ms Plinton, not a *false* belief about Ms
Clinton. This restores the connection between her beliefs and the
world by establishing their proper reference$_3$; namely, the person
who actually gave rise to them.[5] Consider another example: let's
imagine that the adventures of the fictional character Indiana Jones
are based very closely on the real-life exploits of one Mark Miner.
One can imagine the headlines: 'English academic is *the real* Indie!'
Now presumably there is no confusion here: we would take it that
'Indiana Jones' refers$_1$ to the adventure-strip hero and 'Mark Miner'
to the dotty don. Now imagine the situation in (say) 500 years' time,
when the roles of fact and fiction have become confused and the
real-life exploits of Mark Miner are attributed to Indiana Jones
(Mark being long forgotten). Would we say that 'Indiana Jones'
refers$_3$ to Mark Miner, because he did most if not all of the things
attributed to the fictional character, or that 'Indiana Jones' can't
refer$_3$ to anything because he never existed?

Rorty's diagnosis is that only a background concern with ensuring that beliefs or language hook on to the World would incline one
to analyse these abnormal occurrences in this way. In the case of
the two Hillarys, the common-sense approach is to advert not to
reference$_3$ but to reference$_2$. We can maintain that when Rachel
refers$_1$ to Hillary Clinton she's *really* talking about (referring$_2$ to)
Hillary Plinton. That is to say, her remark about Clinton relies on
the existence of Plinton, but is not truth-evaluable in Plinton terms.
The procedure is heuristic insofar as it tells us how we should go
about dealing with someone who says odd things. We don't conclude that what Rachel says is true because she's *really really* talking

about (referring$_3$ to) Plinton, who does have black hair; rather, we instruct her to drop Clinton-talk and join us in Plinton-talk, which is going to be much more useful when it comes to discussing what happened at the party. Likewise, in the case of Indie, Rorty's thought is that we can split the difference and keep things at the reference$_1$ level. We can say that 'Indiana Jones' refers$_1$ to Indiana Jones (the fictional character) and 'Mark Miner' refers$_1$ to the forsaken scholar. If it's the historical exploits themselves that are important, then as with the Hillarys we can fall back on reference$_2$ and suggest that people stop talking about Indiana Jones and talk about Mark Miner instead, because in that context that's what Indie-talk is *really* about.

It is important to note that in these 'abnormal' examples the move towards a philosophical account of reference$_3$ – one that ensures thoughts latch on to the World – is driven by an epistemological asymmetry between different standpoints: 'when we know something that [others] don't' (*PMN*: 289). Rorty's analyses are intended to show that the epistemological issues (the particular asymmetries) they raise can be handled by the 'casual' and 'heuristic' uses of 'reference' without encouraging the adoption of the Realist Attitude. Of course, the more challenging question is why such a temptation persists; and to understand Rorty's response one must recall that these examples, like the eliminativist's approach to sensations, represent the more general problem of conceptual change. In this bigger picture, the concern is with how we regard the cognitive achievements of our predecessors; and in particular how these more general cases of 'our' knowing something that 'they' don't know relate to our understanding of our own cognitive achievements. The intuitive view (Rorty 1976: 321) here is that while they pursued their inquiries with honesty and diligence, and were thus justified by their own lights, nevertheless numerous things that they thought existed turned out not to, and (as a result or cause) many of their beliefs were false. However, this distinction between justification and truth provokes a problem: if *their* beliefs were merely justified and not true; and, as a cause or consequence, *they* were wrong about what sorts of things exist; then when and how did *we* come to get things right about the way the World really is? Moreover, if no satisfactory answer is forthcoming, how do we know that we're anything other than *merely* justified in believing what we do, and that what we as a cause or consequence take to exist really does? How do we know that our own thoughts or beliefs make contact with the World? On this characterization we can see RM and SEM as exemplifying two possible responses: either our predecessors referred$_3$ to what we do, but had mostly false beliefs about it; or they failed to refer$_3$ at all because the things *they* talked about don't exist. In each case the danger that *we* fail to make contact with the world is ruled out by privileging the one (materialist) vocabulary that *is* taken to refer$_3$.

On Rorty's diagnosis it is the sort of epistemological picture that dramatizes the possibility that our thinking *could* fail to hook on to the World that impels us towards the view that the truth of our beliefs is measured by our success or failure to refer$_3$ to it. The implication is that there's something vertiginous about contemplating the vast conceptual changes that have taken place in the West, and the differing ways in which people elsewhere conceive of the world. This induced sense of epistemic fragility inspires the fear that our thinking as a whole might simply get the world wrong; but also the conviction that a standpoint on our beliefs *as a whole* is required to obtain the reassurance we crave. In brief, then, the view Rorty develops from his critique of materialism – including his own – is that the attempt to understand the plasticity or revisability of our concepts in the light of our ongoing (causal) encounters with the world finds itself situated in the classically Cartesian debate about whether the World is or is not within our cognitive reach, and that both doubts and assurances to that effect presuppose that a 'god's-eye' (Putnam 1981), or 'side-ways on' (McDowell 1994) view of our beliefs is available to the philosopher. The invocation of reference$_3$ is just one attempt on the part of the philosopher to overcome the *fear* of epistemological scepticism – of losing our grip on the world – by adopting something like the Realist Attitude.

We'll return to this larger topic in chapter 4, but for the time being let's focus on aspects of Rorty's initial 'turn' that relate to the rejection of the Realist Attitude and to the redescription of the philosophical concepts (like reference$_3$) that underpin it. Evidently a great deal here turns on the extent to which truth and justification can be understood in a way that neither threatens scepticism nor tempts Realism. Since much criticism of Rorty's work centres on the way he deals with these concepts we need to proceed circumspectly. To that end, recall for a final time Lycan and Pappas's argument. In effect, Rorty rejects the temptation to invoke reference$_3$ by rewriting

1   'There are Xs' is true just in case 'X' is a referring$_3$ term, as
1'   'There are Xs' is justified just in case 'X' is a referring$_1$ term.

According to Rorty, 'on this pragmatical view, "truth" would just mean "What ought to be believed"' (1976: 322). This 'relaxed and unphilosophical view' (ibid.: 323) presents no problem when characterizing the errors of our ancestors: what they believed was justified by their lights, and thus (by that measure) *true*. Moreover, since existence-qua-reference$_1$ is indexed to the justificatory practices of a time and place, what their mostly true beliefs are of is what comprises the world. Since our beliefs are subject to the same epistemic criterion, when we convict them of holding false beliefs we are not judging them to have failed where we have been successful; namely, in refering$_3$ to the World. Rather, we are judging their beliefs by our own (better) epistemic criteria and finding them wanting, wherein lies the content of the claim that 'we' know more than 'they'. So *we* can say to the Nortians that demons don't exist; but this is because (common-sense) existence is fixed by *our* standards of justification, not by our having (finally) referred$_3$ to what they failed to refer$_3$ to; and the same goes in the case of a Sortian victory over the Terrans concerning sensation-talk.

This seems like a quick fix against scepticism: if truth *means* justification then the traditional sceptical attempt to drive a wedge between justification ('it looks like a chair') and truth ('but I might be an envatted brain') becomes otiose.[6] However, if we cannot go beyond existence-for-us to really real *existence*, nor beyond justified-for-us to *truth*; that is to say, if denials/affirmations of existence are to be explicated in terms of what is and what is not 'justified by our lights'; then we seem to be left with relativism. In this context scepticism and relativism are flip sides of the same coin. The thought that truth transcends our practices of justification – that it is a property of beliefs or sentences that refer$_3$ – seems to endanger our grip on the world; but epistemically deflating truth to justification implies that there may be coherent but incompatible ways of conceptualizing the world. As a result, truth is relativized to the particular world-view one occupies and we appear to be left with no rational basis for favouring it over another.

Nothwithstanding the problem of relativism, any attempt to *define* truth in terms of justification or warranted assertibility confronts the fact that the following seems to make perfect sense:

(Z) S might be perfectly justified/warranted in believing/ asserting that P and we cannot imagine any way of challenging P, but nevertheless P might not be true.[7]

This challenges the view of truth at the heart of classical pragmatism, imputing to it a version of the 'naturalistic fallacy' in ethics. Although Rorty flirted with the (related) idea of analysing truth along Peircean lines (as 'that to which inquiry will converge' (*CP*: xlv, fn.25), by 1976 the retreat from such a view is well under way. Since justification 'is relative to time and place, and truth is not' (ibid.: 322–3), the meaning of truth per se is not taken to be 'what ought to be believed'. Indeed, he observes that one should resist 'the temptation to offer a definition of truth' (p. 336). Given his militancy against Realism, whatever motivates the claim that 'there is no special relationship between justification and truth' it is clearly not the desire to place truth beyond our grasp. However, if truth is not 'relative to time and place' *because* it 'is a relation to something unchanging out there' (p. 322), more needs to be said about why truth-talk cannot be wholly assimilated to justification and consequently why we have good reasons for rejecting relativism (*without* reinstating scepticism).

Although Rorty discusses truth in *PMN* (pp. 295–311), the fullest statement of his views is in 'Pragmatism, Davidson and Truth'.[8] This paper aims to redescribe the pragmatical view of truth so that it no longer involves a commitment to a *positive* account (as, say, warranted assertibility) but operates merely *negatively*:

> We can . . . isolate a sense for the term 'pragmatism' which will consist *simply* in the dissolution of the traditional problematic about truth. (*ORT*: 127)

The attempt to 'eliminate' the assumption that the truth of a belief *explains* its success is one of the defining ideas of *neo*-pragmatism. For Rorty the idea that 'truth' has an explanatory use is intimately connected to the rejection of what Davidson calls 'the third dogma of empiricism', the distinction between scheme and content:

> The picture . . . of disparate ontological realms, one containing beliefs and the other non-beliefs . . . [which] permits us to imagine truth as a relation between particular beliefs and particular non-beliefs which (a) is non-causal in nature, and (b) must be 'correctly analyzed' before one can rebut (or concede victory to) the epistemological skeptic. (*ORT*: 129)

Acceptance of some version of the scheme–content distinction approximates to the Realist Attitude, and it should be evident how it features in Rorty's response to the threat of relativism. The classical pragmatist analysis of truth as justification is motivated by the threat of scepticism, but its adoption invites relativism. Since, for Rorty, adherence to some version of the scheme–content distinction makes scepticism intelligible, the task becomes clear; namely, to offer a redescription of the 'uses' of 'truth' that satisfies two requirements:

(1) It undercuts the scheme–content distinction, rendering the standpoint from which *both expressions and rebuttals* of scepticism look less attractive. The bonus here is that if one can avoid the need for an epistemic analysis of truth, the temptation towards relativism is obviated.
(2) It offers some diagnostic insight into – or a new way of thinking about – the sources of the appeal of (Z).

The burden of (1) devolves to Rorty's interpretation of Davidson's attack on the scheme–content distinction, which he winningly entitles 'a transcendental argument to end all transcendental arguments' (1979: 78). The upshot of this is that since we must regard most of anyone's beliefs as true, evaluating concept change is just a matter of evaluating the small area of a subject or culture's beliefs that we find unjustified by our lights. Since this does not bring into question the global validity of their (and, by extension, our) beliefs, scepticism and relativism do not arise. This will be the topic of 2.3.

Turning to (2), let's look briefly at Rorty's account of the 'uses' of truth. The aim, recall, is to deflate the *philosophical* assumption that the truth of a belief *explains* its success: a view suggesting a correspondence relation between words and World (reference$_3$). His suggestion is that 'true' has three uses:[9] the *endorsing*, the *cautionary* and the *metalinguistic* (*ORT*: 128). Although Rorty makes no such association, these mirror nicely his treatment of 'reference' so I'll add subscripts, as shown in table 3.1.

The disquotational use of 'truth' has a precise technical use and should be excluded from epistemological considerations for fear of polluting them with dogmatic Realist metaphysics.[10] As with reference, the thought is that truth$_1$ and truth$_2$ can handle any real-life cases without inviting a questionable metaphysical use of truth$_3$, which would explain the success of beliefs that refer$_3$ to the World. Although (1″) might look a little odd, it should hopefully be clear how reference$_2$ and truth$_2$ go together. The possibility that future inquirers might eliminate some entity that we presently take to exist

Table 3.1 Truth and reference

Reference$_1$	Truth$_1$ *Endorsing* or commending (normative) use, relating to what people can 'warrantedly assert'. The sense in which 'true' *means* justified, and in which beliefs are 'rules for action'	Normal use: (1') 'There are Xs' is true$_1$ just in case 'X' is a referring$_1$ term
Reference$_2$	Truth$_2$ *Cautionary* use. Used in sentences like 'You are perfectly justified in believing that P but it might not be true' (P is true$_1$ but it might not be true$_2$)	In cases of conceptual difference/elimination: (1") 'There are Xs' is true$_2$ just in case 'X' is a referring$_2$ term
Reference$_3$	Truth$_3$ *Disquotational* use. Used in sentences like 'P' is true iff _____.	'Pure' philosophical use: (1''') 'There are Xs' is true$_3$ just in case 'X' is a referring$_3$ term

(and about which we have justified beliefs) suggests that what they *might* say to us is what we say to ourselves when we remind ourselves that our justified beliefs (true$_1$) might turn out to be false. In other words, rather than (Z) drawing attention to the justification-transcendence of truth,

(Z')   P is justified doesn't imply P is true$_3$,

we get the deflated version,

(Z")   P is true$_1$ doesn't imply P is true$_2$.

The cautionary use reminds us that just as we deprecate the demon-beliefs of the Nortians because we are 'better at coping with the irradiations' (1976: 323) than they, some Sortian might come along and ride roughshod over our own cherished beliefs. Of course, that won't be because they have discovered the truth$_3$ through identifying the 'ideal' vocabulary of representation, or by inhabiting the end of inquiry. Pragmatically speaking, then, to envisage such a possibility is simply to conceive of a concrete community of inquirers whose beliefs have been modified 'in the interest of greater predictive power, charm, or what have you . . . [which is] philosophically innocuous' (*CP*: 12–13).

This view of concept change or difference is held to be 'philosophically innocuous' because it is thought not to engender fears of relativism or scepticism: for Nortian, Sortian and Terran alike, most of our beliefs are true. This last point takes us back to Davidson again, so it's worth pointing out now a further aspect of his significance for neo-pragmatism. It was noted above that Rorty's treatment of the problem of reference is paradigmatic. The extent to which this is the case becomes clear if one observes that, metaphilosophically speaking, the deflation of substantive (Realist) reference$_3$ amounts to the following *eliminative* suggestion:

(Y″)   When you talk about reference$_3$ you're really talking about (referring$_2$ to) reference$_1$.

Like (Nortian) demon-talk, then, reference$_3$-talk can be regarded as part of a larger set of descriptive practices. These belong to an epistemologically centred philosophy that sees *how* our minds make contact with the world as problematic, and consequently ourselves as in need of philosophical reassurance. Viewing reference$_1$ and reference$_2$ as adequate devices for understanding concept change (and the 'abnormal' cases) goes part-way towards replacing that conception of philosophy's purpose. The task is to offer explications of the concepts that underpin the (old) picture in order to eliminate them in favour of those that conduce better to specified purposes. From this perspective we can see why eliminativism is a dialectically unstable form of materialism, and offer a speedy characterization of Rorty's *Kehre*. In the early work, Rorty was aware that revisionary suggestions made now oughtn't to be evaluated from the standpoint of *present* practices, because if those suggestions were taken up the normative standpoint would change. The options, then, are either:

(A)   Offer an account of conceptual change in terms that don't lose their specificity; or
(B)   Offer an account of conceptual change in terms that are themselves offered in a revisionary manner.

MBIPC propounds a version of (A) using an inter-paradigm (Realist) account of reference, which renders Rorty's position functionally indistinct from Reductive Materialism. The 'turn', then, was towards the adoption of (B) as a strategy: an appreciation of the fact that what require redescription or elimination are the concepts that comprise the underlying 'picture that holds us captive'. We could, for example, write:

(U″)   'There's no such thing as the truth$_3$ and that's the truth$_1$'.[11]

The concepts we use to determine what concept change consists in are themselves targets for revision, and such revisions have to be judged from the perspective of the revised standpoint.

Much will turn here on what content we can give to this revised standpoint. If Rorty is to say more than just 'Lo, look at things the way I recommend and you'll see that right now I'm right!', there has to be a strong sense that the interests and purposes we value here and now are to be well served by that recommendation. This is an exacting requirement when the recommendation in question relates to the very concepts (truth; reference) that (under the influence of Realism, perhaps) we ordinarily use to *evaluate* such recommendations.

We'll examine what interests Rorty has in mind, together with associated criticisms, in chapters 5 and 6. It is now time to return to (1), which turns on Rorty's attempt to bring Davidson into the big pragmatist tent. Rorty's *assimilation* of Davidson's views on language and truth become central to his thinking from the early 1970s onwards. Since his interpretation of Davidson's work is contested, the extent to which the neo-pragmatist project hinges on its coherence is significant. With that in mind, let's look at how Rorty aims to use Davidson to avoid the horns of the relativism–scepticism dilemma.

3   Scepticism, relativism, truth

In 3.2 I indicated that, for Rorty, relativism is the result of the pragmatist's attempt to rescue the normativity of belief from the threat of epistemological scepticism by *analysing* truth as justification. His view is that a prior commitment to Davidson's third dogma of empiricism (the dualism of scheme and content) is required to dramatize such a threat, and to motivate the conviction that the normativity of beliefs has to be *explained* in terms of their truth₃. Without it the pragmatist needn't offer an analysis of truth, remaining satisfied with assembling non-metaphysical reminders of how the word 'true' is used to justify ourselves to others. As noted, Rorty's slogan for his appropriation of Davidson's work in this area is his proposal that 'On the Very Idea of a Conceptual Scheme' offers 'a transcendental argument to end all transcendental arguments'.

To see how this paradox-mongering maxim ties in with the foregoing, recall that what is under consideration is conceptual relativism: the idea that there might be innumerable internally consistent ways of 'carving up', 'interpreting' or 'experiencing' the world. Importantly, the key feature in each of these is of a 'scheme' that constitutes or defines the world-as-it-is-experienced: 'Reality itself is relative to a scheme: what counts as real in one system may not in another' (Davidson 2001a: 183). In this sense 'the dominant metaphor of conceptual relativism [is] that of different points of view' (p. 184): to *have* a 'world' is to occupy or possess (or perhaps even be trapped in) a scheme. Accordingly, the possibility that the concepts of one scheme could be deployed outside that scheme to criticize those of another – to say, for example, what is really real or true – is rendered senseless.

In this paper Davidson sets himself the task of demonstrating that, although 'a heady and exotic doctrine' (p. 183), conceptual relativism relies on a series of metaphors that cannot be cashed out. To demonstrate this, he suggests that a necessary condition for the intelligibility of the idea of alternative conceptual schemes (p. 190) is of a language that we cannot translate, and then goes on to consider the possibilities of complete and partial *failures* to do so. Making sense of such failures is associated with the possibility of adverting to a standard of reference against which to give content to the idea of an *alternative* scheme. Davidson's strategy is to deny the intelligibility of such a standard, and thereby the possibility of a standpoint outside language from which a failure to translate – and hence the 'scheme concept' – could be articulated.

In the case of a complete failure of translation, the standard of reference is the world or experience (some 'given'), 'a fixed stock of meanings' or 'a theory-neutral reality' (p. 195), and a language is seen as something which stands in relation to it (p. 191). This, then, is the third dogma of empiricism: 'the dualism of scheme and content, of organizing system and something waiting to be organized' (p. 189). To make this distinction intelligible, Davidson argues, we must clarify the relationship between the terms, which requires getting outside our theory or language in order to see if it *organizes* or *fits* as proposed. If, on the one hand, we think of language as *organizing* the given (be it experience or objects), we seem to require the individuating resources (predicates, quantifiers, variables, etc.) of our *own* language (pp. 192–3), and the criterion of language we are seeking is one that *does not* depend on translatability. On the other hand, if we think of language as *fitting* the world, we re-encounter the Quinean position outlined in 1.3:

> A sentence or theory fits our sensory promptings . . . or copes with the pattern of our surface irritations, provided it is borne out by the evidence. (p. 193)

For Davidson this presupposes that surface irritations, as intermediaries between beliefs and world, can play an evidential role in the justification of beliefs as well as a causal role in their formation (p. 194). Although Quine dismisses the idea that one can distinguish between sentences true in virtue of meaning alone, he nevertheless cleaves to the view that we can hold constant (as a standard) the contribution of the world (the empirical content), and conceive of the scheme as organizing it in different ways. In this regard, the scheme–content distinction is for Davidson the foundational dogma of empiricism, making the dogmas of reductionism and the analytic–synthetic distinction possible. As the diagnosis of Quine's position makes clear, then, a rejection of the latter is not in itself sufficient to remedy the relativistic and sceptical failings of empiricism.

If we cannot make sense of language 'fitting' something, because we cannot make sense of a something (the given) *making* our sentences true, can we nevertheless make sense of a conceptual scheme being (largely) true and yet not translatable? To put it more pointedly, can we detach the concept of truth from the concepts of translatability or interpretability? It is at this juncture that Davidson invokes Tarski's Convention T, expressed in such theses as:

> (T)   'Snow is white', spoken by an English speaker, is true just in case snow is white.

For Davidson, Convention T 'embodies our best intuition as to how the concept of truth is used'. Since it makes 'essential use of the notion of translation' (p. 195), he can find no support for the idea of a conceptual scheme in the suggestion that there might be (say) sets of truths that are a priori beyond our comprehension (i.e. untranslatable). In the case of a partial failure of translation, then, the standard of reference turns on the possibility of an overlap between schemes *against which* divergences can be made intelligible (p. 197). The previous challenge was to make sense of a language that did not involve translation, which required a 'given' standing distinct from the organizing or fitting scheme. The object now is to make sense of the overlap by formulating a theory of translation or interpretation that makes *no* assumptions about shared concepts, beliefs or meanings, since this is potentially the common part required.

Central to this part of the argument is the idea of a 'radical interpreter' trying to understand an unfamiliar language. The problem is that 'Meaning and belief play interlocking and complementary roles in the interpretation of speech' (p. 141). The attribution of beliefs and the interpretation of sentences are interdependent aspects of interpretation: we cannot imagine making sense of a speaker's utterances without knowing a great deal about what his beliefs are, any more than we can imagine finely individuating his beliefs without knowing what many of his words mean (p. 195). What the radical interpreter needs, then, is some way into the system that avoids the putative circularity of presupposing access to either. Davidson's suggestion, following Quine, is the notion of 'prompted assent' (cf. 1986: 315): looking at those occasions when what the speaker says seems causally linked to worldly saliences (saying 'that's a rabbit' in the presence of rabbits, for example).

Applying this method, we have to suppose that the speaker is expressing a genuine desire to communicate, and holds or accepts as true the sentences they assent to. This tells us nothing specific about the attitudes the speaker expresses, or about his beliefs: *if*, for example, I know in advance that the speaker *believes* that rabbits are brown, have long ears and go hoppety-hop, I can hazard that when, in the presence of a brown, long-eared hoppety-hopper they say 'that's a rabbit' (or 'grqaesf gsttawer'), I should interpret their sentence accordingly. But the fact that they say 'there's a rabbit' with a sober and sincere look on their face does not by itself advance the radical interpreter's project.

So what does? In short, the answer is that we must assign 'to sentences of a speaker conditions of truth that actually obtain (in our own opinion) just when the speaker holds those sentences true' (Davidson 2001a: 196). According to what is sometimes called the 'principle of charity' the assumption that we must count our subjects 'right in most matters' (p. 197) is built into the radical interpreter's pursuit of a theory of truth for a language at the ground-floor level. Charity, then, 'is not an option' but 'is forced on us; whether we like it or not' (ibid.). It is a condition of possibility of the task of radical interpretation; one that issues from the nature of belief:

> a belief is identified by its location in a pattern of beliefs; it is this pattern that determines the subject matter of a belief, what the belief is about. Before some object in, or aspect of, the world can become part of the subject matter of a belief (true or false) there must be endless true beliefs about the subject matter. (2001a: 168)

This does not imply that the interpreter cannot view their subjects as having false beliefs; rather, we can only begin to make these finer discriminations having supposed a shared 'background of largely unmentioned and unquestioned true beliefs' (p. 168). This, then, extends naturally to the case of conceptual relativism: since disagreements can only be brought into sharp focus against a backdrop of shared belief, the concepts required to maximize such agreement are likewise read into the linguistic performances of the interepreter's subjects. But this just means that lacking a criterion for distinguishing a disagreement arising from a difference in belief from one arising from a difference in concepts (meanings), the possibility of dramatizing the idea of alternative conceptual schemes by reference to a common core is similarly unmotivated. Since we can make sense of the idea of *alternative* conceptual schemes neither by complete nor by partial failures of translation, we have failed to make the idea of a conceptual scheme per se intelligible (p. 198).

To deny that one can make sense of the dualism of scheme and content is to deny the possibility of a standpoint other than that of the radical interpreter. The notion of a world 'outside all schemes and science' (ibid.) is unintelligible, and consequently so is the idea of conceptual relativism. The 'world' in this sense is one that, in his earliest response to Davidson's work, Rorty described as 'Well Lost' (*CP*: 3–18): the World Realist philosophers claim our true beliefs 'represent', or 'correspond' or refer$_3$ to. A word of warning, however: for Davidson the concept of truth that we are left with after we dispose of the scheme–content distinction is 'objective truth' (Davidson 2001a: 198) not something equivalent to truth$_1$. The Davidsonian conclusion that 'most of our beliefs must be true' is for Rorty the conclusion that most of our beliefs must be true$_1$; that is to say, justified by our lights. This is the crucial difference between Rorty and Davidson, and although it will not come centre-stage until chapter 6 it's worth saying a little about it now, since it illustrates their respective attitudes to scepticism.

Consider what seems to be an obvious problem with Davidson's account. We are offered an argument to the effect that, when we take up the only standpoint available to us, we must see our subject's beliefs as mostly true 'in our own opinion'. In other words, the principle of charity presupposes that we can readily identify the relations between a speaker's utterance and the worldly saliencies that typically cause it. But, as Davidson observes later, 'Why couldn't it happen that speaker and [radical interpreter] understand one another on the basis of shared but erroneous beliefs?' (Davidson 2001b: 150). For Rorty, this sceptical threat is obviated by insisting firstly that, on the appropriate use of the word, the (shared) beliefs cannot be erroneous because, being justified (as belonging to a mostly coherent set), they are true$_1$; and, secondly, that the notion of global falsity is due to metaphysically inflating the 'cautionary' use into some philosophical use, which can only be cashed out in terms of the scheme–content distinction:

> to say that truth and knowledge can only be judged by the standards of the inquirers of our own day . . . is merely to say that nothing counts as justification unless by reference to what we already accept . . . that there is no way to get outside our beliefs and our language so as to find some test other than coherence. (*PMN*: 178)

Although Davidson concurs with the first part of this, he regards the latter part as adequate for a variety of realism: 'Where [Rorty and I] differ . . . is on whether there remains a question how . . . we nevertheless can have knowledge of, and talk about, an objective public world which is not of our own making' (2001b: 141).

Davidson's response to this question is to 'find a reason for supposing most of our beliefs are true that is not a form of evidence' (p. 146), and centres on the less-than-divine idea of an 'omniscient interpreter'. The omniscient interpreter has access to whatever in the world does and would cause a speaker to assent to any of the sentences they do, and so applies in an optimal way the same method as the radical interpreter. Unlike Descartes' deity (or malevolent demon), then, she is subject to the same constraints in her attributions of content as her limited counterpart. When the omniscient interpreter turns her attention to the speaker, then, she finds that he is mostly true by her own lights. But since, by hypothesis, that is 'objectively true', he is mostly true *simpliciter*. Similarly, when interpreting the (radical interpreter), she finds that he too has mostly true beliefs. The radical interpreter can't share mostly false beliefs with the speaker because they both have mostly true beliefs according to the only opinion that matters! With this conclusion in place, the promised non-evidential reason for believing that our beliefs are mostly true comes quickly: when I reflect upon the nature of belief, and upon the related concepts of objective truth and causality, I realize that 'most of [my] basic beliefs are true, and among [my] beliefs, those most securely held and that cohere with the main body of [my] beliefs are most apt to be true' (p. 153).

For Davidson, then, the idea of the omniscient interpreter reinforces the view that when we take up an 'outside' perspective on a subject's dealings with the world it is not by adopting the traditional Cartesian standpoint, wherefrom the assumption is that beliefs can be individuated independently of how the world is and therefore might possibly all be false. Where Descartes' *defence* against the threat of such global scepticism hinges on God's not mis*leading* us, Davidson considers an omniscient interpreter who cannot see us as grossly mis*led*. Now, the suggestion that Davidson offers us a non-metaphysical way of looking at 'our language-game . . . from a distance' (*ORT*: 132) is central to Rorty's conscription of Davidson into the pragmatist camp (ibid.: 139). It constitutes what he calls 'the philosophy of language of the field-linguist' and he claims that 'this is all the philosophy of language (and, in particular, all the doctrine about truth) which Davidson has, and all that he thinks anybody needs' (ibid.). As Rorty notes, however, he does indeed disagree with Davidson about whether or not his is a *good* question (ibid.: 136, fn. 23). On the face of it, this disagreement comes down to whether or not Davidson provides an argument against the sceptic; but as we'll now see it expresses a rather deeper disagreement, ultimately centring on the uses of philosophy.

To approach this issue, consider that an obvious way of characterizing Davidson's view is that he offers a transcendental argument. These are traditionally associated with the 'deductions' offered by Kant. A typical view is that they are 'anti-sceptical arguments which seek to justify their conclusions by exhibiting them as necessary conditions for experience, or knowledge, or language; or for experience, knowledge, or language of some general type' (Walker 1989: 56). Their form is something like this:

(TA) P_1, P_1 *only if* C, *therefore* C,

where (P_1) is the 'bare premise that . . . there is experience, knowledge or language of some very general kind' (ibid.: 59), which is *accepted by the sceptic*, and (C) is what the sceptic doubts. We encountered this approach as an objection to eliminativism, where the basic claim is that certain suggestions for conceptual revision, such as the elimination of sensation-talk, are unintelligible because they violate the norms of *our* conceptual scheme. Since Davidson disdains the idea of conceptual schemes, this cannot be the right way to think about *his* transcendental argument; but the general statement of their form seems appropriate. On this understanding, what Davidson demonstrates is that a condition of possibility of using the concept of truth to articulate a sceptical or relativistic thesis makes impossible their formulation. If we cannot have truth without interpretation, and we cannot have interpretation without charity, which compels us to ascribe mostly true beliefs to any subject, we cannot help ourselves to the concept of truth without presupposing the falsity of global scepticism (all our beliefs might be false) and relativism. Now, many philosophers have found this glib rejection of the intelligibility of scepticism implausible, not least because it seems to be unashamedly verificationist.[12] It appears to reduce the world to what most of our true beliefs are true of and thence to 'what we could in principle think about' (Nagel 1986: 9) by rejecting as meaningless (or senseless; or unintelligible) any claim for which we lack empirical criteria.

This sort of objection to transcendental arguments goes back to Stroud's (1968) influential critique of those offered by Strawson (1959) in his neo-Kantian response to the revisionary metaphysician-cum-sceptic.[13] In brief, he tries to show that such arguments show at best what we must *believe* things to be like. In other words, Stroud argues that although such arguments aim to (*immodestly*) establish:

(i)   In order for 'X' to have meaning there must be criteria for identifying Xs, so the sceptic cannot deny the existence of Xs on fear of contradiction.[14]

All they in fact establish is (*modestly*[15]):

(ii)   In order for 'X' to have meaning we must believe that there are Xs.

To go beyond (ii) is to show that the *ordo essendi* is fixed by the *ordo cognoscendi* – that how things must be believed to be is how they in fact must *be* – and that requires adherence to the old-fashioned verification principle. According to this, *meaning* and *knowing* are prescriptively tied together on the grounds that something makes sense only if it can in principle be known to be true or not; that is to say, only if knowledge claims are restricted to an empirical domain which is circumscribed by a (reductive) understanding of what constitutes 'actual or possible experience'. With respect to Davidson's argument against the relativist, then, Rorty's thought is that at best this shows us 'that the field-linguist must assume that the natives believe mostly what we do' (*ORT*: 135), which leaves it open to the sceptic to insist that, since believing something does not make it so, all our beliefs might nevertheless be false. In other words, the sceptic is under no obligation to see the philosophical standpoint restricted to the resources required by the field-linguist and is therefore under no philosophical compulsion to see belief as 'in its nature veridical' (Davidson 2001b: 146). To insist that it is requires that the verificationist claim that 'translatability into a familiar tongue . . . [is the] criterion of languagehood' (2001a: 186) is a substantive philosophical doctrine, and Rorty early abandoned the idea that such substantive claims could be put beyond sceptical doubt (cf. *TLT*; 4.2).

To return to Davidson's question, then: the reason why for Rorty it is not a good one is that it presupposes that there is a problem about 'knowledge and talk of an objective world not of our making'. The implication is that regarding oneself as having *answered* the sceptic commits one to the view that theirs is a good question in the first place, that the 'connection between coherence and objectivity has become unperspicuous' (*ORT*: 137) and needs bringing into focus. From Rorty's perspective, to advance the claim that the field-linguist's standpoint is the only external perspective one needs is tantamount to telling the sceptic that since one is no longer required to play her game – there being a better one in town – one is no longer under the standing epistemological obligation to win it. Since there is no direct rebuttal here, for Rorty the full force of Davidson's response to scepticism is carried by whatever arguments he has for maintaining that the external standpoint of the field-linguist is the only one required. And, again, that position cannot be advanced as a result of a philosophical thesis about truth, which a sceptic can dispute. So what are those arguments? The answer, in brief, is that Davidson *is* advancing a transcendental argument; indeed, *the* transcendental argument to end all transcendental arguments. But if transcendental arguments are subject to Stroud's critique, how can this be regarded as a *virtue* of Davidson's argument?

A preliminary step here is to determine what Rorty thinks a transcendental argument achieves. In Rorty (1971) Stroud's criticism of Strawson[16] is addressed. Recalling (i) and (ii), Rorty argues that the belief–existence distinction exploited by Stroud is functionally irrelevant. As with the response to Davidson, the implication is that only if one takes the sceptic's rift between mind and world seriously in the first place would one think that a transcendental argument had the *immodest* aim of *healing* it. Once one has allocated the sceptic the resources to make such a rift intelligible, it will appear inevitable that one is either stuck on the belief side – being unable to go beyond drawing conclusions about what one must (albeit coherently) believe – or left looking for a brutally verificationist quick-fix that makes it appear that the world is answerable to our beliefs. If one denies the sceptic the a priori right to the mind–world gap then (ii) doesn't look problematic since 'belief that there are Xs' amounts to little more than that there is 'talk about' Xs. 'Sherlock Holmes' and 'Cold Dark Matter' are, on this account, both meaningful because there are up-and-running language games involving the terms. Equally, this means that there is *something* to the verificationist charge; though (again) since a mind–world gap is not being presupposed it is not of the crudely metaphysical sort presupposed by Stroud, but of the deflationary Wittgensteinian variety: 'to know meaning is to know inferential relationships . . . you couldn't know about anything unless you could talk about quite a lot of different things' (Rorty 1971: 14).

As noted above, a transcendental argument aims to demonstrate the necessary conditions for something general that the sceptic accepts, like understanding, language or experience. For Rorty, Quine's attack on the analytic–synthetic distinction leaves us with nothing more to say about what a necessary truth is than 'a statement such that nobody has given us any interesting alternatives which would lead us to question it' (*PMN*: 175). As with his Sellarsian account of incorrigibility, the normative force of such statements derives not from acquaintance with a special mental object like a sensation, or in response to the laws of logic, but is expressive merely of the extent to which a social practice is entrenched. If a transcendental argument is to be construed along the lines of identifying necessary conditions, then, it is according to this conception of necessity. If the tip-off to necessity cannot therefore come in the form of a metaphysical principle, all that seems to remain is the suggestion that a transcendental argument puts us in a position to rule out all the *conceivable* candidate alternatives to a certain concept. But the only non-dogmatic way of construing this is that it involves comparing the candidate necessity with all its competitors, which is to ignore the fact that 'nothing in heaven or earth *could* set limits to what we can in principle conceive' (Rorty 1979: 83), and therefore when the candidate necessity is 'justified' as opposed to when we had just run out of ideas or got bored. Accordingly, for Rorty, transcendental arguments are not *general* demonstrations to the effect that certain concepts are impossible to do without, but rather show that *particular* revisionary-sceptical alternatives are *parasitic*[17] on the linguistic resources we do in fact use. They serve, as it were, as 'reminders' assembled by the philosopher for the 'particular purpose' of dealing with the revisionist-sceptic (Wittgenstein 1953: §127). It is in this sense (TA$_p$), then, that Davidson's argument is transcendental; and it is to the rejected sense of what he calls 'realist' transcendental argumentation (TA$_r$) that it supposedly brings an end.[18]

To see the significance of this for Rorty's project, we now need to learn a little more about the discredited use, and what, as a result, the end of such a use presages. According to Rorty, transcendental arguments as traditionally understood (as 'realist') are perhaps the last weapon in the armoury of those who think 'there is such a thing as philosophical criticism of the rest of culture – that the philosopher can say something which science cannot about the claims to objectivity and rationality to which various parts of culture are entitled' (1979: 77). By aiming to establish concepts without which thought, experience, understanding or language *in general* would not be *possible*, they offer succour to those who see philosophy 'as an autonomous critical discipline' (ibid.) that has something authoritative to say about human knowledge. It is central to this self-arrogated authority that demonstrating the necessity of such concepts renders *legitimate* their usage. Since no other area of culture aims to identify concepts that are applicable to all areas (and at all times), this project to legitimate human knowledge in general is specific to philosophy and cannot be expropriated by 'psychophysics on the one hand' or 'history and sociology of knowledge on the other' (ibid.). For Rorty, then, the authority of philosophy as a 'non-empirical criticism of culture' depends entirely on the Realist conception of transcendental arguments, and abandoning them means 'abandoning philosophy' in this sense (p. 78).

For Rorty, a *Realist* argument is one that aims 'to guarantee correspondence of logic, or language, or the practice of rational inquiry to the world', for which he offers the following sufficient conditions (p. 79):[19]

1   A distinction between scheme (concept, thought, language) and content (intuition, objects of thought, 'given', World) is assumed.
2   The coherence of the scheme is not thought to warrant a knowledge claim – further *legitimation* is needed which can be viewed as neither 'empirical' nor 'verificationist'.

In addition to these, a Realist *transcendental* argument requires:

3   The legitimating knowledge that the scheme will correspond to the content is made possible by the fact that the former is better known to us than the latter, and creates it.

Given Rorty's Sellarsian analysis of privileged access (first-person reports), it is clear that he rejects the idea that 'better known to us' can be analysed in any way other than as 'the sorts of claims that most people will take as justified on the grounds of personal testimony'; no different in kind to one's claim to know better where the spare fuses are kept. Consequently little sense can be made of 'our' creating anything public (statuary and nuisance notwithstanding). We thus arrive at the suggestion that all that remains of the originally Kantian idea (3) is that the non-empirical (armchair) knowledge that legitimates the use of a concept in all knowledge claims is determined by ruling out all candidate alternatives to it. But once the *form* of transcendental arguments is determined as 'parasitic', there is no longer any obvious connection with the *motive* behind Realist arguments per se. Thinking back to Rorty's early piece, then, the belief–existence gap, that Stroud presupposes is the shared assumption of both sceptical and (Realistic) anti-sceptical arguments, is now elaborated in terms of (1) and (2), and the form of transcendental arguments, freed from that context, takes on the mildly verificationist air implied by their parasitic function. What remains are Realist arguments that look beyond coherence for something non-evidential to *legitimate* knowledge and thus prove scepticism false; and transcendental arguments that operate as *ad hominim* arguments 'against a certain proposal by showing that the proposal tacitly presupposes what it purports to deny' (p. 82).

This gives us some sense of why Davidson's search for 'a reason for supposing most of our beliefs are true that is not a form of evidence' is interpreted by Rorty as coming too close to asking for the sort of legitimating principle that the sceptic says we require and that motivates 'Realist' arguments. It is to insist that the cautionary use of 'true' is insufficient to dissolve an imputed 'naturalistic fallacy' about truth; that the question 'Is our best explanation *true*?' (p. 84) makes sense above and beyond reminding us that we may later come up with a better one, one whose success is *explained* by its truth. As we've seen, Rorty does not want to find a dogmatically metaphysical quick-fix by defining truth as justification, for that simply leads one to play the game at the meta-level: one now has to legitimate one's metaphysical claim in the light of scepticism about how to justify such knowledge.[20] The fact that pragmatism disdains the epistemological see-saw between Realism and scepticism does not, however, suggest that it 'is simply turning its back on a tradition'; it can still 'bring forward arguments to show the futility of epistemology – of projects of legitimation' (p. 85). So Davidson's argument to the effect that 'most of our belief must be true' is 'a transcendental argument to end all transcendental arguments' in the sense that it shows the futility of Realist attempts to legitimate our knowledge, and in doing so the futility of the associated image of philosophy as an autonomous discipline seeking to legislate with respect to other areas of culture. Now the slogan is appealing, but since (3) has been discounted it in effect amounts to a parasitism argument against *Realist* arguments:

> the aim of his argument is to make impossible the whole Cartesian and Kantian dialectic which makes scepticism and anti-skeptical arguments possible. (p. 78)

Given the restrictions on what a transcendental argument can achieve, this talk of making something *impossible* might sound like a piece of modal hysteria. However, the point is to make a certain way of talking or thinking impossible by undermining the context (or picture) required to sustain it (compare 'make it impossible for anyone to ask questions like "how many angels can dance on the end of a pin?" or "is he better qualified for the job because he's white or because he's male?" ').

To see how a transcendental argument might work against the desire to ask Davidson's question, let's examine a related concern. It seems natural to think that when we make the judgement that (say) present-day science (and perhaps morals) are better than those of the past, the evaluative criteria invoked are not just 'local'. One reason for thinking this is a certain underdetermined notion of progress – either of advancing towards some desirable goal or at least away from something undesirable; another is the sense that if we judge the past harshly, we may come to be judged likewise in the future. Together they bespeak a fear that there is a standpoint from which present thinking might be judged and found wanting; a standpoint from which the question is not 'how do our theories work?' but 'why do they succeed?' To answer *this* question, of course, one cannot invoke norms operative in one's theories/world-views: what is required is some sort of device for evaluating theories/ world-views themselves. To take an example, although Sellars accepts that (in Rorty's terms) truth$_1$ and reference$_1$ are view-relative concepts, he nevertheless thinks that we need the concept of 'picturing' to capture the sense that (say) our version of the scientific image is better than that of our predecessors.[21] A more common version of this is the idea that our theories are in some way 'maps' of reality. Just as successive maps can more accurately represent geographical features, so the science of our day is better at representing the topology of the world.

The problem here, of course, is that the sort of conventions or transformations one uses for making (and thus judging) maps or pictures are specific to the purposes they are intended to serve. It seems otiose to ask whether a photograph of Dora Maar is a *better* 'picture' or representation per se than a Picasso portrait because no one expects there to be criteria for making such judgements. Likewise, while one map might be better for navigational purposes than another, it may not be better at representing relative land mass or levels of carbon emission. Most visitors to London have no problem finding their way around using the map of the tube, but it's of little use above ground. The philosophical thought here, then, is that if there are no best-in-show awards for maps and pictures, one would be better off using the categories employed by judges at Crufts than metaphors taken from cartography and art criticism. In other words, along with the ordinary and correct use of words like 'picture' and 'map' go certain discursive obligations, which the philosopher pretends to accept but in fact rejects when they talk of Mind 'picturing' or 'mapping' the World.

The latter formulation should give a clue as to how this sort of conservative Wittgensteinian critique relates to transcendental arguments: what the latter do is show that *particular* philosophical suggestions for the usage of certain words are parasitic on sublunary employment and cannot sustain the sorts of inferential connections that constitute that use. Accordingly, to use 'picture' and 'map' talk to make sense of the standpoint from which one can talk of the relationship between (coherent) inquiry and the world is to put faith in unsustainable metaphors that only linger in the philosophical imagination because of their association with customary use. Of course, customary use is not *necessary* use: the argument is effective only against *specific* counter-proposals. So what of Davidson's *sui generis* transcendental argument? The point, it will be recalled, is that 'the dominant metaphor of conceptual relativism' is that of 'differing points of view . . . of different observers of the same world who come to it with incommensurable systems of concepts' (Davidson 2001a: 184, 187). To cash out this dualism of scheme and content, the philosopher deploys the notions of a scheme organizing (systematizing, or dividing up) or fitting (predicting, accounting for, facing, corresponding to, representing) the world or experience. However, metaphors around 'organization' just remind us that the term relates to a unity only when pluralities are involved: you can't organize a sock-drawer that is empty. Likewise, although Eskimos of lore have ways of organizing their snow-experiences that we don't, the fact that we can say *that* demonstrates that there's nothing marvellous here beyond the wonders of human adaptation. As with the examples of mapping and picturing, the ordinary uses of terms like 'organize' cannot sustain their philosophical (mis)employment.

In the case of 'fitting' and its cognates, the parasitism is not on the ordinary usage of the relevant term but on the ordinary use of 'truth': 'the notion of fitting the totality of experience, like the notion of fitting the facts or of being true to the facts, adds nothing intelligible to the simple concept of being true' (Davidson 2001a: 193–4). Since what remains is the question whether or not we can make sense of 'largely true but untranslatable' (ibid.), the argument comes down to whether or not we can find a use for truth that goes beyond the intuitions embodied in Tarski's Convention T. Since, for Rorty, this is 'the everyday, philosophically innocuous, sense of truth' (Rorty 1979: 98), what Davidson has given us is not a direct argument *for* Tarski, but a recipe for dealing with any attempt to say *more* about truth by attempting to cash out the various metaphors that might be used to make sense of the scheme–content distinction. From the standpoint of the field-linguist, then, 'unless one is willing to postulate some intermediary between the organism and its environment . . . [he] knows . . . which objects most of [the natives] beliefs are true of' (*ORT*: 134). It is a transcendental argument to end all *Realist* arguments, not because a philosophical thesis about the nature of truth has been deduced, or the truth or our beliefs demonstrated, but because no sense can be given to the scheme–content distinction without employing terms in ways that are parasitic on their ordinary uses. Without some sense being given to such uses of terms like 'represent' and 'correspond to', no *explanatory* use can be found for 'true' that would give content to the project of legitimation, of thoughts being true because they represent or correspond to reality. And without this no sense can be given to the notion that philosophy has a task to perform that requires a standpoint on our beliefs in general in order to go beyond coherence to *legitimate* our thinking about the world.

For Rorty, then, Davidson has offered a conception of the external standpoint on belief that neither tempts nor answers scepticism. According to the 'pure' conception, the question of 'how language works' (*PMN*: 259) is answered by understanding how 'true' is used to construct a Tarskian theory of meaning for a language, which issues from an investigation of 'the causal roles played by [the natives] linguistic behaviour in their interaction with their environment' (*ORT*: 148). To see beliefs 'from the outside' (p. 139) in this way – as descriptions of causal transactions – is to see their role in the identification of the truth conditions that give 'truth' its disquotational use. But for Rorty this activity has nothing to do with the question 'how knowledge works', and to imagine it does conflates the 'inside' normative story – where beliefs are seen as 'rules for action' (ibid.) – with the external, descriptive one (and do 'impure' philosophy of language). The temptation to run these two accounts together derives from the desire to *legitimate* the inside story – to look for a reason that goes beyond the coherence that characterizes it. For Rorty, then, the scheme–content distinction is the dogmatic, philosophical presupposition that leads one to think that one can make sense of the possibility of running the accounts together by thinking of truth in a way that satisfies the conditions for neither 'pure', external, use nor 'relaxed and unphilosophical' use. To think that way is to regard truth as an explanatory concept and maintain that it could be offered discursively as a non-circular reason for holding the beliefs one does. That in turn requires that to the question 'why do you believe it?' the answer 'because it's true' would notch-up a norm and thereby advance one's epistemic standing in one's community rather than serve merely as a place-holder for genuine 'inside' explanation in the form of a social practice that authorizes the belief.

On Rorty's appropriation, Davidson's argument to the effect that attempts to cash out metaphors relating to the intelligibility of the conceptual scheme idea show that an explanatory concept of true (of true$_3$, relating to reference$_3$) is parasitic on the 'unphilosophical', 'normative' use (of true$_1$) and so on a distinction between the normative and descriptive stories. It requires the picture of a relationship between two realms such that the success of one side is explained by its adequacy to the other. With the end of such a story goes the possibility of framing or answering scepticism and thus, for Rorty, the idea that philosophy can legitimate knowledge claims across the breadth of our culture. The conclusion that the elimination of a particular project signifies the end of philosophy as traditionally conceived clearly turns on the plausibility of Rorty's account of truth, and we'll return to it with a more critical air in chapter 6. For now, it's time to look in more detail at what adherence to that project means for Rorty's conception of the future of philosophy, and what interests and purposes a successor activity might be expected to promote.

4

Overcoming Philosophy

1   After philosophy?

Chapter 3 examined how Rorty's revision of his eliminativist views led him to a more radical assessment of the significance of concept change for the authority of philosophy. The Quinean over-privileging of the 'ideal language' of scientific discourse led to the assumption that criteria for establishing the identity of reference were transparent to inquiry, and that assertions of identity war-ranted a *positive* ontological conclusion. Rorty comes to see this view of reference is in tension with his analysis of incorrigibility, which invests normative authority in language viewed as a social practice. It is therefore part of the same epistemologically centred picture which, as early as 1965, he regarded as responsible for the insistence that mental terms cannot be eliminated because their *intrinsic* nature is known only to the introspecting subject. The view Rorty develops from his critique of materialism (including his own) is that the revisability of our concepts, in the light of our ongoing (causal) encounters with the world, conflicts with an inherited sense of the world or (the logic of our) language dictating to us what we can and cannot justifiably believe.

This conflict provokes a sort of existential-epistemological anxiety about what sort of creatures we are. Of course, everything here turns on the scope of that 'we'. As we've remarked, the dominant trope to be 'deconstructed' is the dualism of scheme and content. On Rorty's borrowing of Davidson's critique, that distinction comes to encapsulate the problematic inheritance of the Cartesian-Lockean-Kantian tradition (*PMN*: 3–4) as expressed through the visual metaphor of 'the mind as a great mirror, containing various representations . . . capable of being studied by pure, nonempirical methods' (ibid.: 12). If there is no empirically isolated standpoint from which the philosopher could convict a proposal for linguistic reform of in-principle impossibility, then the very idea of philosophy-as-first-science is undermined, and along with it the philosopher's self-appointed role as cultural critic. Absenting this standpoint and its concomitant role for the intellectual, the question naturally arises as to what philosophy might otherwise be, and how 'we' philosophers might otherwise conceive of our intellectual task. However, the 'we' has a potentially much broader scope. The mind-as-mirror imagery may help furnish philosophy with an image of non-empirical inquiry, but it is an image for philosophy insofar as it is an image of and for humankind.

In this important respect Rorty's 'therapy' (cf. *PMN*: 7) differs from the 'ordinary language' model. On a simple rendering of the Wittgensteinian approach to philosophical problems, they represent the 'bewitchment of our intelligence' (Wittgenstein 1953: §109). When he adds that 'what *we* do is to bring words back from their metaphysical to their everyday use' (ibid.: §116) by 'arranging what we have always known' (ibid.: §109), the latter 'we' denotes the understanding of the philosophically innocent, while the former 'we' refers to the philosophers who must seek within themselves that pre-lapsarian state of apprehension. The 'explicatory' pragmatism Rorty takes from Quine (2.2) acknowledges no absolute 'isolation' of the (deviant) philosophical 'we' from the (legitimate) uses 'we' make of ordinary language. Consequently, he is apt to emphasize that it is common sense – and not philosophical deviations from it – that is 'irredeemably Cartesian' (1970a: 406, fn. 11; cf. *PMN*: 84, fn. 5).

Viewed thus, the philosophical debate about the epistemic authority of sensation-talk reflects the *meta*philosophical debate about the authority philosophers arrogate to themselves when they make claims to a privileged standpoint on culture as a whole. Incorrigibility about our minds' representations is the singular expression of the philosopher's trans-individual incorrigibility about *the* Mind's representations: if man's essence is to *know*, it is the essence of philosophy to know about *knowing* (cf. *PMN*: 357). Since Rorty analyses incorrigibility per se along the lines of a social practice, the normative standing of what we have to say both as philosophers, claiming to know non-empirical truths, and as sentient creatures, claiming to feel pain, depends on what our peers will let us get away with saying (with what is true₁). The concern, then, is not with what we *are* but of how we might come to talk and be talked about: what we might *become*; or, perhaps, of what we might *hope* to become, and of what interests and ends should guide us in that process. What would be the task of the intellectual in a world where human nature is not a given but is creatively up for grabs? If that task is not to be carried out by the philosopher, is it nevertheless the discipline's job to carry us beyond philosophy-as-epistemology?

These questions recall Rorty's autobiographical musings 'about what, if anything, philosophy is good for' (*PSH*: 11). Hitherto I have emphasized his 'turn' at the slight cost of downplaying the continuity of these metaphilosophical concerns. To remedy this, we'll begin with the bold statement of Rorty's early metaphilosophical views from his introduction to *The Linguistic Turn* (1992).[1] The dialectical evaluation this presents of the two dominant variants of linguistic philosophy offers an important insight into Rorty's conception of the role philosophy can play in bringing about a post-philosophical culture. What emerges is the conviction that the primary function of linguistic philosophy is to engage with the philosophical tradition in a critical (negative; deconstructive) capacity, in order to create a discursive space for the sorts of reforms that will help shape the future. *PMN* (4.4–4.6) and *CIS* (ch. 5) differ in their emphases on what is important in conceptualizing that future. However, the idea that the intellectual must be Janus-faced, both confronting the philosophical present and gesturing towards the post-philosophical milieu, is key to the structure of both. With that in mind, let's look at his evaluation of the importance of the linguistic turn in philosophy.

2 The linguistic turn

Kant (1993) evokes powerfully the pessimism many feel about the possibility of philosophical knowledge:

> Human reason, in one sphere of its cognition, is called upon to consider questions, which it cannot decline, as they are presented by its own nature, but which it cannot answer, as they transcend every faculty of human reason. It falls into this difficulty without any fault of its own. It begins with principles, which cannot be dispensed with in the field of experience, and the truth and sufficiency of which are,

at the same time, insured by experience. With these principles it rises, in obedience to the laws of its own nature, to ever higher and more remote conditions. But it quickly discovers that, in this way, its labours must remain ever incomplete, because new questions never cease to present themselves; and thus finds itself compelled to have recourse to principles which transcend the region of experience, while they are regarded by common sense without distrust. It thus falls into confusion and contradictions, from which it conjectures the presence of latent errors, which, however, it is unable to discover, because the principles it employs, transcending the limits of experience, cannot be tested by that criterion. The arena of these endless contests is called *metaphysics* (Avii).

For Kant and, as Rorty notes, many others (*TLT*: 1), such feelings have frequently been the rallying call for a new method of inquiry, which will finally establish the discipline's scientific status by elucidating a criterion for philosophical knowledge. Unfortunately, proposals seem vulnerable to the sort of question posed by the ancient sceptics:[2] how does the philosopher know that their criterion of philosophical knowledge is the correct one? If they offer a *new* criterion then the same question can be raised, and the prospect of a vicious regress opens up. The alternative response is to claim that by an application of *their* criterion it constitutes the criterion of philosophical knowledge, but now truth in philosophy is reduced to self-referential consistency. So one either makes sense of a standpoint, neutral with respect to competing philosophical theories, from which one's presupposed criterion does not need justifying, or one must conclude that all consistent philosophical theories are at best elaborations of ungrounded presuppositions. Since these determine what counts *as* philosophical knowledge, they are likely to take the form of substantive and therefore controversial philosophical claims.

As Rorty notes, then, it is reasonable to ask of any new philosophical method, two questions (*TLT*: 4):

(1) Does it presuppose (the truth of) any substantive philosophical theses?
(2) Does it offer either (a) a criterion of philosophical *knowledge*, or (b) a criterion of success or progress?

Before looking at (1) it's worth noting that, for Rorty, sceptical considerations rule out an affirmative answer to 2(a), so the significance of the linguistic turn devolves to 2(b). To see the importance of this, note that a feature of Kant's diagnosis is that philosophical perplexity is a perfectly *natural* expression of human reason. His new transcendental method addresses the 'confusion and contradictions' into which we fall when we undertake metaphysical inquiry, but it does not aim at ridding us of the view that there *is* such a thing as a criterion of metaphysical knowledge. Philosophical speculation is not a glass-bead game, pursued for aesthetic ends alone, but arises out of natural and perplexing engagements in and with the world. This is 'the notion of philosophy as a discipline which attempts the solution of certain traditional problems – problems generated by certain commonsense beliefs' (*TLT*: 23). There is much to say about whether or not philosophical problems are timeless; and, if not timeless, whether they are nevertheless 'real'. For now, note that Rorty's rejection of 2(a) goes along with a dismissal of the Kantian assumption that philosophical questions are *ipso jure* questions that we cannot rationally decline to answer. In the broadest sense, they are not *scientific* problems.

Turning to question (1), Rorty offers the following definition of linguistic philosophy:

> the view that philosophical problems are problems which may be solved (or dissolved) either by reforming language, or by understanding more about the language we presently use. (*TLT*: 3)

The distinction between 'reforming' and 'understanding' language marks the familiar (2.2) contrast between those philosophers who look to an 'Ideal Language' (ILP) to dis/solve problems, and those who look to 'Ordinary Language' (OLP). Bergmann brings out their common feature:

> All linguistic philosophers talk about the world by means of talking about a suitable language. This is the linguistic turn, the fundamental gambit as to method, on which [OLP and ILP] agree. (Bergmann 1964: 177; quoted *TLT*: 8)

As Bergmann goes on to note, 'Clearly one may execute the turn . . . The question is why one should' (1964: 177). Amongst the reasons he gives, the first is the most important for our purposes:

> Words are used either ordinarily (commonsensically) or philosophically. On this distinction, above all, the method rests. The prelinguistic philosophers did not make it. Yet they used words

philosophically. Prima facie such uses are unintelligible. They require common-sense explication. The method insists we provide it. (ibid.)

Being able to distinguish between philosophical and commonsensical uses in order to convict the former of 'unintelligibility' has an obvious appeal: one need no more feel obliged to answer questions that turn on 'needles usages' than to search for the Snark. However, the distinction seems to require theoretical resources. This was evident in the early version of ILP we encountered in 1.2 where Hempel et al. maintained that an 'ideal language' comprises statements which are either analytic or have clear procedures for verification or confirmation (synthetic). Here the ordinary philosophical contrast presupposes a substantial but reflexively unstable thesis about when a statement is meaningful or significant.

This failure suggests a more nuanced approach to (1): can one make the common-sense-philosophy distinction without presupposing such an egregiously metaphysical thesis? Posed differently, is there a way of conceptualizing the 'ideal language' idea that satisfies the following desiderata:

(i)   It does not presuppose the existence of the sort of neutral standpoint from which a substantial metaphysical thesis might be identified.
(ii) It enables us to draw an invidious distinction between philosophical and common-sense usage.

How is one to think of an 'ideal language' if not as one that allows us to legislate with respect to meaning? In his response to Carnap, Bergmann (1960) suggests that rather than aiming for the (as it were) *ideal* ideal language, the task is to sketch a language in which all *commonsensical* uses of terms are transcribed adequately, but no *philosophical* uses are. For Rorty, the key insight here is that a philosophical question is vocabulary-relative, not expressive of some fundamental human need or obligation to the world or to reason. If such an 'ideal' language were *possible*, the burden would fall on the traditional philosopher to make a case for continuing to ask the kinds of questions that the transcription has shown needn't be asked *if* one wants to ask any of the questions of common sense and science.

As Rorty observes (*TLT*: 6–7), Bergmann's pragmatic take on the metaphilosophy of the *Tractatus* also gives us a way of accounting for what philosophers were doing in the past, rather than merely dismissing their pronouncements as nonsense. On this Hegelian account philosophy is the history of attempts to construct an ideal language in which the questions of one's predecessors can no longer be asked because they cannot be transcribed into it. If one adopts Humean as one's 'ideal language', one cannot transcribe Leibnizian questions about the principle of sufficient reason (they are dis/solved); and one cannot transcribe Cartesian problems about the interaction of mental and material substances into the vocabulary of the *Monadology* or of Spinoza's *Ethics*.

For Rorty, then, Bergmann's method avoids the reflexive instability of presupposing a criterion for distinguishing sense from (philosophical) nonsense. If philosophy is to be regarded as 'linguistic recommendation' (p. 8) it is clearly consistent with this view that one is offering a new use for the term 'philosophy' that renders otiose certain metaphilosophical questions about the relative status of philosophical discourse. With a passing glance at (2), this method also suggests a criterion of success: a philosophical vocabulary {PV_2} is better than a competitor {PV_3} at dealing with philosophical problems presented by {PV_1} if (*ceteris paribus*) it can transcribe more fully the common-sense uses of language and thus more effectively exclude the philosophical uses. As things stand this is only a temporizing move: {PV_2} will invariably trade on metaphysical presuppositions that subsequent generations of philosophers take as their target in the (next) formulation of an ideal language. So, although Bergmann's suggestion throws down the gauntlet to someone who denies that this characterization of philosophy is plausible, it refers us back to the relationship between the ideal language and philosophical presuppositions. As Rorty notes, Bergmann's own suggestions concerning the 'ideal' language are far from being metaphysically innocent (ibid.). Can one retain some sense of 'ideal' talk without any such presuppositions? Crucially, the answer for Rorty is no.

To see why, consider the weakest interpretation of ILP, which maintains that there can be no in-principle failure of 'transcription' in a *specific* area of ordinary discourse. When we've transcribed all our ordinary uses of particular terms into 'idealese', nothing remains unexpressed. To hold such a view is to be what Rorty calls a 'methodological nominalist', an abbreviation for what he takes from Sellars and Wittgenstein:

> the view that all the questions which philosophers have asked about concepts, subsistent universals, or 'natures' which (a) cannot be

answered by empirical inquiry concerning the behaviour or properties of particulars subsumed under such concepts, universals, or
natures, and which (b) can be answered in *some* way, can be answered
by answering questions about the use of linguistic expressions, and
in no other way. (*TLT*: 11)

Although he later describes this as amounting to no more than the
pragmatic thesis that we should only ask questions that we have
criteria for satisfactory answers to (p. 14),[3] this is confessed to be 'a
substantive philosophical thesis' (p. 11). Indeed, it is a thesis we saw
put to work in previous chapters, and it appears in mantric form
throughout Rorty's subsequent work. Likewise, we have seen examples of the only way in which it can be defended; namely, by
demanding examples of questions that *cannot* be answered in this
way and yet for which there *are* some adducible criteria for what
would count as an answer. So, on this account, 'idealese' is simply
that vocabulary into which present ways of talking that raise philosophical concerns can be 'transcribed' so that nothing relating to
our aims and purposes is lost. Recalling Quine, the 'problematic usages' will be *eliminated* through explication. The question
is whether this 'thin' conception of ILP is sufficient to give us a
criterion of philosophical success. The problem is that unless
we are willing to inflate our metaphysical commitments, 'transcribe'
amounts to no more than 'can be interpreted or described as'. Nominalism, which at best can be defended only via critique of alternatives, does not legislate with respect to what is the correct account
of usage, and therefore cannot tell us when a philosophical question
is abandoned *legitimately*.

The intuition that no stipulated reform of language could secure
the criterion of philosophical success guaranteed to convince us
(confronted with our peers) that abandoning traditional philosophical questions is warranted motivates the counter-reformation in
linguistic philosophy, OLP. For philosophers like Strawson, the
ideal language required to secure agreement is one already in our
possession: English (Chinese, Xhosa, etc.) as used by competent
speakers. The aim, then, is to 'describe the complex patterns of
logical behaviour which the concepts of daily life exhibit' (Strawson
1961: 313) as a preliminary to demonstrating how philosophical uses
deviate from them. Since we are describing the shared fund of linguistic experience, there ought to be no problem establishing the
consensus required for empirical success. If Smallweed is inclined
to describe genteel ladyfolk as 'bachelors' one's success in diagnos-

ing his error would derive from the 'description' of common usage. Likewise, if 'cause' or 'doubt' or 'reference' or 'truth' have a certain 'logical behaviour' that can be described, any deviation from that usage *should* be recognizable to a competent speaker.[4]

This talk of 'logical behaviour' made many post-positivist philosophers queasy; and we've encountered Quine's objection to the analytic–synthetic distinction, which seems required to give the idea bite. If the 'logical' part is discarded as a vacuous attempt to suggest the philosopher has a privileged standpoint on 'our language', we are left with 'linguistic behaviour', which seems to be as open to the problem of interpretation/description as an *ideal* language. Imagine that you are being advised on how to act in a difficult situation on the basis of a description of the context you find plausible. Did you already have that description in mind, or has your interlocutor *convinced* you of something? Imagine that the description is 'you're projecting your desire to kill your father and take your mother as wife on to your relationship with your employer'. With Freudian stage-setting in place this might strike someone as convincing, but it is unlikely that is because the description is available to *any* competent speaker of English. Given any vaguely interesting description of usage, there will be no clear criterion for distinguishing between what one always-already understood and an imaginative suggestion one has been persuaded by. Which is to say that neither OLP nor ILP can draw on the sort of neutral standpoint that would be required to legislate in this area.

Rather than offer descriptions of 'logical behaviour' one might aim lower and try to identify conditions of possibility. We've already encountered Rorty's opposition to this 'transcendental' approach. What Rorty wants to press here is that the primary purpose of all forms of OLP is dis/solving traditional philosophical problems (*TLT*: 31). In response he suggests that the ILP simply grant that their alternative (ideal) language, in which the problems cannot be stated, is 'merely as sketch of a "form of life" that is logically possible, though pragmatically impossible' (p. 17). Since such things are not logically *im*possible, the OLP can at best maintain that they are unenlightening with regard to present linguistic practices. But this acknowledges that the so-called necessary conditions serve merely to remind us that our linguistic practices do not at present sanction certain moves in a linguistic game. To take our oft-utilized example, the fact that we cannot *now* issue challenges to a person's authority in the case of sensation-reports does not mean that the structures of linguistic authority might not change in the future. Accordingly, all that remains of OLP is the claim that we can contrast the uses made of certain words in ordinary contexts with the special uses made by philosophers (p. 22). Given the intuitive appeal of the idea that philosophical perplexity arises naturally from our ordinary concepts, this is not trivial. It does, however, set limits on how one can respond to the expression of a philosophical problem. On the whole, this will require noting that a premise used in its formulation trades on an ambiguity, piggy-backing a philosophical *use* (not *mis*use) of a term on the ordinary one. As to any new uses that a philosopher may care to suggest, the methodologically nominalistic aim would be to show that they give rise to silly questions – questions for which 'no procedure of answering' them 'suggests itself naturally to users of the language' (p. 31).[5]

On Rorty's dialectical presentation of ILP and OLP, 'ideal language' serves two ends. First, it is anticipated that sketches of such 'may . . . lead us to abandon the attempt to solve certain traditional philosophical problems' (p. 24) by presenting a vocabulary in which they cannot be formulated. Although he notes the criterion for such a partial substitution is 'no greater cost than inconvenience' (p. 18) he says nothing more about this, preferring instead to switch attention to the shortcomings of OLP. It is, however, clear enough that since Rorty has his own eliminativism of the mental in mind, the question of inconvenience devolves to the idea that the 'ideal language' maintains the 'continuity of purpose', which, as we have seen, at the time presupposed that we privilege scientific purposes when establishing the identity of reference. The second end is to show that if one cannot reject such an 'ideal language' suggestion on the grounds of logical impossibility, one must conclude that this is because one's norms are constituted by contingent linguistic practices that might in principle change. Given the realization that 'necessity' is used to flag a lack of imagination, we arrive at the conclusion that linguistic philosophy is merely a *critical activity*.

Returning to Rorty's two questions, his answer to the first is that linguistic philosophy presupposes methodological nominalism, while acknowledging that it cannot be defended directly. Although that may sound weak, it is at least consistent with Rorty's own view to the effect that it is 'an essentially critical activity' (p. 31). Given this characterization, his answer to the second question is clear enough: (linguistic) philosophy is 'an activity whose success is measured by its ability to dissolve' the problems that constitute the 'great philosophical tradition of finding out the essence of X's' (ibid.). Of course, if finding the essence of X's reduces to looking at how the word 'X' is used, and accounts of usage are just *more uses*, philosophy thus conceived could never be a contribution to that tradition. Since there is no standpoint from which to identify an ideal language (including an ideal *ordinary* language), progress is simply to be measured by the linguistic philosopher's success in demonstrating that a *'particular formulation* of a given problem' is such that, given current linguistic practices, no one has any idea how to answer it (p. 32). If there is any alternative to methodological nominalism it must operate critically to demonstrate what it is that *it* fails to get right (with respect either to normal usage or to any other stipulated criterion[6]).

Recalling our two desiderata relating to the ideal language idea, it appears that although (ii) is satisfied insofar as one can draw the philosophical/common-sense distinction locally,[7] (i) is answered incompletely. Just as Bergmann's own 'ideal language' is permeated with 'controversial philosophical theses' (p. 8), Rorty's materialism implies possession of a philosophically privileged standpoint. However, that presupposition is not required to defend linguistic philosophy and the 'ideal language' idea. Indeed, as we've already noted, it is undermined by the underlying commitment to a 'social practice' based account of normativity. The question therefore remains of what more can be made of the ideal language idea, and of the Bergmannian thesis that 'philosophy is linguistic recommendation'. To see what possibilities might be opened up and the extent to which these illuminate Rorty's later work, let's turn to the conclusion of Rorty's paper where he discusses the prospects for the future of philosophy.

3   The future of philosophy

For Rorty 'the critical thrust of the linguistic movement in contemporary philosophy is against philosophy as a pseudo-science; it has no animus against the creation of a new art form . . . consciously rejecting the goal of "solving problems" ' (*TLT*: 23). Since it can make no 'scientific' knowledge claims, it has a 'merely critical, essentially dialectical, function' (p. 33). This naturally leads to the question, 'would philosophy come to an end if linguistic philosophy as so conceived were successful insofar as the activity of asking certain sorts of philosophical questions were no longer possible?'.[8] Rorty proposes six possibilities for the philosophy of the future, each of which he associates with a paradigmatic practitioner (table 4.1).

Table 4.1 The philosophy of the future

		Are there criteria of philosophical truth (success, progress, etc.)?	
		Yes Philosophy-as-discovery	*No* Philosophy-as-proposal
Is methodological nominalism accepted?	*No*	(1) Husserl	(2) Heidegger (later)
	Yes	(5) Austin (6) Strawson	(3) Waismann (4) Wittgenstein (later)

Insofar as Husserlian phenomenology combines a commitment to the existence of some criterion of philosophical knowledge with the renunciation of methodological nominalism, it represents the continuation of the philosophical tradition, not a break from it. We've already noted that the Austinian approach to philosophical problems rests on an empirical description of linguistic usage, which might not be regarded as sufficiently neutral to carry the weight of philosophical consensus, even if every philosopher were to sign up for the programme, which they haven't. Likewise, Rorty inducts Strawson into the merely critical phase of the linguistic method by claiming that his transcendental demonstrations serve only to remind us of the actual use made in common life of such terms as 'experience' and 'knowledge' and that *particular* proposals for philosophical uses are parasitic on the ordinary uses they seek to displace.

Rorty's positioning of the later Heidegger shows where the real concern is. The advocate of (3) is the true heir of the 'ideal language' tradition, for they have abandoned any attempt to conceive of the criterion of the 'ideal' in terms of the dis/solution of philosophical questions. If the questions that constituted the philosophical tradition are no longer present to dictate the criteria by which an ideal language is to be judged – questions deriving from the notion that philosophy is a descriptive endeavour to get the world right – then philosophy is open to the possibility of new criteria relating to 'the creation of new, interesting and fruitful ways of thinking about things in general' (p. 34). From the perspective of (3), then, even Heidegger's attempt to return us to a non-quasi-scientific questioning of Being (2) *could* be regarded as contributing to 'understanding how things in the broadest possible sense of the term hang together in the broadest possible sense of the term' (Sellars 1963: 1).[9] What then of (4), the Wittgensteinian option? For Rorty, it seems that the only difference between (3) and (4) is that whereas (3) relates its project sympathetically to the philosophical tradition, (4) does so through repudiation. From the perspective of the latter, the end of the tradition is the end of philosophy *tout court*. Henceforward, whatever world-view is required will be elaborated not by philosophy, but by 'the arts, the sciences, or both' (p. 34).

So where does Rorty himself fit into this schema? Clearly, his sympathies lie with (3) and (4); but, despite the family resemblance, it's difficult to identify the two. There clearly *is* a difference, but it's hard (metaphilosophically speaking) to determine if it's a difference that makes much of a difference. If the philosophy of (3) bears no relation but 'sympathy' to the tradition, the contrast comes down to whether those who strive for the new vision call themselves philosophers (3), or think of themselves as bringing to an end the very thing that necessitates their activity (4) in order to make room (culturally speaking) for those who would come after. What we seem to have here is merely a disagreement about how the word 'philosophy' is used (cf. *CP*: 29–33). From the standpoint of (3), philosophy is an honorific we give to intellectual endeavour of the most expansive order, and there is no reason to restrict it to whatever thinkers the academe sees fit to crown. From this perspective, one assumes that the 'sympathy' the philosophers of the future feel with the traditional problems of philosophy is akin to a Bergmannian respect for those sketches of ideal languages that self-deludingly masqueraded as descriptions of the nature of reality. From the standpoint of (4), philosophy is a disparaging term to characterize a senseless distraction from the real business of coming up with ways of thinking about the world.

Given the shared conviction that the task of the intellectuals (whatever they're called) is to see philosophy as engaged in world making, not World *description*, what would make the difference between (3) and (4) *seem* more important to the philosophers involved? No direct answer is given to this question, but Rorty's concluding remarks hint at one and point towards the metaphilosophical strategy he proceeded to pursue. He notes that it is not linguistic philosophy itself that has been the most important post-war philosophical development, but 'the beginning of a thoroughgoing rethinking of certain epistemological difficulties which have troubled philosophers since Plato and Aristotle' (p. 39). Without the 'spectatorial' account of knowledge, according to which mind is conceived of as an inner eye contemplating what is pre-linguistically given to us, the very problems that constitute the philosophical tradition would not have arisen. As he observes, opposition to this account is a concern shared across the philo-sophical divide, and methodological nominalism is the anglophone expression of it (ibid., fn. 75; cf. *CP*: xx). More importantly, 'over-throwing' this account of knowledge will, Rorty contends, affect the very vocabulary in which the metaphilosophical dispute bet-ween philosophy-as-describing (of finding) and philosophy-as-making is framed.

The clear implication is that the options outlined on the basis of the dissolution of the traditional philosophical questions are 'con-trolled' by a metaphilosophical assumption that is the residual legacy of what gave rise to those problems in the first place; namely, the image of the mind 'as a sort of "immaterial eye"' (*TLT*: 39, fn. 75). That assumption is that the distinction between philosophy and science is constitutive of the metaphilosophical choices on offer. That is to say, the view is that philosophy either *can* be a science, because it collects empirical facts about usage *à la* Austin, or is defined *in opposition to* science and therefore must end or continue as something *lacking* criteria of truth but nevertheless serving to 'picture' or 'show' what cannot be said. Despite having embraced methodological nominalism, then, the putative philosophers of the future have failed to escape the epistemological problematic, which continues to dictate the terms of the metaphilosophical struggle between philosophy-as-making and philosophy-as-finding. One assumes that it is 'blindness' to this deeper similarity that leads the philosophers associated with (3) and (4) to conclude that their dif-ferences are more significant than they are; but this purported failure tells us a great deal more. The implication is that Rorty's own metaphilosophical position will be contrasted with (3) and (4) on the basis of this deeper insight. At the same time, this diagnosis suggests that, despite their commitment to methodological nomi-nalism, the *methods* of linguistic philosophers are insufficient to address the allure of the spectatorial picture of knowledge. Despite Rorty's prognostications, then, it seems unlikely that such methods would indeed bring about the ultimate dissolution of philosophical problems.

Writing in 1990, Rorty confesses himself embarrassed by the efforts of his younger self to 'persuade himself that the disciplinary matrix in which he happened to find himself . . . was more that just . . . one more tempest in an academic teapot' (*TLT*: 371). If the metaphilosophical kernel of linguistic philosophy is the view that the problems of philosophy are problems of language, Rorty now finds himself dissenting from his earlier views in two ways:

> I am no longer inclined to view 'the problems of philosophy' as naming a natural kind ... [and] I am no longer inclined to think that there is such a thing as 'language' in any sense which makes it possible to speak of 'problems of language' (ibid.)

He goes on to note that if the phrase 'the problems of philosophy' has any sense it applies to those problems deriving from an epistemological tradition that has the mind or language representing something outside or external to itself. We saw in 3.3 that Rorty regards Davidson's attack on the scheme–content distinction as marking a decisive victory against the view that true sentences are made true by, and therefore represent, Reality. If one concludes with Davidson (1986: 46) that there's no such thing as language, if by language one means a medium of representation, then there are no concerns relating to language's adequacy to the world, and consequently no correlated philosophical problems. The point of *PMN*, he tells us, is to demonstrate that post-Cartesian problems about representation were the product of a 'bad' and, as it turns out, 'optional and replaceable ... description of human knowledge' (*TLT*: 372), which disappear once that description is replaced by an alternative suggested by Quine, Sellars, Davidson and Wittengenstein. The end of representationalism will (probably) mark 'the death of philosophy as a discipline with a method of its own' (*TLT*: 370); but since not all the problems discussed by philosophers are directly linked to representationalism, philosophy will not be brought to an end by this redescription: 'philosophy ... is too vague an amorphous a term to bear the weight of predications like "beginning" or "end" ' (*TLT*: 374).

Despite the bemused tone of Rorty's retrospection, the gap here does not seem quite so wide. The earlier speculation on philosophy's future took for granted that amongst the six possibilities canvassed, that for which 'Husserl' stood as an eponym was no longer viable. However, we've already noted that Rorty registered doubt that linguistic philosophy would bring about a post-philosophical paradigm, and perhaps the majority of contemporary philosophers continue to engage in activities that are 'representationalist' in character. From this perspective, the 'bad' description of knowledge detailed in *PMN* is but an elaboration of the 'spectatorial' account (with its 'immaterial eye') referred to in the earlier piece; and the anti-representationalist alternative derived from Sellars et al. is the one that aims at 'overthrowing' the former, opening up a new way of thinking about the philosophy-as-finding versus philosophy-as-making dispute. Nevertheless, we've remarked the extent to which Rorty comes to think of the image of the 'immaterial eye' as standing proxy for an entire picture that holds us captive: 'of man as mind, or spirit . . . [and of] his knowledge as a special relationship between his mind and its object' (*CP*: 32–3). Indeed, it was a feature of what we called Rorty's *Kehre* that he came to regard his eliminativism as still controlled by such a picture, and the changes this brought about in his views about reference and truth were outlined in 3.2. Moreover, we can see why this supports doubts about the utility of linguistic philosophy: if this epistemological picture is so embedded in common life that the latter is 'irredeemably Cartesian', the linguistic philosopher is hard-pushed to argue that the traditional philosopher is departing from 'ordinary linguistic practice' (*TLT*: 32).

From the 1970s onwards, then, Rorty was engaged in elaborating an alternative description of human knowledge. With the strategic and increasing 'use' of Davidson's work, this involves the label 'methodological nominalism' being dropped, first in favour of epistemological behaviourism (in *PMN*) and subsequently 'anti-representationalism'. These preferred 'descriptions' are proposals for a Bergmannian ideal language, wherein the problems relative to the vocabulary of representationalism will disappear with it. This is a *negative* use of the ideal language idea, intended to help bring an end to 'the entire cultural tradition which made truth – the successful crossing of the void which divides man from the world – a central virtue' (*CP*: 32–3, 35) by presupposing a representationalist picture of knowledge. What, then, of the *positive* use of the idea? As we left it, the vocabulary in which *making* was to be championed metaphilosophically over *describing* was unformulated. It was, however, evident that, if it is to pick up the 'ideal language' idea, a vocabulary of making will no longer be constrained by the requirement that it shows how philosophical questions needn't arise, and neither will that end furnish the criteria of success. It will answer to a much broader array of interests and purposes.

These two realizations of the 'ideal language' idea can be pursued separately. We've already noted that much of Rorty's work contributes to the delineation of an anti-representational standpoint.

Equally, books like *Achieving Our Country* (1998), as well as collections like *Philosophy and Social Hope* (1999) and essays gathered elsewhere, are engaged with 'social hopes, programs of action, prophecies of a better future' (*PCP*: x). Metaphilosophically, however, the two projects are intimately related. As we saw in 3.3, the anti-representationalist account of knowledge promotes a standpoint on what it is to find something justified from which both itself and any post-representationalist 'vision' is to be judged. But as we began this chapter by observing, to take the anti-representationalist gambit is to abandon an image of ourselves as in some way cosmically privileged, both as individual *knowers* whose essence is to 'represent' the true nature of reality and as philosophers who exemplify that essence through our intellectual calling. The purpose of the second project, then, is to provide a reason to take that gambit. In this *positive* use the ideal language is an alternative vision of ourselves, both as individuals and as intellectuals aiming to give collective expression to that identity. In what remains of this chapter, we'll therefore look at the first text in which Rorty integrates his negative account of an ideal language and his alternative vision for intellectual life. Let's turn, then, to the book that 'though disliked by most of [his] fellow philosophy professors' nevertheless brought him 'success among nonphilosophers' (*PSH*: 12).

4 Whither epistemology?

For Rorty, the still dominant conception of philosophy is 'as a discipline [that] . . . sees itself as the attempt to underwrite or debunk claims to knowledge made by science, morality, art, or religion . . . on the basis of its special understanding of the nature of knowledge and mind' (*PMN*: 3). Its claim to such legislative authority is based on the view that only philosophy can elucidate the criteria of accurate representation, and thus distinguish between those discourses that deliver up objective truths about the world – the usual paradigm being natural science – and those that serve more decorous ends. This suggests that rather than philosophers showing understanding of the relevant subject matter, these areas must demonstrate their competence in the *philosophical* idiom. This 'representationalist' paradigm reached its fullest cultural expression in the nineteenth century, when intellectuals could take pride in the fact that their subject was in the vanguard of the secularizing forces in Western culture. Since then, philosophy has declined relentlessly in status, to find itself sandwiched between 'occult' and 'self-help' on the shelves of most bookshops.

Although a self-respecting intellectual would no longer be expected to turn to philosophy for 'an ideology or a self-image' (p. 5), most practitioners of the subject operate with the same 'Cartesian-Kantian' conception of its legislative role. Here the mind–body problem stands proxy for an image or picture of man, both in the world and with others, that unites concerns about knowledge and personhood through the concept of consciousness. This gives philosophy both a model and a method. The world is mirrored in the minds of knowers, the elect amongst whom can determine a priori those representations 'which are the touchstones of truth' (p. 210) and thus constitute the normative framework for all empirical inquiry. Without the idea of such a 'permanent, neutral framework' (p. 8), the notion of philosophy being distinct from science or from culture in general would make little sense; and it is part of the task of *PMN* to elucidate and undermine the image of the mind and the world that holds it in place. To this end, Rorty draws on the constructive efforts of philosophers like Quine and Sellars to advance an anti-representationalist critique of the analytic (indeed, the post-Kantian) philosophical tradition.

This critique of the 'spectatorial' account of knowledge is not restricted to recent analytic philosophy: Heidegger, Dewey and Wittgenstein 'are in agreement that the notion of knowledge as accurate representation, made possible by special mental processes, and intelligible through a general theory of representation, needs to be set aside' (p. 6). One might therefore ask why bother with the constructive efforts of those whom Rorty descries as working within a 'frame of reference' he is 'trying to put in question' (p. 7)? The answer lies in part with the fact that for Heidegger et al. the critique of the ontotheological tradition is set in the context of envisaging a post-Kantian culture, a standpoint *from which* Rorty wishes to articulate his glimpse of a culture no longer in thrall to a master-discourse. At the same time, the audience for the book consists of the selfsame philosophers who, while they would regard Quine, Davidson and Sellars as authoritative voices in the conversation of analytic philosophy, would reject Heidegger (if not Wittgenstein) with Carnapian scorn.[10]

Before proceeding, it's worth remarking an apparent inconsistency in Rorty's motivation. Since it has been acknowledged that few take the philosopher's self-arrogated role as guarantor of objectivity seriously, why should we aspire to a glimpse of an age that no longer sees the philosopher in such a role? A quick response highlights one of the themes that, for Rorty, unites Heidegger with Dewey and Wittgenstein: each of them came to see their own efforts to retain a foundational role for philosophy as 'self-deceptive' (p. 5) and thence reached the conclusion that such inclinations required therapy 'to make the reader question his own motives for philosophizing' (ibid.). The implication, then, is that just as Rorty managed to overcome his own self-deceptively Carnapian view 'that philosophers should . . . try to become more "scientific" and "rigorous"' (*PSH*: 177–8), so too might his analytic audience.

The foregoing emphasizes that *PMN* is a book for philosophers. But who else would it be written for? And why, if it was written for philosophers, did it prove so unpopular with philosophers and a 'success among nonphilosophers'? Stating that a book on quantum theory is for physicists hardly makes a substantial point. Of course, the thought is that although the contents aren't accessible to everyone, they nevertheless apply to a common world of physical entities. Likewise, most analytic philosophers publish scholarly papers presupposing that their findings are no less 'scientific'. Needless to say, *PMN* is not intended to be a contribution to science. Its therapeutic ambition is that by becoming convinced that the strains *within* the specified 'frame of reference' were resolvable into the thesis of epistemological behaviourism, its readers might then be able to relate to Heidegger et al., not as philosophers 'holding view on subjects of common concern' (*PMN*: 372) but as edifying philosophers who can help them find 'new, better, more interesting, more fruitful ways of speaking' (p. 360). That would be to give philosophy a new self-image, which puts it beyond the desire to legislate with respect to other areas of culture. Not surprisingly, this view is likely to appeal more to those 'nonphilosophers' whose activities already seem more edifying than scientific to those being asked to relinquish the privileges of epistemological rank!

Notwithstanding the confessedly limited conception of its audience, one might still wonder why one would bother trying to wean analytic philosophers off the idea that their subject had cognitive authority long after the rest of the culture has ceased to hold such a view. The issue here relates to what exactly it is that Heidegger et al. glimpse. Clearly, this future culture hitherto dimly perceived is done so from a perspective wherein the rejection of the mirror of nature 'picture' is seen in a *positive* and not merely negative light. Only certain elements of this are developed in *PMN*, but Rorty makes it clear where, from his metaphilosophical standpoint, the respective strengths of Heidegger et al. lay. Where Wittgenstein has a 'flair for deconstructing captivating pictures', it is Heidegger who allows us to ' "distance" ourselves from the tradition' by giving us an 'historical awareness . . . of the source' of the mirror imagery that is central to it (p. 12). Since both men are concerned with 'keeping oneself apart from the banal self-deception typical of the latter days of a decaying tradition' (p. 13), they flatter us into thinking that we philosophers might too escape the herd and become Nietzschean free-spirits.

However, this existential glimpse of freedom from Plato's self-deceiving promise of power through knowledge only has appeal if the herd is similarly self-deceived; otherwise one is merely one of the last to be let in on an ill-kept secret. This, then, is where Dewey is required: he gives content to this 'glimpse' for he 'lets us see the historical phenomenon of mirror-imagery . . . within a social perspective' (ibid.). Of the triumvirate, then, only Dewey wrote with an end in view that wasn't merely self-transformative, because only he has a vision of what a culture might be like once such imagery is abandoned. So, for Rorty, although philosophy's influence has withered, the 'picture' of the human subject it bequeathed the world survives, leaving a culture (self-deceptively) 'dominated by the idea of objective cognition' (ibid.) and vulnerable to a similar decline. The task of the book, then, is to transform its readers' understanding both of their subject and of themselves, qua practitioners (and subjects) of that subject, in order that they might play a role in freeing up culture for the post-objectivist age.

Carrying out this transformation will take philosophy 'From Epistemology to Hermeneutics', the title of the opening chapter of Part III of *PMN*. To be open to this redescription of philosophy one needs to have one's faith in the epistemological project shaken, and that is the combined task of the first two parts of the book. In Part I, Rorty aims to reduce the problem of consciousness (in the form of the mind–body problem) to the problem of privileged access. What emerges is the by now familiar view that the norms governing reports of pains and other 'mental events' are equated with moves warranted in a linguistic game. Since the rules of the game can change, 'we' subjects have no conversation-transcending *authority* to assert knowledge in this area, and 'we' philosophers are unable to legislate with respect to what determines the correct usages of relevant terms. Part II expatiates on this attack on the authority of both 'subjects'. In chapter 4, Rorty details the Bergmannian version of the ideal language idea, the quest for a redescription of human knowledge in which the post-Cartesian problems about representation cannot be stated, and so can be regarded as having been 'eliminated'. In 3.2–3.3 we outlined some of the important features of Rorty's 'substantive philosophical' alternative, but it's worth lingering over the key idea, and examining how the transition towards hermeneutics is advanced through a critique of Quine.

For Rorty, 'the basic confusion contained in the idea of a "theory of knowledge"' (p. 161) comes from eliding 'the causal process of acquiring knowledge with questions concerning justification' (p. 209). In simple Lockean terms this is the notion that (for example) I am justified in believing that there's a pint of beer in front of me because my 'pint of beer' impression is a representation of its worldly object in virtue of being caused by that object. The counterposed thought is that when something is grasped conceptually, this occurs within a context or web of linguistically articulated inferential linkages. This is what distinguishes my seeing a pint of beer *as* a pint of beer (as something desirable, or as being one too many) from an animal's or a pre-linguistic infant's ability to respond differentially to such an object in their environment. The latter is a causal relation, and has no bearing on the nature of judgements made about the experience. As Sellars famously notes:

> In characterising an episode or a state of knowing we are not giving an empirical description of that episode or state; we are placing it in the logical space of reasons, of justifying and being able to justify what one says (1963: 169)

Relations of justification, then, are orthogonal to causal interaction. As we saw in 2.4, for Rorty the former run along lines established by the norms authorized by social practices. Epistemological behaviourism – 'which might be called simply "pragmatism"' (*PMN*: 176) – is the generalization of his Sellarsian account of sensation-reports, 'explaining rationality and epistemic authority by reference to what society lets us say, rather than the latter by the former' (p. 174). On this account, the gap between mind and world is not the metaphysical abyss of the Realist and the sceptic but a causal gap; and the beliefs that philosophers regard as privileged representations are just the items society, in the form of ongoing language games, won't at present tolerate deviation from.

One way to think about epistemological behaviourism is as an alternative standpoint to the one presupposed by 'traditional philosophy'.[11] For Rorty, the latter requires that one make sense of 'the

idea that truth consists in correspondence to, or accurate representation of, reality' (*TP*: 25), itself invested in an imagined escape from
finitude that has us able to 'step outside our skins . . . and compare
ourselves with something absolute' (*CP*: xix). To accept the former
is to embrace our (as it were) species-being and revert to the 'community as source of epistemic authority' (*PMN*: 188). It also delivers
up the anti-representationalist apothegm; to wit, that only a belief
can justify another belief. Here's Davidson's version of it:

> All that counts as evidence or justification for a belief must come
> from the same totality of belief to which it belongs. (2001b: 153)

Although they share this disregard for truth-makers, we've heeded
the lack of complete accord between them on the topic of truth and
will return to it in chapter 6. For now, recall that for Rorty this
maxim goes along with the rejection of the view that 'truth' has any
use other than to remind us that *this*, here and now, is what the
community sanctions (truth$_1$), but that they might nevertheless
come to sanction something else in the future (truth$_2$). Referring
back to Quine's attack on the analytic–synthetic distinction (1.3), the
point is that a concept or distinction is only as good as its utility in
giving an explanation of what people do and say. There is nothing
wrong with talking about 'raw feels, a priori concepts, innate ideas'
(*PMN*: 177) as long as it's understood that these terms have no
special source of *authority*. Without the accompanying epistemological picture, these are ordinary uses and not *philosophical* uses. Like
'electron', 'justice' and 'the unconscious', they take their chances in
the free-market that is the social realm of language. Since they do
not tap into a deeper ontological vein, neither their elimination nor
their retention has any ontological significance: ontology disappears along with reference$_3$ and an 'explanatory' use for truth.[12]

It is for this reason that Rorty comes to disdain Quine's rejection
of intentional idioms as a failure of pragmatic nerve. Quine's commitment to the philosophical importance of the distinction between
the language of physics (which treats of matters of fact) and the
lesser idioms leads him to conclude that 'if we are limning the true
and ultimate structure of reality, the canonical scheme knows . . . no
propositional attitudes but only the behavior of organisms' (Quine
1960: 221). The important distinction here is between under-
determination and indeterminacy. Under-determination of theory
by the evidence relates to the fact that, even when all the facts are
in, the choice of theory is still open: 'In a word, [physical theories]

can be logically incompatible and empirically equivalent' (Quine 1970: 179). However, 'the indeterminacy of translation it not just an instance of the empirically underdetermined character of phys- ics . . . [it] is additional' (ibid.: 180). If, from two equally consistent physical theories A and B, we adopt A, we would still be free to (radically) translate a foreigner as believing A or B (or neither). For Quine, it is of the nature of the indeterminacy of translation that even when there is agreement on the physical facts, the translation of intentional statements and acts is undecided:

> The question whether . . . the foreigner *really* believes A or . . . B, is a question whose very significance I would put in doubt. This is what I am getting at in arguing the indeterminacy of translation. (ibid.: pp. 180–1)

As Rorty argues (1972c), Quine's distinction between indetermi- nacy and under-determination rests on a prior commitment to a physicalist ontology.[13] Unless one has a stable realm of 'matters of fact' with which to contrast the wobbly realm of the intentional, there are no grounds for suggesting that indeterminacy is anything other than under-determination. Without that distinction, however, all descriptive resources are on a par with regard to their ontologi- cal status. It is at this point (*PMN*: 205–9) that Rorty turns to David- son. In 'Mental Events', Davidson attempts his own 'solution' to the mind–body problem by undermining the possibility of (psycho- physical) laws that generalize relations between intentional and physical terms and thus make possible a naturalistic reduction of the former to the latter. For Rorty, this suggests that, although we can formulate remarks that bring together terms from different realms of language like the mental and the physical, we cannot build these up into comprehensive theories. So, for example, there are (homonomic) theories that run together talk of atoms, neutrons, protons and electrons, with that of spin and quanta of energy, but we don't have (heteronomic) theories that mix this talk up with talk of justice, aesthetic bliss and the experience of pain. The point is that these distinctions have no ontological significance; all are simply ways of coping with that 'unit of empirical inquiry' that is 'the whole culture' (*PMN*: 201): 'an intentional vocabulary is just one more vocabulary for talking about portions of the world which can, indeed, be completely described without this vocabulary' (p. 207).

Rorty does not need to invoke Davidson here, and in general he looks with greater favour upon Dennett's treatment of intentionality, where the adoption of the idiom is to be thought of as a strategy for better prediction and control of certain sorts of things (people, chess computers, some animals).[14] It is important to note, then, that Rorty disputes the way Davidson motivates his attack on the possibility of laws linking the intentional with the physical. As he observes, Davidson explicitly associates the non-assimilation of physical and mental terms to the differing sources of evidence appropriate to the two linguistic realms. For Davidson, 'we cannot intelligibly . . . attribute any propositional attitude to an agent except within the framework of a viable theory of his beliefs, desires, intentions, and decisions' (Davidson 1980: 96; quoted favourably at *PMN*: 206) precisely because of normative constraints implied by 'the central role of translation in the description of all propositional attitudes, and to the indeterminacy of translation' (Davidson 1980: 97; quoted unfavourably at *PMN*: 207). Since Rorty rejects the idea that indeterminacy is anything other than under-determination, he cannot see what the 'philosophically interesting' difference is between the irreducibility of, on the one hand, biology (or geology) to physics and, on the other, that of meaning and belief likewise. The constraints 'on psychological explanation *are* simply the familiar constraints of holistic explanation' (1998: 393) which apply across the board.

We will return to the question of whether or not there is a difference that makes a difference between the constraints placed on intentional discourse and the familiar under-determination of theory in 6.4. Turning to the future of philosophy as hermeneutic, however, we'll observe in passing that it emerges in a different idiom.

5   The reappearing 'we'

In 4.4 we saw Rorty deploy the negative use of the ideal language idea to show that *if* this alternative description of human knowledge is plausible, *then* the 'way of thinking of knowledge' that stands at the heart of the representational model 'is optional . . . and so is philosophy as it has understood itself since the middle of the [nineteenth] century' (*PMN*: 136). Purging Quine of his ontological bias towards one particular discourse – theoretical physics – allows for the culmination of what Rorty finds most amenable in his work: 'his strictures against . . . attempt[s] to divide philosophy from science' (p. 208). In 4.3 it was observed that for Rorty an anterior commitment to this division delimited the options for post-philosophical thinking. The 'overcoming' of this distinction redeems the intentional idiom and restores to respectability the *Geisteswissenschaften*. So the alternative description of knowledge that renders otiose the problems of epistemologically centred philosophy simultaneously gestures towards its successor, hermeneutics, by placing its subject matter on the same footing as the subject matter of the *Naturwissenschaften*.

Readers familiar with the hermeneutic tradition will be forgiven for finding this compliment problematic.[15] That sense of dislocation is heightened when one considers that one of the central characters in Rorty's hermeneutic turn is Hans-Georg Gadamer. After all, on the traditional account, hermeneutics contrasts the *explanations* natural scientists seek of the phenomena of nature with the *understanding* aspired to by social scientists of the objects that constitute their fields of investigation.[16] Whereas the *Naturwissenschaften* treat of a brute, purposeless, intrinsically meaningless world, the phenomena of the *Geisteswissenschaften* are presented to inquiry within a normative framework constituted by the values, projects and presuppositions of 'self-interpreting'[17] creatures like ourselves. To interpret such phenomena – to grasp their meanings – requires that one take up to a certain degree the participatory standpoint of the agents involved. However, this activity is not orientated towards some uncritical identification with another. When we try to understand what demon-talk means for the Nortians, we do so for our own purposes. To 'understand' in this sense is to bring their world, their understanding of things including themselves, into our own: to fuse the normative horizons of (engaged) participant and observer.

In 1.2 we observed that hermeneutic inquiry thus construed presents a barrier to the aspiration to unify the sciences under the aegis of a common methodology, which in Hempel's time was broadly deductive-nomological.[18] Moreover, insofar as the realm of the 'intrinsically meaningful' was equated with the mental, it aligned the apparent inescapability of certain philosophical problems with a vision of man divided ontologically between disparate realms. Along with the project of unifying the sciences, then, goes the imperative to bring us metaphysical peace by placing man *in* nature as a proper object of empirical investigation. However, it turns out that, in order to defeat dualism, philosophy is required to legislate with respect to what is and is not cognitively significant. This seigneurial attitude towards science came under attack from the likes of Quine, Kuhn, Feyerabend, Hanson and Hesse. The upshot was a post-positivist account of science that emphasized how the results of inquiry are under-determined by the evidence, and constituted likewise within 'paradigms' that express a full range of disciplinary norms. From this perspective, the natural sciences begin to look a little more like the hermeneutic activities they were supposed to contrast with.

Of course, hermeneutic 'inquiry' on the Heideggerian-Gadamerian approach is as avowedly anti-Cartesian as postivism; but in any event the fear that edging towards a globalized herme-neutics presages a lapse into mentalism is mitigated by the fact that on Rorty's Sellarsian account the normative structures are socially mediated, not expressive of the 'private' states of individual minds. In this sense, one might think of Gadamer's thought as a sort of hermeneutic counterpart to Sellars's. Compare the latter's famous apothegm about psychological nominalism with the following:

> All understanding is interpretation, and all interpretation takes place in the medium of language that allows the object to come into words and yet is at the same time the interpreter's own language. (Gadamer 1975: 389)

As noted in 3.3, Rorty's principle objection to Sellars is the latter's desire to retain something of the Realist's practice-transcending intuition about truth through the notion that scientific theories 'picture' extra-linguistic reality more or less adequately.[19] Likewise, for Gadamer, philosophical hermeneutics is concerned with an understanding of truth that is non-methodological and therefore presumed distinct from that aspired to by the natural sciences as traditionally construed. In both cases, then, there is an assumed contrast between philosophy and science, an opposition Rorty (4.3) contends 'controls' the terms in which the metaphilosophical strug-gle to articulate a view of philosophy-as-making are made. The suggestion is that once one abandons the attempt to disambiguate philosophy from science by attempting to legislate with respect to the criteria that determine the latter, the grounds for motivating a distinction between human and natural sciences disappears for *both* hermeneuticists *and* their former positivistic opponents.

It is in this light that Kuhn's role in Rorty's appropriation of hermeneutics becomes clearer. Kuhn helps undermine the episte-mological picture thought to sustain the distinction between phi-losophy and science by offering a redescription of the nature of theory change. This leaves Rorty free to interpret hermeneutics[20] in a way that does not presuppose a distinction in kind between the natural and the human sciences. Central to Rorty's use of Kuhn is his application of the latter's concept of incommensurability.[21] In 1.3 we examined briefly Kuhn's distinction between 'normal' and 'revolutionary' science. The principal point was that, since the 'disciplinary matrix' that constitutes the activity of normal science fixes the norms of scientific rationality, there is no higher, neutral standpoint from which shifts *between* paradigms can be evaluated. When a scientist comes up with a revolutionary theory of nature, no algorithm is available for deciding in advance whether or not her suggestion is or is not 'rational'. It is in this sense that successive paradigms are said to be *incommensurable*. Although Rorty chastises his lapse into idealism (*PMN*: 324–5), implying that in this respect he is, like his opponents, still 'held captive' by the traditional epistemological project, he goes on to endorse Kuhn's observation that if there are no independently specifiable rules that *determine* the choice of theory, the relevant criteria are 'values, which *influence* it' (Kuhn 1977: 321, quoted at *PMN*: 327; emphasis added). This implies that it is only if one had a prior commitment to the idea that there are specifically *scientific* values – values that 'influence' the choice of scientific theory but operate across no other stretch of discourse – that one would draw a line between the sort of deliberative process involved in switches between scientific paradigms and that involved in 'for example, the shift from the *ancien régime* to bourgeois democracy, or from the Augustans to the Romantics' (*PMN*: 327).

It is Rorty's contention that such a prior commitment is expressive of a deeper fidelity to 'the image of scientific theory as Mirror of Nature' (p. 333). Without it we simply have the contingent emergence of the values that were hammered out during science's turf wars with religious authority, which, given the normal model we *now* have of (normal) science, are canonical.[22] This leads to two important claims. The first is that the distinction between 'normal' and 'revolutionary' discourse 'cuts across the distinction between science and nonscience' (p. 333), allowing Rorty to co-opt Kuhn's terminology into his redescription of hermeneutics. The second claim is that, although the 'moral and scientific . . . ideals of the Enlightenment', which are 'our most precious cultural heritage' (ibid.) and 'made us what we are today' (p. 331), came attached to this questionable epistemological picture, it is not required to keep them intact. Indeed, they will look 'more attractive' (p. 333) without it. We'll return to that second point in the next chapter. For the time being, let's examine how this Kuhnian vocabulary is put to use in advancing beyond epistemology and towards hermeneutics.

Rorty's uses of the term 'hermeneutic' are extremely diverse, and it oftentimes seems to register little more than a 'hurray!' to epistemology's 'boo!' After *PMN* Rorty scarcely used the term again, no doubt for the simple reason that it becomes merely a name for the desire to escape the epistemological problematic, the use of which invites the sort of disputation Rorty wanted to gesture beyond. Nevertheless, even if an interpretive unity cannot be brought to his 'abnormal' use of the term, it plays an important role in the discursive economy of *PMN* as part of the attempt to 'change the subject' of the philosophical conversation. At one level of usage, then, the suggestion is that traditional epistemology operates on the basis that since all rational discourse is constrained by rules accessible to the philosopher – the 'neutral framework of inquiry' – all present and future ways of talking about the world are commensurable. No matter how great the conceptual innovation, any future suggestion will be subject to rules that show how agreement can be reached. It amounts to the assumption that from a certain standpoint there is only *normal* discourse. This parallels the view of scientific method that Kuhn set out to oppose. Mapping Kuhn's normal-revolutionary distinction on to the culture as a whole, Rorty contrasts normal discourse, where criteria for resolving disputes are readily available (be they moral, aesthetic, scientific or political), with *abnormal* (revolutionary) discourse, where inter-discursive norms (rules for commensuration) are not apparent. As conceived, hermeneutics is the name given to attempts to come to terms with abnormal discourse. This *might* relate to new ways of talking about humans or to encountering humans who talk about themselves and their world in ways radically different from our own – those who believe in demons, for example, or disbelieve in the mind – but it might equally relate to new scientific theories.

From this perspective, the term has a sort of flag-waving, troop-rousing generality: it is a 'struggle against [the] assumption' that all discourses are commensurable (*PMN*: 318); 'an expression of hope that the cultural space left by the demise of epistemology will not be filled' (p. 315). It is, however, intended to give a certain prophetic shape to the considerations that emerge from the eliminativist approach to concept change, and to the revisionary accounts of truth and reference we examined in 3.2. When we encounter abnormal discourse, we are meeting recommendations that we talk in a different way. When the Sortians tells us that ' "Sensations" refers to brain-processes' (reference$_2$) or that 'there are no sensations' (true$_2$) they are doing what others did when declaiming that 'all people are born equal', or that 'the id is the source of all creativity': suggesting that claims not authorized presently by the social norms of the day be assented to nevertheless. The aim is to get us to see challenges to present ways of thinking, not as more grist for the epistemological mill, to be ground down to reveal the concepts or structure that underpin all knowledge claims, but as offering the promise of better achieving what we want. To accept the hermeneutic gambit is to redescribe what goes on when we operate *within* a normal discourse. That is to say, it is to adopt the following 'eliminative' suggestion:

* When you refer$_1$ to epistemology, what you're *really* talking about (referring$_2$ to) is 'discourse about normal . . . discourse. (*PMN*: 346)

This account should not obscure the fact that 'hermeneutics' has a more 'ground-level' use. On this, 'we have to practice hermeneutics' (p. 358). It is 'a fact about people which the epistemological tradition has tried to shunt aside' (p. 358). As we've noted, Rorty's story turns in part on the way the mandate the philosopher claims with respect to other discourses reflects a model of the self that centres on the authority each of us claims over the contents of our own minds. If adopting the hermeneutic standpoint presages the end of epistemology, whither the *subject* of epistemology? This brings us to the *existential* aspect of the hermeneutic gambit. On the epistemological behaviourist account, 'we' reappear in the guise of what one might call a describing – or *re*describing – animal. Descriptions are ways of giving salience to the causal patterns that an otherwise brute and disenchanted nature delivers up to our sensory organs. Given this view, the concern with self-interpretation that Rorty identifies as being at the heart of the desire to redeem the particularity of the human sciences is recast as the 'existential' claim that 'redescribing ourselves is the most important thing we can do' (pp. 358–9).

Of course, no single account or set of vocabularies is (philosophically) privileged in this respect; to maintain the contrary – to search for truths (truths$_3$) – is the expression of bad faith. When Rorty redescribes epistemology as dominated by the idea that 'to be fully human . . . we need to find agreement with other human beings' (p. 316), the implication is that 'we' look outside ourselves for

sources of normative authority that would ensure the desired agreement and thus absolve us of the responsibility for creating it.
Indeed, Rorty appropriates Sartre's use of the *en-soi/pour-soi* distinction to suggest that the desire for the one true account is nothing
less than the desire to flee from the responsibility of having to
choose[23] which 'vocabulary' one will *be*, to deny simultaneously
both the sociality of normal discourse and the challenge of abnormal discourse. Recall (4.4) the thought that the key insight upon
which epistemological behaviourism is based is the (Sellarsian)
claim that causation is confused with justification. For Rorty, this
goes along with the idea that the world and not our peers authorize
our norms. What we have here, then, is the *existential* diagnosis of
this mistake, and a *naturalized* version of its import: to want to
become an object is simply to want to 'programme' oneself once
and for all with a way of coping with the world. It is to deny our
finitude, and the consequent contingency of our descriptions; to
blind ourselves to our ability to come up with better ways of dealing
with the world, with realizing more efficiently our ends by coming
up with new saliencies, to what can 'aid us in becoming new
beings' (*PMN*: 360).

   On Rorty's story, then, to step up to the hermeneutic mark is to
overcome a certain immaturity of the will. When we think of ourselves in this new way we embark on the quest for edification, not
knowledge. To educate ourselves is to strive for new descriptions,
not seek out the one true description. To this end, Rorty invokes
Gadamer's concept of *wirkungsgeschichtliches Bewusstsein*. On his
pragmatic appropriation, this is a kind of historicized counterpart
to Sellars's psychological nominalism, according to which we cul-
tivate 'the sort of consciousness of the past which changes us'
insofar as we come to see it as something presented 'for our own
uses' (p. 359). Edifying discourse presents a challenge: it takes us
outside ourselves, demanding of us the hermeneutic effort required
to come to terms with what is abnormal. To see ourselves as the
kinds of creatures that should be open to this renewal through
adaptation[24] is to embrace the existential freedom to choose our
own projects.

6   In conversation

The new 'use' that, in the spirit of Bergmann, Rorty aims to give
to hermeneutics can be elaborated by considering the crucial role

of the concept of 'conversation'. This in turn will lead us into Rorty's concluding thoughts about the future of philosophy. Ironically, adverting to Kant's later work may be of assistance. Clearly, the lack of an algorithm for rendering discourses commensurate is at the heart of Rorty's attitude towards the phenomenon of concept change. This is also one of the concerns of the *Critique of Judgement*. Defining 'Judgement in general' as 'the faculty of thinking the particular as contained under the universal', Kant contrasts what he calls *determinate* judgement, 'where the universal (the rule, principle, or law) is given', with *reflective* judgement 'where only the particular is given and the universal has to be found for it' (1987: Introduction, IV). Kant's focus is on aesthetic and teleological judgements as illuminating instances of reflective judgement, but the details need not detain us. The issue is with how sense is made of things that are presented not as familiar, classifiable and rule-governed, but as requiring the use of imagination if they are to be made part of the unity of thinking. In composite terms one might say that while determinate judgements operate within normal discourse, where decision procedures are apparent, reflective judgement is required when, during encounters with abnormal discourse, there are no rules for how to proceed and the work of imagination is required.[25] In this sense, hermeneutics can be thought of as the study of the work of reflective judgement: for the 'study of an abnormal discourse from the point of view of a normal discourse' (*PMN*: 320).

One further aspect of judgement is that the sort of imaginative activity one finds in operation in reflective judgement is the more fundamental.[26] In this light, consider Rorty's description of the 'hermeneutical notion of knowledge', according to which:

> we cannot understand the parts of a strange ... practice ... unless we know something about how the whole thing works, whereas we cannot get a grasp on how the whole works until we have some understanding of its parts. (*PMN*: 319)

This characterization of hermeneutics seems to add little to the holistic, socialized normativity of epistemological behaviourism (cf. pp. 170–1, 181, and *passim*). Indeed, it suggests that what goes on when we encounter abnormal discourse, when the requirement for reflective judgement becomes paramount, is a natural extension of what takes place in the context of normal discourse. This connection between the one use of 'hermeneutics' (as 'another way of coping' with the world (p. 356)) and its higher-level designation as an attitude is reinforced when one considers the role of conversation. Characterizing epistemological behaviourism as seeing 'knowledge as a matter of conversation' (p. 171), Rorty likewise maintains that the 'hermeneutic' notion of knowledge described above 'fits well with . . . the notion of culture as conversation' (p. 319). If this is plausible, 'conversation' might be thought of as the socialized form of reflective judgement. On the one hand, it relates to the way in which individuals comport themselves with respect to the discursive practices that authorize what can and cannot be said; that is to say, with normal discourse, with what is $true_1$ ('justification is . . . a matter of . . . conversation' (p. 170)). On the other hand, it is through conversation that (abnormal) challenges to what is customary and habitual are mediated, the way that new norms – new $truths_1$, new 'determinate judgements' – are forged. In effect, Rorty weds Sellars's 'space of reasons' talk with Gadamer's *wirkungsgeschichtliches Bewusstsein* to characterize 'culture as the "conversation of mankind" '. As such, hermeneutics proposes an alternative view of human flourishing, one which sees incommensurate discourses as 'strands in a possible conversation' between people 'united by civility' (p. 318). Culture is the space wherein our fledgling selves become orientated to the norms of the day before seeking out the conversations that edify by provoking us into rewriting ourselves, in the hope perhaps of contributing a new voice – a new abnormal discourse – to that conversation.

So where does this leave philosophy? Referring back to table 4.1, *PMN* offers some slight variation, as shown in table 4.2. The primary contrast is between systematic and edifying philosophers. The former in effect answer 'yes' to one of the questions that divided up the proper names in *TLT*: in the parlance of *PMN*, they 'search for universal commensuration in a final vocabulary'. On the other hand, the latter have kept alive the 'historicist' and 'relativist' idea that, since truth is just 'conformity to the norms of the day' (p. 368), the purportedly final vocabulary is just the latest dream of reason. The distinction formerly made between those that are and are not methodological nominalists is no longer regarded as significant. Since epistemological behaviourism is meant to be the result of the dialectical resolution of tensions in the thought of (in particular) Quine and Sellars, one might feel that it is important to distinguish them from (say) Kant and Descartes. For Rorty's metaphilosophical purposes, however, that is not the case. Whereas in *TLT* one could subscribe to methodologi-

Table 4.2 The future of philosophy

		Are there criteria of philosophical truth (success, progress, etc.)?	
		Yes	*No*
Epistemologically behaviourist?	*No*	*Systematic philosophers* Descartes; Kant; Russell; Habermas; Apel; Sellars; Quine; Davidson; Ryle; Kuhn; Putnam	
	Yes		*Edifying philosophers* Heidegger (later); Wittgenstein (later); Dewey. Also: Nietzsche; Kierkegaard; Sartre; Freud; Marx; Derrida; William James, etc.

cal nominalism and still be 'systematic', on this redescription all and only edifying philosophers are epistemological behaviourists whether or not (and of course none do) they formally embrace anything like this particular 'substantial thesis'.

The contrast between Heidegger and Wittgenstein (and the latter and Waismann) disappears because the sense in which any of these thinkers contribute to a *positive*, post-philosophical conception of the ideal language idea (in the non-Bergmannian sense) has (largely) gone. Their task now is (almost) entirely negative. As purveyors of edifying discourse, their abnormality lies in their refusal 'to present themselves as having found out any objective truth (about, say, what philosophy is)' (p. 370). As intellectuals, who feel most acutely the desire to redescribe themselves, edifying philosophers exhibit an existential 'dread (of) the thought that their vocabulary should ever be institutionalized' (p. 369). They wish to remake themselves in terms that invite no systematization: articulate a vocabulary that gives rise to no School, no project, and no merry band of tenured acolytes. Since one cannot be edifying on this account unless one is abnormal, the edifying philosophers' authenticity lies in the fact that their work is (qua philosophy) entirely reactive: it 'loses its point when the period they were reacting against is over' (p. 369).

Needless to say, this is not a characterization destined to flatter the reputation of any 'edifying' philosopher. It does, however, hint at where to locate Rorty's own text. The formal task of the edifying philosophers is to write against the tradition while avoiding the imputation that what they *say* as a consequence is claimed to be *true*. Now the charge that any attempt to escape metaphysics and make space for 'postmetaphysical thinking' is caught up in the logic of the very discourse it seeks to free itself from is one of the defining problematics of what used to be called 'postmodernism'.[27] In this respect it's an example of what motivated Rorty's (eliminativist) concern with concept change; namely, how to take up a (future) standpoint on the past or present and avoid it being judged by familiar standards. By characterizing the edifying philosopher as giving intellectual expression to the desire for authenticity, Rorty adds an existential twist to the reflexive problem: *being* a philosopher – not just *doing* philosophy – obliges one to remake oneself in terms that invite the very systematization that authenticity demands one avoid. Rorty's solution to the reflexive problem, then, is to see the struggle between edifying philosophers and systematic philosophers from the *outside*. The former don't articulate a post-metaphysical thinking; they mark the limits of the metaphysical. Their role as edifying *philosophers* makes sense 'only as a protest' against the thought that 'all discourse could be, or should be, normal' (p. 377).

To think that would be to deceive oneself. In this sense, then, edifying/existential philosophers help us overcome our bad faith: the 'cultural role of the edifying philosopher is to help us avoid the self-deception' (p. 373) that we might be known completely under a single description. They 'make the reader question his own motives for philosophizing . . . help their readers, or society as a whole, break free from outworn vocabularies' (pp. 5–6, 12). When philosophers aim to 'surpass' their predecessors, when they see themselves as *seeing* what others did not see, as opposed to just questioning the idea of such 'seeing', they themselves are falling into self-deception (p. 378). The only way they can avoid this and authenticate their vocabulary is to desire not to want to perpetuate philosophy (as a science). Or, rather, these texts can only be *read as* escaping the reflexive problematic if they are situated as conversational partners whose task is to keep open the conversation, not as making claims to truth₃. From the perspective of *PMN*, then, what these philosophers glimpse is the need to 'keep space open for the sense of wonder which poets can sometimes cause' (p. 370), to 'send conversation off in new directions' (p. 378). The 'gift' of the text is to invite 'we' philosophers to think that by doing that we are giving as full an expression to our self-interpreting selves as ever did the systematic philosophers of yore, and thereby embracing what should be of 'more concern': 'continuing the conversation of the West' (p. 394).

5

New Selves for Old

1 From epistemology to politics

In *TLT* Rorty suggests the metaphilosophical options on offer for formulating the philosophy-as-finding versus philosophy-as-making distinction are 'controlled' by an assumed contrast between science and philosophy (4.3). In *PMN* that contrast is undermined by using Kuhn's attack on scientific method to extend the epistemological behaviourist's 'socialized' account of the sources of normative authority. As a result, it is no longer clear what the 'philosophy' in 'philosophy-as-making' *means*, and as a consequence how one is to conceive of the *positive* conception of the 'ideal' language idea (of philosophy-as-linguistic-recommendation when the latter is not determined by the need to 'dissolve' traditional philosophical problems).

We can get a better sense of where this leaves us if we recall that those edifying philosophers who pitch themselves against the epistemological tradition can at best glimpse the view we post-epistemological readers of *PMN* are offered of a rhapsodic celebration of the abnormal in its multifarious forms. Making is abnormal; but abnormal philosophy has utility only while there is normal philosophy to oppose. The payback for the edifying philosopher is that by striving to be abnormal they give expression to the *existential* idea that freedom is the ability to re-create ourselves; or, on the less seductive, naturalized account, the capacity to 're-programme our dispositions to better enable us to achieve our goals'. At the same time, by their example, they help us ward off the temptation towards self-deception and nudge us towards the creative possibilities for the self in a post-'representational' culture.

The problem is that the self-image of the intellectual that Rorty aims to promote obliges us to play our part in freeing up culture for the post-objectivist age (4.4). Here it is not *self*-deception (of the sort Heidegger and Wittgenstein are good at uncovering in their readers) that is the issue, but the deception of *others*. That is where Dewey came in; yet, despite being heralded as one of the triumvirate of 'heroes' of the book, little specific use is made of his work in *PMN*. Similarly, although Rorty makes reference to the values of the 'West'/'the Enlightenment', and philosophers are emboldened to advance publicly their hold on us by 'continuing the conversation', that terminating declamation has the air of a homily. What exactly are we philosophers supposed to do? If those precious values are no longer 'tied to . . . shopworn mirror metaphors' (*PMN*: 333), what metaphors *ought* they to be tied to and who is to do the tying? If redescriptions of ourselves, of concept change, of truth and objectivity, are advanced on the basis, not of values and interests construed narrowly ('scientifically'), but in this expanded sense of what we like best about where we are now (and what other values and interests could motivate us?), how does this Bergmannian 'ideal' language relate to the *positive* conception of the 'ideal', the conceptual space for which *PMN* aims to open?

Perhaps, as Rorty observes, *PMN* is haunted still by the need to find out 'what, if anything, philosophy is good for' (*PSH*: 11).[1] Indeed, on this account, he was held captive by the desire to 'hold reality and justice in a single vision' (ibid.: 12). This image is the central metaphor of *Contingency, Irony, and Solidarity*, the book in which Rorty tries to make good on the lacunae in *PMN* by offering a vision of intellectual life that is no longer held back by that need to find a place for philosophy. In doing so it aims to resolve the problem outlined above. Rorty's first acknowledgement of this came soon after the appearance of *PMN*. The concern, he notes, is that since pragmatism holds truths to be *made* rather than *found*, and thus treats 'both science and philosophy as . . . literary genres' (*CP*: 141), it challenges the philosopher's moral self-image as someone who seeks the truth (political, moral) on behalf of humanity in the name of progress. In its place it seems to offer no more than the aesthete's romantic desire for self-creation, for making a poem of themselves, for constructing their own truth. But this search for 'sacred wisdom is purchased at the price of his separation from his fellow-humans' (p. 158), the results of which might range from aesthetic withdrawal, through Nietzschean revulsion, to totalitarian politics.

To put this another way, the 'existential turn' appears to set no limits on what people might want to be, and the extent to which that might impact on the requirements and freedom of others; and conversation seems all too thin a concept to set in place the safe-guards required to promote those precious Enlightenment values. So how are we to think of freedom when those who claim it do so in the name of a view of humans that we don't like? As Rorty notes, 'accommodation and tolerance must stop short of a willingness to work within any vocabulary that one's interlocutor wishes to use, to take seriously any topic that he puts forward for discussion' (*ORT*: 190). Rorty takes it that such an attitude is equivalent to having dropped the idea that 'a single moral vocabulary and a single set of beliefs are appropriate for every human community everywhere' (ibid.). In other words, the potentially amoral element in romanticism is another expression of that 'controlling' desire for a 'single vision'.

The task, then, is to offer an image for the intellectual that insu-lates the moral commitment to oneself from the 'sense of our common human lot' (*CP*: 158) by sketching a (*positive*) 'ideal lan-guage' that does not give rise to the temptation towards that 'single vision'. The primary purpose of this chapter is to offer an account of how Rorty goes about doing this, ending with an evaluation of his new self-image for the intellectual, the liberal ironist. Since *CIS* represents a turn towards the moral and political concerns of Rorty's 'philosophical hero' (*PCP*: 79) John Dewey, it will be helpful to start with a brief account of one of the latter's own attempts to synthesize, in the context of his own time, the concerns of *PMN* and *CIS*.

2   Dewey's redescription

Reconstruction in Philosophy (like *CIS*) began as a series of lectures, summarizing the version of pragmatism developed under the name of 'instrumentalism'. The book's principal aim is to make a case for the contemporary relevance of philosophy by opposing 'the classic notion' of its nature:

> Philosophy has arrogated to itself the office of demonstrating the existence of a transcendent, absolute, or inner reality and of reveal-

ing to man [its] nature and features. It has therefore claimed that it was in possession of a higher organ of knowledge than is employed by positive science and ordinary practical experience, and that it is marked by a supreme dignity and importance. (Dewey 1988: 92)

Dewey rejects the idea that such a conception of 'Reality' is the 'appropriate sphere for the exercise of philosophic knowledge' (p. 93). Pragmatism represents the moment of disciplinary self-consciousness: when it is recognized that 'under disguise of dealing with ultimate reality, philosophy has been occupied with the precious values embedded in social traditions' (p. 94), the content of philosophical discourse is redeemed:

> That which may be pretentiously unreal when it is formulated in metaphysical distinctions becomes intensely significant when connected with the drama of the struggle of social beliefs and ideals. (ibid.)

Philosophy's task is thus to 'clarify men's ideas as to the social and moral strifes of their own day' (p. 94). The reward for subject and practitioner comes with the hortative conclusion to the first lecture:

> Philosophy which surrenders its somewhat barren monopoly of dealings with Ultimate and Absolute Reality will find a compensation in enlightening the moral forces which move mankind and in contributing to the aspirations of men to attain to a more ordered and intelligent happiness. (ibid.)

Dewey's reconstruction of philosophy turns on his redescription of the concept of experience. Hitherto regarded as passive, and opposed to and standing in an inferior relation to reason, experience has now become 'an affair primarily of doing' (p. 129), of the active integration of 'reason in experience' (p. 127), and thus 'a guide in science and moral life' (p. 125). This presages a change in the way experience is conceived *and* experienced: 'the thought of experience follows after and is modeled upon the experience actually undergone' (p. 133). Moreover, it is not arbitrary but results from experience having 'undergone a profound social and intellectual change' (ibid.). Firstly, this is due to biological insights into the sorts of creatures we are:[2]

> The true 'stuff' of experience is . . . adaptive courses of action, habits,
> active functions, connections of doing and undergoing. (pp. 131–2)

Environmentally orientated activity is for Dewey 'the primary fact,
the basic category' (p. 129), not the passive reception of sensations
'representing' the *ordo essendi*. The implication is that cognition is
'derived . . . secondary in origin . . . involved in the process by which
life is sustained and evolved' (ibid.).[3]

Before continuing with Dewey's epistemology, let's take up the
second cause of experience having changed. On Dewey's historicist
account, this involves the transition from a Platonic account of
experience as 'enslavement to the past' (p. 132) to the Baconian
revolution that regarded it as a 'liberating power' (p. 133) that puts
nature to the test. According to this new experimentalism, experience is dynamic, in process, responsive to and generative of new
ends; it comes to 'include the process by which it directs itself in
its own betterment' (p. 134). Consequently, reason is 'experimental
intelligence' (p. 135). Concrete possibilities for the future arise as
a result of past experiences and present aims and values. These
are put to the test, evaluated for success and failure, and new
methods devised accordingly. Although this dynamic, fallibilistic,
experimentalism is drawn from the method of the new sciences,
it is not restricted to them: the 'intelligent administering of experience' that it suggests is equally applicable to moral and political
goals (ibid.).

On Dewey's naturalized Hegelian account of the concept of experience, the liberal and progressive forces of the Enlightenment were
held back and frustrated by the failure of philosophers to articulate
this account of experience. Our collective historical failure to integrate reason and experience 'played into the hands of the reaction-
ary and obscurantist' (p. 137) by giving common folk no option but
to fall back on philosophically disreputable common sense, which
embodies the very hierarchies and class privileges that the Enlightenment aimed to unsettle. The 'moral concern' of philosophers is to
promote the philosophical reconstruction of experience that will
liberate those forces.

Returning to cognition, on this naturalistic view it is no longer
conceived of as attendant on the 'spectatorial' picture: 'knowing . . . means a certain kind of intelligently conducted doing' (p.
149). Necessarily, then, philosophy must alter its nature to remain
in sympathy with the 'authorized spirit of science' (ibid.). Traditionally, the opposition was between the (empirically investigated)

ready-made *real* and the (rationally scrutinized) ready-made *ideal*. On the new conception the contrast is between 'the material of change' (ibid.) and the 'intelligently thought-out possibilities of the existent world which may be used as methods for making over and improving it' (p. 150). Philosophy is thus set free to:

> concentrate its attention upon ... projecting an idea or ideal which ... would be used as a method of understanding and rectifying ... the great social and moral defects and troubles from which humanity suffers. (p. 151)

Given that philosophy is to subserve moral and political ends, the reconstruction of logical theory is of primary importance (cf. p. 157). For Dewey, thinking 'takes its departure from specific conflicts in experience that occasion perplexity and trouble' (pp. 159–60). Since logic concerns the ways in which thinking proceeds according to some intelligent method, he rejects the idea that it is normative *as opposed to* descriptive, or that the 'form' of logical thought can be liberated from its content.[4] Logic is both art and science, the methodological sedimentation of what has worked in the past and might be relied upon to work in the future, but always subject to revision in the face of new experiences and new tasks. '[C]onceptions, theories and systems of thought' are 'tools', the value of which resides 'in their capacity to work' (p. 163).

Dewey's account of truth 'wholly depends[s] upon' (p. 170) his account of thinking, which itself extends his view of experience. The central claim is that 'the adverb "truly" is more fundamental than' 'true' or 'truth'. We plan to act in a certain way in order to deal with a particular problem, and that way guides us either truly or falsely depending on whether or not the desired outcome is achieved. In this sense, 'true' is a derivative success word applied to 'that which guides us truly' (p. 169), to the useful 'tool'. The challenge, then, is to see that an account of truth must be *deduced from*, and not be assumed antecedent to, the realignment of thinking brought about by the changes in the physical sciences. Diagnostically, resistance to this redescription on the part of the traditionalist is ascribed to an ill-fated alliance between the conception of Reality vouchsafed above and deference towards traditional sources of social and political authority (the priest, the prince). On the pragmatic view of truth, there is no authority external to whatever norms derive from concrete experimentation with experience. Consequently, the great task confronting the philosopher is to extend logic qua intelligent method from where it is already well developed to 'moral and political affairs' (p. 159).

Unsurprisingly, Dewey regards the idea that there is a 'single, final and ultimate' moral good or law as a hangover from feudalism (p. 172). The extension of the scientific challenge to the pre-Copernican celestial hierarchy issues in a moral and political particularism.[5] Like truth, justice, benevolence, health and friendship are derived from their adverbial forms and are not the names of Platonic universals. Similarly, the distinctions between natural and moral goods, between intrinsic and instrumental values and between politics and morals collapse. The emphasis, then, is on the difficult task of reconciling possibly conflicting goods, of thinking through concrete situations and not avoiding responsibility by assuming the existence of some supernatural order that is guaranteed in advance to make the task achievable.

Since no 'Reality' fixes possibilities, 'Growth itself is the only moral "end"' (p. 181). Indeed, 'freedom for an individual means growth, ready change when modification is required' (p. 198). It is here that education comes to the fore. For Dewey, the purpose of education is not training children for the demands of adult life but the continuous development of human capacities. It is the 'heart of the sociality of man' (p. 185), the means by which goods, which 'exist and endure only through being communicated' (p. 198), are circulated and tested so that each individual is empowered to utilize their capacities in making things better. Since 'social arrangements, laws, institutions . . . are means of creating individuals' (p. 191), the only moral meaning of democracy is found in resolving that the 'supreme test' of all such institutions 'shall be . . . their effect in furthering continued education . . . the contribution they make to the all-round growth of every member of society' (p. 186).

Towards the end of the book, Dewey notes that, although 'freedom for an individual is growth' (p. 198), this is not a freedom purchased at the expense of social interests. To assume this is to reify the concepts of 'Individual' and 'Society'.[6] Rather, the future development of society requires that its members can fulfil their potentialities. Indeed, since institutions derive their legitimacy precisely from this, the only moral 'end', society must allow for 'a leeway of experimentation beyond the limits of established and sanctioned custom' (p. 199). For Dewey, the results of this experimentation – of this 'abnormal discourse' – will eventuate in public goods (be 'normalized'). It is with this framing task in mind that we turn to Rorty's own attempt to reconcile the (private) 'growth of the individual' with those (public) 'social interests'.

3 Contingency, irony and solidarity

Contingency, Irony, and Solidarity (1989)[7] attempts to redescribe the trajectory of Western thought as an endeavour to bring theoretical unity to two 'constellations' of values: our individual need to fulfil, create or perfect ourselves (to exercise private autonomy), and our desire for solidarity with others, manifest in a commitment to the language of justice and of the commonweal. For Rorty, on the founding narratives of the West – the Platonic and the Pauline – and in their various footnotes, this reconciliation is effected through an account of human nature, of the essential self.[8] The historicist and contextualist decentring of the self and the associated attack on the 'Real' have helped to shift the burden of inquiry from a concern with Truth to a concern with Freedom. However, this has tended to emphasize one aspect of freedom (either the personal or the social) at the expense of the other; even, at the limit, regarding one as a threat to the other's existence. The suggestion, then, is that a collective error abides: the search for a 'single vision' that will either bring the two into focus or warrant the disavowal of one in favour of the other.

Rorty's alternative is to regard these values as incommensurable at the level of theory.[9] This is not intended to indicate some timeless, metaphysical division; rather, these values are our starting point, a matter of where *we* are *now*. The alternative view is that these present values are best served, not by a theory that grounds them but through a narrative that facilitates their elaboration and expansion. Consider this contrast in the light of two different models of justification. On a *metaphysical* conception, something is justified if it can be reduced to or shown to be dependent upon something else; on the *pragmatic* model something is justified through being extended in use. Imagine a situation in which free speech is valued but there are no newspapers. One might aim to legitimate free speech by grounding it in some more fundamental concept; alternatively, one might provide an edifying narrative through which a proposal for newspapers comes to be regarded as a 'natural' extension of the valued concept, an extension which when realized 'justifies' free speech.[10] In this latter sense there is no implication that by justifying a value one is looking 'outside' it and therefore simultaneously *de*valuing it.

A central feature of Rorty's own narrative is the encouragement of this 'turn against theory and toward narrative' (p. xvi), which is reflected in a methodological shift from philosophy to literary criticism. This shift is reflected in the structure of the book, which moves from the philosophical concerns of Part I to the more heterogeneous readings that comprise Parts II and III; and it requires a conception of philosophy as itself 'a kind of writing' (cf. *CP*: 90–109; *EHO*: 85–106), not something with a specific and clearly circumscribed set of problems. This conception in turn facilitates a different way of dividing up texts; specifically between those that serve as 'illustrations of what private perfection . . . can be like' and those that we read as 'fellow citizens . . . engaged in a shared social effort . . . to make our institutions and practices more just and less cruel' (*CIS*: xiv).[11] Regarding different sorts of texts as different tools for achieving the goals of justifying (in the *pragmatic* sense) incommensurable values allows philosophical texts to fall on different sides of a more pragmatic divide. 'Existential' thinkers are thus rescued from the liminal state, to which they were consigned at the end of *PMN*, to play a part in the *private* projects of anyone with a taste for the genre.

If texts subserve their respective values then philosophy's successor need no longer carry its theoretical burden. Literary (or cultural) critics, unfazed by disciplinary boundaries, play genres off against each other to produce new sorts of narratives. They therefore act as 'moral advisers' (*CIS*: 80) to Rorty's 'ideal' readers. These recognize no temptation to strive for that 'single vision', engaging with texts in pursuit of their (distinctive) private and public projects. Rorty terms such 'ideal' readers 'liberal ironists'. 'Ironists' embody the latest iteration of the (nominalistic, etc.) Bergmannian 'ideal language' idea we examined in chapter 4, for which the new catchword is 'contingency'. They have embraced the idea that the truth (qua truth₁) of their most cherished commitments stands on no firmer foundation than the social practices of their 'community' because there is *nothing* firmer. 'Ironist' is the intellectual genus; as such, some of its members (like Foucault, Heidegger and Nietzsche) are potentially dangerous. Seduced by the ideal of a single vision, they allow their 'search for sacred wisdom' to take 'precedence over the common moral consciousness' and thus feel no solidarity with their 'fellow-humans' (*CP*: 158). Being both a liberal *and* an ironist requires that one refuse this temptation by 'making a firm distinction between the private and the public' (*CIS*: 83).

The 'political' content of Rorty's liberalism is purposefully unexciting, involving an allegiance to typical 'bourgeois liberal institutions' (*ORT*: 199) like 'freedom of the press, educational opportunity, opportunities to exert political influence, and the like' (p. 67). As with Dewey, these institutions are warranted insofar as they help realize the singular goal of 'an ideal liberal society': 'freedom' (p. 60). What liberals apprehend is the need for a corrective to the ironist's sense that 'persons and cultures are . . . incarnated vocabularies' (p. 80): recognition that 'incarnation' implies the shared capacity to feel pain and suffer humiliation (p. 192). Their concern with the growth of freedom under its *public* as well as its private aspect is expressed through the sentiment that 'cruelty is the worst thing we do' (p. xv). This is not something the ironist thinks can be grounded, of course; but it forms the basis of their commitment to the public project of increasing human solidarity, expressed through 'the hope that suffering will be diminished, that the humiliation of human beings by other human beings may cease' (ibid.). As one becomes increasingly attuned to the suffering and humiliation of others, one's sense of community deepens and the ambit of one's *ethnos* expands. At the limit would be a 'liberal utopia', in which 'ironism . . . is universal' (ibid.) and it is fully recognized that solidarity is 'achieved not by inquiry but by imagination' (p. xvi).

Although the conception of a 'liberal utopia' evokes the *positive* (post-Bergmannian) notion of the 'ideal language' idea, its status is ambiguous. In the first instance, it is for 'we' intellectuals already tempted by 'post-metaphysical thinking' and looking for the new vision of our activities promised in *PMN*. Cultural critics are our moral advisers because they show us how to go about devising a 'final vocabulary', the 'words in which we formulate . . . our long-term projects, our deepest self-doubts and our highest hopes' (p. 73). And as we reap, so might we hope to sow: purged of the desire to see philosophy as an attempt to unify our public and private concerns, we can put 'philosophy *in the service* of democratic politics' (p. 196). So understood, 'philosophy is one of the techniques for reweaving our vocabulary of moral deliberation in order to accommodate new beliefs' (ibid.), thus contributing to Rawls's 'reflective equilibrium'. It indicates that the liberal ironist successor to the metaphysician might revive a role for 'philosophy as cultural politics'.[12]

The background to this is that 'the mass of mankind . . . are still committed either to some form of religious faith or to some form of

Enlightenment rationalism' (p. xv) and consequently view the ironist's attack on these sources of normative authority as an assault on the idea of community with our fellow human beings. One might therefore conclude that the liberal ironist's task is to help universalize irony, and thereby assist her fellow citizens to see that rejecting an inherited faith in some antecedent rational or divine order need pose no threat to those precious Enlightenment values. The threat of illiberal ironists is defused by demonstrating that it's their illiberalism, not their ambition for personal freedom, that's dangerous. But now we hit an apparent contradiction. Having noted that Rorty characterizes liberal utopia as 'ironism . . . is universal', he goes on to assert that 'citizens of my liberal utopia . . . would be liberal ironists' (p. 61) and that embracing the contingency of language (and, by extension, of self and of community) is equivalent both to being 'nominalist and historicist' and to being an ironist. However, he later remarks that:

> In the ideal liberal society, the intellectuals would still be ironists, although the nonintellectuals would not. The latter would, however, be commonsensically nominalist and historicist. (p. 87)

Before we can address this apparent contradiction we need to know more about Rorty's account of contingency, and how it helps facilitate a culture in which the priority of narrative over theory is 'emblematic of' our having given up the quest of a 'single vision' idea (p. xvi). In the next section we'll look at how Rorty exploits Davidson's account of metaphor to reformulate the metaphilosophical picture familiar to us from *TLT* and *PMN*.

4 Metaphorlosophy

In 'What Metaphors Mean', Davidson (2001a) examines a variety of theories that analyse metaphors in terms of their possession of some concealed cognitive content, either in the form of some special ('figurative') supplementary meaning taken on by some of the words used (in the 'metaphorical context') or by the sentence taken as a whole; or by encoding or condensing empirical claims about the world. So Melville's phrase 'Christ was a chronometer' might turn on the divergent meanings of the word 'chronometer', or on the fact that the sentence is elliptical for the simile 'Christ was *like* a chronometer', which explicates the figurative content. Alternatively, the sentence 'gasses are collections of massive particles' 'selects, empha-sizes, suppresses and organizes features'[13] of gasses by applying statements appropriate to particle-talk to them. Davidson's response extends his Quinean antagonism towards the reification of mean-ings, implying that such analyses suppose a metaphor to possess a definite and potentially explicable content that their author 'wishes to convey and that the interpreter must grasp if he is to get the message' (2001a: 262). In critical mode, Davidson attempts to dem-onstrate that the ascription of such a content contributes nothing to an understanding of their distinctive function.

On the positive side, metaphors clearly have meaning. 'Tim's heart sank at the news' is not nonsense: 'its meaning is given in the literal meaning of the words' (p. 259). However, whereas 'Tim's heart sank' is a metaphor, 'the boat sank' is not, so wherein lays the metaphoricity of the former? Since it does not reside in *meaning*, it must turn on *use*. To highlight this point, Davidson notes that one of the curious features of metaphors is that they are either literally false ('the sky was on fire'; 'time stood still'), or their (literal) truth is taken to be irrelevant ('business is business'; 'no man is an island'). Indeed, this flagrant disregard for the norms of utterance tips us off to the intended use. When informed that Tim's heart sank at the news, something *happens*. You suspect that Tim is no longer a happy puppy; that some recent occurrence was not merely part of the passing show, but involved a loss that may bear on his future projects.[14]

Insofar as they have meaning, then, metaphors mean what they say. In this regard, 'a metaphoric use of language is parasitic on literal language, and so on ordinary rational thinking' (Cavell 1986: 506). But since their truth or falsity is largely beside the point, it is the work they do *on* us that is important. On this account, meta-phors and similes direct us 'to what language is *about*' (Davidson 2001a: 252; emphasis added). They are just 'two among endless devices that serve to alert us to aspects of the world by inviting us to make comparisons' (p. 256). Theorists of metaphorical content have confused effect with cause by projecting onto a metaphor 'the insight' it 'inspires or prompts' (p. 263). Since there is no limit to what a metaphor might intimate – to what in the world it might call our attention – no closure could even *in principle* be brought to the process of listing what it does. Moreover, the insights gained through exposure to metaphor are examples of 'seeing as . . . not seeing that . . . Not entirely, or even at all, recognition of some truth or fact' (p. 263). Since no truths or facts are prepared for communication, no truths or facts are grasped in their unpacking. On this anti-cognitivist account 'metaphor is the dreamwork of language . . . Understanding a metaphor is as much a creative endeavour as making a metaphor, and as little guided by rules' (p. 245).

Although Davidson's work comes out of the analytic philosophy of science tradition, he restricts himself to literary examples of metaphor. However, one of his targets – Max Black – writes specifically about the use of metaphor in science, and the topic was important in the transition towards a post-positivistic philosophy of science. Hesse (1980), for example, synthesizes Black's treatment of metaphor with Quine's non-deductivist account of scientific explanation to suggest that metaphor plays a crucial role in theorizing concept change. When it comes to the introduction of 'novel theoretical concepts', she writes, 'explanation can be interpreted as metaphoric redescription of the domain of the explanandum' (1980: xvii; cf. 120–3). A later piece concludes that the 'radical challenge' metaphor poses to 'contemporary philosophy' must be met by revising 'ontology and the theory of knowledge and truth' (ibid.: 40) to account for their cognitive function (as outlined by Black). Only then do we acknowledge fully that 'metaphor remains the necessary mode of speech . . . in the practical interest of personal communication and the emancipatory interest of critique of ideology' (Hesse 1984: 39).

This latter formulation connotes Hesse's admiration for Habermas (Hesse 1980: xxii; 206–30). Like Habermas, she retains a distinction between the natural and social sciences, the former identified by their satisfaction of something like Quine's 'pragmatic criterion': 'the criterion of the successful prediction and control of the environment . . . of empirical test and self-corrective learning' (ibid.: 188; xviii). As we've seen, the rejection of this distinction is central to Rorty's redescription of hermeneutics, part of the motive for which is a Deweyan, experimentalist extension of a 'pragmatic criterion' to *all* discourse. Not surprisingly, then, Rorty elaborates *his* version of Hesse's 'radical challenge' in the context of a redescription of 'ontology and the theory of knowledge and truth' that aims to *undercut* the distinction.

Rorty's initial (*ORT*: 162–72) appropriation of Davidson's anti-cognitivist account of metaphor comes in the form of a response to Black (1979). Picking up Davidson's anti-subjectivist[15] motive, he notes that if one supposes that we need to 'throw light on what meaning is' (Dummett 1986: 464; quoted at Rorty *ORT*: 165), it will seem natural to look for a theory of meaning in terms of the conventions that show how communication is possible. It will also seem natural to think of metaphorical meaning in terms of a subject's prior grasp of those conventions, which ensures in advance that the meaning is communicable. Davidson's account of metaphor is pursuant to his conviction that 'we should give up the attempt to illuminate how we communicate by appeal to conventions' (1986: 445–6) and therefore on the idea that we need a theory of meaning at all. In the first instance, then, Rorty takes Davidson's account of metaphor to buttress the assertion that language is, if not under the full command of a subject, contingent.

To see how this works consider the opposing view, familiar enough from *PMN*. The world and/or the self is taken to have an essence, which philosophy seeks to fit or represent in a vocabulary that expresses timeless truths$_3$. This vocabulary serves as the standard against which other linguistic practices are measured, and alongside which suggestions for conceptual change are evaluated. Following Dewey, Rorty takes this representationalist view of language to be the last gasp of the idea that 'the world is a divine creation, the work of someone who had something in mind' (*CIS*: 21). What Davidson offers is 'the first systematic treatment of language which breaks completely with the notion of language as something . . . standing between the self and the nonhuman reality with which the self seeks to be in touch' (pp. 10, 11). *Denying* that metaphors disclose some predetermined but elusive content, while *asserting* their significance for changing the way we think about things, undermines the notion that language is answerable in advance to what is Real. If the most useful way of thinking about conceptual innovations is in terms of the introduction of new metaphors, and these in turn are ways of world-making, not World-representing, then in an important sense the languages we use are *contingent*.

Rejecting instrinsicality – de-divinizing mind and world – is equivalent to embracing contingency. Since truths are properties of sentences, and the vocabularies they comprise are human creations, truths are 'made' not 'found'. The satisfaction conditions for particular sentences like 'the cat is on the mat' suggest that a worldly fact (the cat's being on the mat) is represented by, and therefore makes true$_3$, the corresponding claim. However, if we think of the relevant unit of language as the 'vocabulary' this intuition weakens. The vocabulary of 'vocabularies' is the successor term to the *PMN*'s 'paradigm' paradigm. To use a complementary metaphor, they denote language games like 'the moral vocabulary of Saint Paul' and 'the jargon of Newton' (*CIS*: 5). Considering these as *made* (true$_1$), rather than as limning the true$_3$ nature of reality, does not make them the results of intramundane committee-work: they are 'tools' developed in response to demands made on some concrete community of individuals by chance and circumstance: ways of coping with the world. This is a world that can *cause* us to have beliefs once we have 'programmed ourselves' with a language (p. 6), so that, for example, in the presence of a Narwhal horn, S believes (justifiably) that there's a Narwhal horn. Of course, programmed with an earlier vocabulary Rachel might well have asserted (truly$_1$) 'Lo, a Unicorn horn!', since worldly saliencies are etched by a linguistic community. Vocabularies change, re-ordering beliefs and consequently the way we're programmed to react to the world.

For Rorty, then, the attack on the idea that language is a medium is 'part of a larger attempt to get rid of the traditional philosophical picture of what it is to be human' (p. 19). The pragmatic self is as thoroughgoingly contingent and as lacking in metaphysical authority as the 'world well lost'. We'll examine the existential import of the self conceived of as 'a network of beliefs and desires which is continually in process of being rewoven' (*ORT*: 123) in 5.5. For the time being, observe that this redescription of the self is intended as a metaphor, which brings us to a broader use of the 'metaphor' metaphor. For Rorty, 'the history of language' (*CIS*: 16), which is to say the history of everything, is 'the history of metaphor' (p. 16). Metaphor thus becomes the *ur*-concept for repackaging and elaborating the metaphilosophical concerns of *PMN*.[16] On this view we are to think of metaphor as the motor of linguistic change – of that growth which for Dewey is the only moral end. From dada to Dada, metaphors are thrown up, challenges to the literalness of 'normal' discourse. They may take the form of one-off sentences, or be extended in the guise of an 'abnormal' discourse. Metaphors are initially parasitic on the normal discourse that gives them their literal meaning, and might become rendered literal – dead – thereby expanding the 'space' of normal discourse. Quite where these innovations come from is of no interest to Rorty (cf. *CIS*: 17); the point is that since they 'disclose' nothing, the only way to keep them coming is to maximize the conditions under which they do. To keep the conversation going is to remain on the look out for these linguistic innovations, to remain open to the possibility that some new moral, scientific or artistic redescription might be spun out of someone's apparently crazy utterance.

As we've seen (4.3–4.5, 5.1), the presupposition vocabularies operate in distinct logical spaces is regarded as the main impediment to the reformation of metaphilosophy. The focus on metaphor extends that analysis from the science–philosophy distinction to all supposed differences between vocabularies. As such, it represents a further modulation of the eliminativist position on concept change. That adjustment is reflected in tone and method – what one might call 'style'[17] – as well as in intended audience. For example, Rorty ceases to think it useful to characterize his opponents as 'confused', 'vague' or 'incoherent' (*CIS*: 8) about some concept or relation that he has more clearly in view (*CIS*: 8. Cf. 2005: 233, 235; *PCP*: 120–30). He becomes insistent that he will offer no arguments against traditional positions, but is merely 'redescribing lots of things' in a way intended to appeal to readers. So Rorty's talk of 'metaphor', 'vocabulary', 'liberal', 'ironist' and the other terms that comprise this 'ideal' language are themselves to be regarded as metaphors: suggestions for ways of talking that, if normalized, will allow us to get on with asking 'new and possibly interesting questions' rather than the 'apparently futile traditional questions' (*CIS*: 9).

This methodological hand-wringing revisits the familiar concern with escaping the problem of self-reference: trying to avoid the suggestion that one is advancing (self-refuting) truths when one denies that there's such a thing as 'truth$_3$'. However, this problematic is as canonical as those 'traditional philosophical questions', and avoiding it is no end in itself. The point, rather, is to tie the possibility of these 'new questions' in with an alternative 'picture of intellectual and moral progress' (ibid.) in the hope that doing so will contribute *to* that progress by promoting the conditions for the increasing freedom it represents. Freedom is associated with maximizing the possibilities for conceptual innovation, and the supposed end of liberal culture is the promotion of freedom. In the 'ideal language' of Rorty's liberal society, external authority is disdained; its users 'content to call "true"' whatever emerges from the 'free and open encounters' that liberal institutions are there to guarantee (p. 52).

With *CIS*, Rorty is no longer preoccupied with convincing the professional Realist that they should embrace pragmatism and acquire a new self-image. The new 'picture' of intellectual life is offered to the liberal intellectual. Perhaps overly impressed by philosophy in the past, these have embraced the contingency of language and seen that the freedom liberalism represents is best served by aestheticizing culture. The 'liberal ironist' will 'build the rhetoric of liberalism around' the thought that 'all vocabularies . . . are human creations' (p. 53), the most innovative being those 'at the forefront of culture . . . art and utopian politics' (p. 52).

The contingency of language underpins the 'metaphor' metaphor. This in turn makes freedom the focus, thereby evoking the central concern of liberalism. Of course, mere use of the word freedom is insufficient to establish a link with the concept of autonomy, which so exercises liberals. To appreciate how the uses of 'freedom' that emerge from Rorty's account of the contingency of language bear on this issue, we need to examine the correlative notions of the contingent self, and of the liberal community associated with it.

5   Two concepts of freedom

Getting rid of the idea that language is a fixed medium disposes of both the mediated items. While the self is left essenceless and decentred,[18] the world becomes divided between the norm-inducing community and a de-divinized causal realm. Advancing the cause of liberalism thus requires conceptions of the self and community that give expression to what expanding the exercise of public and private freedom mean. This must show that neither 'use' of freedom has precedence, and that the ironist's demand for autonomy can be insulated from his commitments to his fellow humans. Since ironists have been in the vanguard of de-divinizing the self, much turns on how this is described. Despite Rorty's strongly Nietzschean tone, then, it is to Freud that he turns when he offers his account of how a post-rationalist account of autonomy might look.

As with metaphor, the starting point for Rorty's reading of Freud is a paper by Davidson. In 'Paradoxes of Irrationality' Davidson argues that we can explain why someone does Ø when their sound reasoning tells them to do not-Ø only on the assumption that there are mental causes that aren't reasons. The mind, in other words, is 'weakly partitioned': there are causally connected areas, which, although taken collectively comprise contradictory attitudes, are locally coherent and so might not come into rational conflict. The clearest examples are of akrasia, or weakness of will. Tim may reason that he ought to give up drinking, given the evidence in favour of its deleterious effects on his health, and yet not do so if there is a supporting (if 'hidden') structure of reasons and beliefs on the side of inaction. Crucially, Davidson concludes that it is *only* on this partitionist assumption that 'our salutary efforts, and occasional successes at, self-criticism and self-improvement' (Davidson 1982: 305) can be explained.

The implication that the self is, in this respect, Legion suggests to Rorty a way of reading Freud's saw about the ego not being master in its own house, but having to content itself 'with scanty information of what is going on unconsciously in its mind' (Freud SE 16: 285).[19] If the unconscious is viewed, not as a 'seething mass of inarticulate instinctual energies' but as 'one or more well-articulated systems of beliefs and desires' (*EHO*: 149), then those systems can be thought to connote 'other persons' with whom one cohabits. One is not master of one's mental abode because the exercise of such authority presupposes the image of a central, essential, rational self exercising control over a base, 'bodily' other (the animal; unreason). Instead we have a picture of decentred mentation, where an ego interacts causally with a confederation of rationally coherent others.[20]

This way of decentring the self allows Rorty to reformulate the notion of morality. As noted, after *PMN*, Rorty extends to morals the conception of the Realist project as the quest to identify the true account of the essential self. Crudely put, on this picture the moral benefit of self-knowledge is to set aside our contingent preferences in order to discern what commands us universally. When Tracy looks inside herself she sees that, although inclined to employ her friend, the dictates of conscience will guide her to the universal principle of fairness. However, if the distinction between essential and inessential parts of the self disappears along (Rorty's) Freudian lines, the moral obligation to 'know thyself' can be redescribed in terms of the exploration of one's *in*essence, of the contingencies that makes one distinct from others. This leads to an account of the therapeutic process as an expansion into inner 'space' of the culture-as-conversation metaphor from *PMN*. When we think of those other selves as 'cooking up our jokes, inventing our metaphors' (*EHO*: 149), we regard them as producers of abnormal discourse, as possible partners in a (mediated) conversation that might help us shape 'a genuinely stable character' (Rieff 1966: 57). Therapy is only one way of doing this: once we stop thinking that a single vocabulary describes the (true, moral) self and see ourselves as 'random assemblages of contingent and idiosyncratic needs' (*EHO*: 155), the moral successor to self-knowledge becomes *self-creation*. This requires keeping one's mind open to the myriad possible ways in which one might find new descriptions of oneself 'whose adoption will enable one to alter one's behavior' (ibid.: 153).

As with Dewey, then, the only moral end is growth: specifically, the growth of the self. Consequently, the content of 'private morality' is 'the search for perfection in oneself'. In this respect, Rorty appears to reverse the essential–inessential distinction, situating the self-creating aestheticized self 'beyond good and evil'. Accordingly, only the being who makes a poem of himself, who places himself beyond the (normal) herd, lives an authentic life. This is the position Rorty associates with Nietzsche. The latter's transformation of Plato's 'true world – attainable for the sage, the pious, the virtuous man'[21] into a fable is the first (explicit) recognition that the intellectual's task is not to discover truth but to *make* it. To this end they must make *themselves*, go beyond the 'higher men' (cf. Nietzsche 1974) in whose terms they have learned to describe themselves, by doing so in a language of their own. In Rorty's Nietzschean terms this is how one 'becomes what one is', embracing one's contingency by creating the language (new metaphors) through which one tells the story of one's self, a story in which the very terms used *necessitate* one's being the way one is and no other way.[22]

As the high priest of ironism, Nietzsche represents the best and worst of the turn towards the aestheticization of subjectivity, and Rorty notes that Freud's moral psychology is compatible with this view (*CIS*: 34). The utility of Freud's metaphors, then, is that they *can be used* to aestheticize the self without exalting the minority, more Frank Bascombe than de Sade. On Rorty's reading, this takes shape in two ways. First, there is the idea, familiar from the time of the Surrealists' experiments with automatic writing,[23] that creativity is the work of the unconscious. Since we all have these inner selves, we are all fantasists in our own minds, working to make sense of the metaphors they tip into consciousness. When we consider the strange thoughts, obsessions and interests that populate our own reveries we come to see that each member of the herd is, appearances to the contrary, 'consciously or unconsciously acting out a fantasy' (p. 36). For Rorty, then, the self-image Freud promoted when he 'democratized genius' (Rieff 1959: 36) is the apotheosis of particularism: any object, event or memory can produce a metaphor around which 'a human being's self-identity' can be given narrative form (p. 37).

On the Freudian extension of the 'metaphor' metaphor, our private fantasies are no different in kind to the crazy theory of a maverick scientist (pp. 37–8). Indeed, his abnormal discourse is just a private fantasy uttered aloud until a public use is found for it and it becomes normalized. On this reimagining of Quine's 'web of belief', we give shape to ourselves as individuals by expanding our narrative resources, just as 'public' vocabularies grow by literalizing the metaphors thrown into the conversation. This brings us to the second perceived advantage of the Freudian self. Morality does not collapse wholly either into the Nietzschean quest for self-creation or into some abstract conception of self-interest. Even though conscience is reduced to the level of narrative, it is not inauthentic; and, although the 'the prudence–morality distinction' is blurred (p. 32), the deliquescence of the self suggests no bite can be given to the idea of a reformulated egoism. Although the 'common moral consciousness' is just another narrative, pity, compassion and sympathy are not to be despised: they remain as features of another adaptive mechanism for coping with ourselves and with the world (p. 35; cf. *EHO*: 151).

Taken alone, then, the metaphor of the 'contingent self' is not anathema to the idea of human solidarity. However, if solidarity is an important normative concept for public morals/politics *only* insofar as its scope is necessarily the community of all rational beings, it is indeed corrosive of such a notion. For the idea of such community is, on Rorty's account, predicated on the idea of an essential self, something laid bare when moral truth, like a knife, excises the contingencies of each individual's preferences. Undermining such a notion of the self makes implausible an account of solidarity based on an appeal to the authority of liberal shibboleths 'such as "human rights" and "autonomy" ' (*EHO*: 162). Just as, in the realm of private morality, the self needs to create itself, so too the commitments that constitute public morality need to be *made*.

For Rorty, which communities we identify with is as contingent a matter as are language and the self. To embrace such a view is to accept that 'one consequence of antirepresentationalism' (*ORT*: 13) is ethnocentrism. The ethnocentrist acknowledges that we 'attach a special privilege to our own community . . . even though there can be no noncircular justification for doing so' (ibid.: 29). Accordingly, if members of your community are bemused by the claim that demons cause illness, or feel revolted by the practice of female genital mutilation, you will not regard yourself as failing to respect their views if you refuse to take them seriously. And neither will you feel that there are adducible, non-question-begging, community-transcendent principles that will demonstrate the correctness of your own views.

On the ethnocentric view[24] the human race is divided 'into the people to whom one must justify one's beliefs and the others' (ibid.: 30). The relevant community is we inheritors of the Enlightenment, 'the community of the liberal intellectuals of the secular modern West' (ibid.); even if some affect having resiled from it (cf. *ORT*: 15). On this view, justice is the 'name for loyalty to a certain very large group' (*PCP*: 44). The liberal's commitment to freedom under its public aspect comes as an obligation to deepen and broaden our existing sentiment of solidarity. Since we are moved by the plight of those whose suffering we have to give an account (not exculpation) of, this necessitates an expansion of the range of people to whom we have to justify ourselves: an extension of 'our sense of "we" to people whom we have previously thought of as "they"' (*CIS*: 192). If we recognize this as an imperative it is only because it rests on values 'we' liberals happen to have developed in the course of our culture's contingent history. When Montesquieu, Paine et al. announced that 'All men are born equal' they expressed not a moral fact about human essence, relating to each rational subject being an 'end in itself', but gave birth to a metaphor that invites us to seek out similarities where we oftentimes find only difference.

To help literalize this metaphor is to follow Dewey in seeing that 'under disguise of dealing with ultimate reality, philosophy has been occupied with the precious values embedded in social traditions'. In Rorty's terms, it is the search for objectivity that has obscured the fact that those values are more usefully served through striving for solidarity (cf. *EHO*: 21 ff.). The most striking use of the notion that objectivity is a danger to solidarity, not its metaphysical passport, comes in his discussion of human rights, which summarizes usefully a much broader conception of the content of our commitment to public solidarity. To summarize, the moral concept of rights comes in two steps. First, there is the idea that since standards of morality are derived from, or entailed by, the nature of the world and of human beings, moral universalism relates to natural law. Since human beings are by nature rational beings, it is morally appropriate that they should behave in a way that conforms to their rational nature: 'the rational creature . . . has a share of the Eternal Reason, whereby it has a natural inclination to its proper act and end: and this participation of the eternal law in the rational creature is called the natural law' (Aquinas 1947: Question 91). The second step is Kant's. As we noted in the introduction, Kant sums up the spirit of the Enlightenment as the 'resolution and courage to use [one's reason] without direction from another' and thereby relocates the governance of reason in the universality of a 'God-like self' (cf. Cooke 1988). Rights are rooted in the concept of duty, which is itself a *purely rational* determinant of action. Such a determination is only rational if it derives from a law that the subject gives itself, and as such it must be a law recognized as binding on and by all rational beings. Human rights are not therefore derived from some substantive sense of human flourishing; rather, respecting the autonomy of self-determining individuals, they are grounded in the authority and universality of reason's acknowledgement of the moral law.

The idea that human rights have a philosophical justification is of course antithetic to Rorty's view. Provocatively identifying Serbian torturers during the Bosnian conflict with moral philosophers and Thomas Jefferson (*TP*: 167–8), he convicts them of sharing a self-image. This mistakes a paradigmatic 'we' for a common humanity and then goes on to categorize the non-we (Muslims, Batutsi, slaves, women, dumb animals, the irrational) as falling short of the standards of admission to 'our' – perceived as *the* – moral community: *not* beings to whom one need justify oneself. The devastating consequence is that people inflict unspeakable cruelties on one another; but the same effect is felt nearer to home when our disgust with the behaviour of one faction or another expresses itself in the judgement that that's what *those* sorts of people do; that if it hadn't been Tutsi killing Hutu, or Serb torturing Muslim, it would have been the other way round.

Phenomenologically, at least, this seems right; at least for many people in the rich democracies. The implication Rorty draws is that there is an intellectual temptation to justify a collective sense of *their* otherness by adverting to the fact that, unlike 'them', *we* respect human rights. Since Rorty dismisses the reasonableness of a genuine cultural relativism, he does not abjure this conclusion (ibid.: 170). He does, however, repudiate the notion that a claim of moral superiority is grounded in (or is evidence for) our knowledge of an essential human nature. The mistake here is to regard our admirable 'Eurocentric human rights culture' (ibid.: 178) as a cognitive as opposed to a sentimental achievement. Mistaking moral luck for moral destiny induces a sort of ethical quietism, a failure to embrace the task of spreading a human rights culture.

Underlying Rorty's objection to foundationalist talk of human rights is his rejection of the idea that *the* universal language of moral deliberation already exists, that unlike science all the concepts required are (and always were) available. Having (1) rejected the idea that divers vocabularies are exhibited in or constitute discrete logical spaces; and (2) redescribed the purported objectivity of scientific inquiry as a paradigm of 'human solidarity' (*ORT*: 39); Rorty suggests that, like progress in science, progress in morals requires an expansion of the 'logical space' of what is sayable (cf. *TP*: 203). Moreover, this requires that moral-talk becomes as much a region of 'free and open encounters' and 'unforced agreement' as science-talk. Just as Phlogiston-talk withered in the face of such 'encounters', so might the human in 'human rights' come to seem provincial, the particular 'rights' claimed parochial.

Rorty's position makes more sense set against the criticism of the metaphysical conception of rights advanced by Burke (1986), Godwin (1842) and (in particular) Bentham. In his *Anarchical Fallacies* (1843), Bentham notes that, although the published 'Declaration of the Rights of Man and of the Citizen' of 1791 purported to identify *universal* rights, there had been some trouble identifying them.[25] In various drafts, the list of rights underwent several radical changes, with the right to equality appearing, disappearing and then reappearing, and the right to resistance to oppression vanishing altogether (cf. p. 525)! His substantive point is that if one conceives of rights in an abstract, metaphysical way then there are no criteria with which to identify them. If the right to liberty means being able to do what you want, then only one person could in principle have that right as any exercise of it would in principle impose restrictions on the liberty of others. The identification of such 'contradictions and impossibilities' leads Bentham to conclude sublimely that 'Natural rights is simple nonsense: natural and imprescriptible rights, rhetorical nonsense – nonsense upon stilts' (p. 501).

Having dispensed with the metaphysical nonsense, however, something positive emerges:

> [I]n proportion as it is right or proper, i.e. advantageous to the society in question, that this or that right – a right to this or that effect – should be established and maintained, in that same proportion it is wrong that it should be abrogated: but that as there is no right, which ought not to be maintained so long as it is upon the whole advantageous to the society that it should be maintained, so there is no right which, when the abolition of it is advantageous to society, should not be abolished. (ibid.)

In work published posthumously, he says more about what a Utilitarian theory of rights looks like:

> A right is . . . a kind of secondary fictitious entity, resulting out of a duty. Let any given duty be proposed, either somebody is the better

for it or nobody. If nobody, no such duty ought to be created: neither is there any right that corresponds to it. (Bentham 1945: 316)

Since rights-talk is linked inextricably to corresponding duties or obligations, and metaphysical ('natural') accounts of rights[26] can make no sense of this idea, a legal framework is required. In keeping with general utility, the right-obligation pairings thus established have moral content only insofar as the interests of society as a whole are at issue. The thought that rights might be held up as 'trumps' or 'side-constraints' is incompatible with – indeed, a danger to – a commitment to the open-endedness of moral progress.

In this sense, Rorty is a 'cultural' Benthamite. Rights-talk takes its content not from enforceable laws, which identify the relevant duties, but from communal norms, which situate relevant bearers. Rights have content independently of being legally enforceable because they are *discursively* enforceable: to participate in the rights culture is to see oneself and one's interlocuters as being bound by the norms such rights represent. Given this association, it is not surprising that Hume is regarded as a 'better adviser than Kant about how we intellectuals can hasten the coming of the Enlightenment utopia' (*TP*: 180). Following Baier (1991), Rorty suggests that what is demanded by a human rights culture is an increased ability to see similarities between people. It is through the education of sentiment, not exercise of reason, that 'our' moral community is expanded.[27] As centreless tissues of beliefs and desires, that inessential self requires reprogramming in such a way that the contemplation of a woman dying alone of AIDS in Zimbabwe moves us in a way that (mere) contemplation of the moral law wouldn't. The method by which one becomes reprogrammed is by exposing oneself to texts, broadly construed. It is 'the novel, the movie, and the TV programme' (*CIS*: xvi) that help overcome the parochial 'we' and make us care about others (cf. *TP*: 185). These stories will help us to see the woman as a mother, no different from our own, whose suffering is as relevant as that of our neighbour. In this sense, a human rights culture remains at the centre of liberalism because to commit oneself to the enlargement of one's sensibility is to embrace the self-image of a liberal, one for whom 'cruelty' and 'sensitivity to the pain and humiliation of others' (*CIS*: 198) are definitive of public solidarity.

The texts one reads as part of one's commitment to a human rights culture comprise one set of those that 'help us become less cruel' (p. 141). These are the works 'which help us see the effects of social practices and institutions on others ... typified by books about, for example, slavery, poverty, and prejudice' (ibid.). The other set 'help us see the effects of our private idiosyncrasies on others ... books which exhibit the blindness of a certain kind of person to the pain of another kind of person' (ibid.). This brings us to an interesting variation on Bentham's position. As we've just observed, one objection was that any particular right might become a constraint on rather than facilitate moral progress, where moral progress was regarded as 'what is advantageous to the society in question'. If, with Rorty, one thinks of what is advantageous to society in terms of what enables the 'growth' of the individuals that comprise it, this gives us another way of thinking about the danger of regarding rights as universalistic. Assume for the moment that one's moral identity is fixed in part by the rights one claims. Considering rights universalistically, the extension of a particular right will be regarded as (perhaps belated) recognition of one's membership of the (universal) 'we'. But what if, rejecting universalism, one views rights as subserving the interests of a particular group? One might then regard their extension not as emancipatory but as a more subtle form of oppression, a way of colonizing the moral identities of those previously excluded from the hegemonic discourse (cf. *TP*: 202–3).

Borrowing Rorty's penchant for exchanging people-talk for text-talk, another way of putting this takes us back to that *second* set of texts. Perhaps the books that unmask the suffering and humiliation of some might be as yet unwritten because their putative authors have yet to acquire a moral identity of their own, and have not as yet invented the words in which to articulate their own sense of exclusion. The problem with analogizing moral growth with the growth of science is that the institutional context of scientific inquiry is, more or less, such that there are inducements to advance one's new metaphors. Although Rorty errs on the side of hope rather than caution, he is not insensitive to claims made by hermeneuticists of suspicion, who see the Enlightenment's heritage as a repressive. He is alert to the fact that even in the bourgeois West, not all groups have had the same access to the public discourse of morals and therefore the opportunity to formulate their own – and as a result enlarge our – 'moral vocabulary'. They haven't been able to contribute to 'the conversation' because they have been deprived of the discursive space required to formulate what their contribution to the public vocabulary of morals might be.

An illuminating example of this concern is Rorty's contribution to the debate about the intersection of philosophy and feminist politics (1993; *TP*: ch. 11), suggested by a line from MacKinnon's *Feminism Unmodified*: 'I'm evoking for women a role that we have yet to make, in the name of a voice that, unsilenced, might say something that has never been heard' (1987: 77). For Rorty, the prophetic moral tone struck here can be recuperated if the notion of moral identity is rethought along pragmatist lines. The 'unsilenced voice', the 'women's role' do not denote lines written and as yet unperformed, but a 'space' of unformulated possibilities: 'as I read' MacKinnon, ' "woman" is not yet the name of a way of being a human being – not yet the name of a moral identity' (*TP*: 205). Rorty in effect concludes that the separatism that some feminists advocate 'has little to do with sexual preference or with civil rights' (*TP*: 223) and more to do with constituting the equivalent of the community of solidarity that scientists have (cf. *ORT*: 21–62); or, rather, the sort of communities always sought by those outsiders who recognize the need to band together if they are to forge collectively a 'moral identity' (*TP*: ibid.). In this way they can start to put together the sort of language that will eventually alert others to the pain and humiliation they've previously experienced only in the form of a mute powerlessness, and thereby contribute to that (moral) progress of the sentiments.

Rorty's view of the relationship between feminist politics and philosophy exhibits the usual combination of postmodernist scepticism and Enlightenment hope.[28] The scepticism derives from the critique of foundationalism he shares with the ironist theorists who comprise the 'Nietzsche-Heidegger-Derrida-Foucault tradition'; the hope from the claim that what is 'politically useful' in this tradition is expressed in the account of contingency offered above (*TP*: 211), which advances the cause of moral growth. Taking up that latter point, it should be evident how closely allied for Rorty is the redescription of liberalism with the account of the uses of truth. Those who wish to 'ground solidarity in objectivity – call them "realists" – [and who] have to construe truth as correspondence to reality' (*ORT*: 22) are failing to confront their own finitude. Although he is aware that the reliance on sentiment will seem like gruel to some – especially the reliance on the kindness of rich, white, male strangers – the imagined alternative is just an expression of *ressentiment* (*TP*: 182): seeking what Nietzsche (1988) calls 'metaphysical comfort' from some imagined 'relation to a nonhuman reality' (*ORT*: 21). Crucially, for Rorty, the restriction of morality to sentiment goes along with the exclusion of theory from politics: rejecting this account of truth$_3$ means giving up the view that there is a standpoint from which one might adduce the theoretical resources required either to justify liberalism, or to mount a fundamental critique of its institutions. What remains is the suggestion that one replace talk of objectivity with talk of solidarity (ibid.: 22).[29]

This has led to the familiar charge of relativism, even from those sympathetic to Rorty's dismissal of truth-as-correspondence, such as Putnam and Habermas. Rorty aims to rebuff this accusation by invoking Davidson's work (3.3): ethnocentrism is a consequence of anti-representationalism because the latter is taken to rule out both Realism *and* relativism. The question this raises is whether all socially probative theory is reliant on a correspondence theory of truth. As Elshtain remarks, 'surely one can reject [that] . . . without opting for the view that truth is solely a property of "linguistic entities" ' (2003: 141). An account of truth and objectivity that neither presupposed the Realist idea of correspondence, nor embraced their pragmatic redescription, might open up the discursive space for an account of rational agency that does *not* identify it 'with membership in *our* moral community' (*TP*: 177).[30] This leaves open the possibility of a standpoint from which the institutions of liberalism might be subjected to a radical critique by a philosophical theory that retains an emancipatory content. Of course, exhortations are cheap, and Elshtain's strategy is the typical Johnsonian manoeuvre of making space for her alternative by casting Rorty as a crude anti-Realist.[31] We will return to this important issue in chapter 6, but before doing so it will be helpful to possess a more detailed appreciation of how Rorty's rejection of theory from politics situates him with respect to contemporary political debate. That will in turn take us back to the proposed self-image of the intellectual as a liberal ironist.

6   Liberalism and the limits of philosophy

The account of the self and of language outlined above is held 'better suited . . . to the preservation and progress of democratic societies' (*CIS*: 44) than the Enlightenment vocabulary of truth, reason and morality in which they were originally described. We can elaborate Rorty's view of the relationship between politics, philosophy and the subject by examining his intervention in two debates. The first is between traditional liberals like Dworkin and

Raz and Communitarians like Sandel and MacIntyre;[32] the second between Habermas and heirs to Nietzsche's critique of the Enlightenment like Foucault, Heidegger, Adorno, Horkheimer and Derrida. Rawls emerges as the hero of the first exchange, though this is the Rawls not of *A Theory of Justice* but of later work (1980, 1982, 1985, 1993; see *ORT*: 175–96). Since 'Foucault is an ironist who is unwilling to be a liberal, whereas Habermas is a liberal who is unwilling to be an ironist' (*CIS*: 61), the hero of the second exchange is easy enough to infer: the liberal ironist. These debates in turn raise two distinguishable concerns. The first relates to the conception of the subject/self presupposed by the relevant stretch of theory; the second to the nature of the link between the particular view taken of the self and the political position being defended. The connection between these can be represented thus:

1 Liberalism is justified *iff* the subject is morally autonomous/ rational.
2 The subject is morally autonomous/rational.
3 Liberalism is justified.

Autonomy has been the ground of principles of justice since Kant, for whom it hinges on a strong conception of the rational self.[33] Indeed, debate about the Enlightenment's legacy usually turns on the status of this view of persons, which in the Anglo-American tradition is represented by versions of liberal theory deriving from Rawls (1971). For Rawls, 'a plurality of reasonable yet incompatible comprehensive doctrines is the normal result of the exercise of human reason' (Rawls 1993: xvi). This implies that for a 'government to treat its citizens as equals . . . as free, or as independent, or with equal dignity . . . it must be neutral on what might be called the question of the good life' (Dworkin 1978a: 127). Since the applicable concept of justice purposefully neglects 'conceptions of what is valuable in human life . . . and much else that is to inform our conduct' (Rawls 1993: 13), it centres on the requirement for a split between the public and the private. The commitments required to express one's sense of solidarity must be held distinct from those (private; incommensurable) values that characterize one's quiddity.

Communitarians (and others; Marxists, for example) take a different view on the demands of equality, subscribing to the perfectionist view that government 'cannot be neutral' on 'the question of the good life' 'because it cannot treat its citizens as equal human beings without a theory of what human beings *ought* to be' (Dworkin 1978a; emphasis added). Although there is much diversity amongst views advanced under its name, the communitarian[34] holds that since the self is social and historical in character, any account that fails to acknowledge that (at least partly) 'the community [is] constitutive of the individual' (Taylor 1985b: 8) will impoverish the resources for thinking about human goods and the political community.

On this simple division communitarians accept (1) but deny (2), which they associate with the idea that an autonomous, private, rational subject stands distinct from the public[35] realm. Given this characterization of the self, for liberals, the argument is valid. However, this 'metaphysical' conception of the subject is one Rorty specifically rejects, while disputing the claim that this necessitates abandoning liberalism. One must therefore distinguish what Rorty calls 'metaphysical liberals' (cf. *CIS*: 75 ff., *EHO*: 175–96) from 'political liberals', for whom Rawls is taken to be the model. The key to the difference takes us to the text framing the above quotation. It is for 'political purposes' that 'Political liberalism' assumes the existence of 'reasonable yet incompatible' world-views, and it is 'within the framework of the free institutions of a constitutional democratic regime' that they emerge (Rawls 1993: xvi).

The conception of justice in question, then, is 'Political not Metaphysical' (Rawls 1985). Contrasting his position with that of 'ethical liberals' (Rawls 1993: 135) like Dworkin and Raz, who seek a rational foundation for liberalism (Hampshire 1978: x; Dworkin 1978a: 142–3 and *passim*), Rawls acknowledges that 'philosophy as the search for truth about an independent metaphysical and moral order cannot . . . provide a workable and shared basis for a political conception of justice in a democratic society' (Rawls 1985: 230). For Rorty, the strength of Rawls's liberalism is its willingness to take 'our' political tradition as its stated starting point and, as the limit of its ambition, the aim of justifying *pragmatically* the convictions that underlie it by organizing 'the basic intuitive ideas and principles' implicit in them 'into a coherent conception of justice' (ibid.). For Rawls, then, the public–private split is 'political' not metaphysical, and it could be taken otherwise only on the assumption that liberalism *requires* some metaphysical account of the subject in the first place.

Returning to our original argument, since Rorty rejects (2) he cannot maintain (3), which implies a notion of justification that is allied to a conception of an essential subject. Rejecting (1), however, he can invoke the appeal of liberalism on the pragmatic grounds that it embodies our convictions about justice. This strategy only works if the alternatives are ruled out. Neglecting the communitarian view, this leaves two of significance:

A(i)   Reconstruct the nature of the rational subject in such a way that the connection in (1) is re-established; or

A(ii) Radicalize the decentring of subjectivity in a way that demonstrates that 'here' is most definitely not where 'we' *ought* to be.[36]

These two options take us to the second debate mentioned. What they share for Rorty is a commitment to the political relevance of philosophy. The origins of A(ii) lie with rejection of Enlightenment rationalism, which issues in the sort of criticism associated with Adorno and Horkheimer (1997). According to this, modernity is characterized by rationality undermining its own purported grounds for a universal human nature, thereby revoking the promise of philosophical foundations for liberal institutions. More proximately, it is represented by Foucault's appropriation of the aestheticized Nietzschean subject.[37] Desirous of authenticity and suspicious of any modality that would seek to circumscribe its autonomy, this rejects the legacy of the Enlightenment and remains suspicious of any 'we' with which it might feel solidarity. The collective attitude is evoked in a lovely piece of Habermasese:

> The accusation . . . [which] has not substantially changed from Hegel and Marx down to Nietzsche and Heidegger, from Bataille and Lacan to Foucault and Derrida . . . is aimed against a reason grounded in the principle of subjectivity. And it states that this reason denounces and undermines all unconcealed forms of suppression and exploitation, of degradation and alienation, only to set up in their place the unassailable domination of rationality. Because this regime of a subjectivity puffed up into a false absolute transforms the means of consciousness-raising and emancipation into just so many instruments of objectification and control, it fashions for itself an uncanny immunity in a form of thoroughly concealed domination. (Habermas 1987: 55–6)

Rorty acknowledges the force of this attack on subject-centred rationality, and it suggests to him that we expel the 'realist' discourse in which the Enlightenment pursued its justificatory project from the *public* realm. Correlatively, since 'the totalizing self-critique of reason gets caught in a performative contradiction since subject-centred reason can be convicted of being authoritarian in nature only by having recourse to its own tools' (Habermas 1987: 185), the appropriate response is to shift the tradition of ironist theorizing to which it has given rise into the *private* realm of self-creation. For those who regard such texts as interesting, Rorty's advice is threefold:

1 Read the texts as attempts on the part of the author to *constitute* their autonomy by *creating* an authentic self.
2 Interpret the tradition they comprise (crudely, the 'existentialists' with which *PMN* ended) as leading to the view *that* they be read this way.
3 View 'the desire to be autonomous' (*CIS*: 65) that they embody as having nothing to do with politics.

In this way, the very texts that lead to the 'death' of the 'centred' subject become part of its rebirth as the self-creating subject.

According to Habermas it is 'with Nietzsche [that] the criticism of modernity dispenses for the first time with its retention of an emancipatory content' (1987: 94). Nietzsche's thought marks the moment at which 'the philosophy of subjectivity' collapses to a point where a purified subjectivity – pure Will – is purged of the values of modernity and has to create new values *ex nihil*. No emancipatory content remains because the political and social institutions of democracy are pervaded with the despised herd's 'morality of *shared* pity' (Nietzsche 1973: §202). For Habermas, the only way to keep philosophy relevant to politics while avoiding the 'performative contradiction' of A(ii) is to embrace A(i): accept the decentring of the subject but reinstate the authority of reason through the idea of domination-free communication. On this view, Rorty's desire to deprive philosophy of such a role by levelling the genre distinction between philosophy and literature (eg. *EHO*: 85–106, and *passim*) derives from his lack of recognition that 'intramundane linguistic practice draws its power of negation from validity claims that go beyond the horizons of any currently given context' and makes itself 'felt in the idealizing presuppositions of communicative action' (Habermas 1987: 206). Rorty fails to see that 'philosophy and literary criticism' mediate in distinct ways between 'expert cultures and the everyday world' insofar as they are 'tailored to a single validity dimension . . . or to a single complex of problems' (p. 207).

This leads to an important dilemma, one side of which is illustrated by some typical critical remarks. Bernstein (2003), for example, chides Rorty's liberalism for its metaphilosophical abstraction, which lacks the 'care, detail, and finesse of Rawls and Habermas' (p. 129) and leads him to conclude that the only choice is between what Fish (1989) calls the 'theory hope' of the 'metaphysical liberal' and the 'antifoundationalist hope' of the cultural left. For Bernstein, this leads to a failure to recognize and encourage 'the type of serious thinking and action required to bring about liberal reform' (2003: 137): the sort of theorizing 'Dewey thought was necessary for *intelligent* social reform' (ibid.). Elsewhere he contends that pragmatism blunts the tools required for 'getting a grip on important differences that make a difference' (Bernstein 1991: 235), leaving Rorty's liberalism not much more than an *'apologia* for the status quo' (p. 233). On this view, Rorty neglects the fact that there is *controversy* about what exactly liberalism is (p. 239); namely, that the content of what he cavalierly refers to as 'political practices' is up for grabs, and requires the sort of critical reflection that only the theorist can provide.[38] The consequence of Rorty's attempt to neuter the political impact of the Nietzscheans et al. is a 'depoliticized theory and a detheorized politics' (McCarthy 1991: 26):

> This privatized, narcissistic conception of radical theory has two important social consequences. First there can be no legitimate cultural politics, no genuinely political struggle for cultural hegemony . . . Second, there can be no politically relevant radical theory, no link between theory and political practice; there can only be apolitical ironist theory and atheoretical reformist practice. Thus both culture and theory get depoliticized . . . and politics gets detheoreticized. (Fraser 1990b: 314–15)

Habermas summarizes nicely this line of criticism against Rorty's liberalism: 'whoever transposes the radical critique of reason into the domain of rhetoric in order to blunt the paradox of self-referentiality, also dulls the sword of the critique of reason itself' (1987: 210). The sword is 'dulled' because Rorty appears to discern a decisive breach between philosophy and politics. Treating these as 'natural kinds' requires that all differences that make a difference are *eo ipso* political *as opposed to* theoretical (cf. Bernstein 1987: 240, 241, 245), thereby relocating theory in the *private* realm.

This suggests that the public–private split is not at all straightforwardly political. Moreover, it seems to run counter to the experimentalism of the authentic pragmatist to exclude the transformative power of metaphor from the political and conclude with Rorty that

'Mill's suggestion that governments devote themselves to optimizing the balance between leaving people's private lives alone and preventing suffering seems to me pretty much the last word' (*CIS*: 63). To side with Rorty on this leaves no space for a theoretically informed social criticism. Indeed, it is from this perspective that we must evaluate the liberal's basic commitment to the view that cruelty is the worst thing that we do. This is not an essentialist claim, as some hold.[39] Having deprived liberalism of the emancipatory insights of theory, Rorty must appeal to something that is both viscerally pre-theoretical and yet capable of the sort of nuance demonstrated in and inculcated through reading novels and what have you.[40]

So far we have considered our dilemma from the side less amenable to Rorty. However, consider the thought that despite talk of his 'cold war' liberalism,[41] this strand of criticism is motivated not so much by political differences as by philosophical differences. In his contribution to Bernstein's *festschrift*, Rorty expresses doubts that the two 'have ever seriously disagreed about what [political] measures to support . . . what disagreements remain might be called "merely philosophical"' (Rorty 2004: 3).[42] Of course, this is more than *mere* rhetoric. If there really is little to distinguish their politics (thus defined), it's harder to motivate Bernstein's claim that *important* distinctions can be made between their respective interpretations of the 'content' of 'political practices' – *content*, that is to say, and not just theoretical froth. Bernstein implies that space can be made for Fraser's 'politically relevant radical theory' only if one finds an alternative to Fish's dichotomy and makes good on A(i). For Habermas, this requires reconstructing the concepts of rationality and truth, and not abandoning them in a frenzy of postmodern *jouissance*. Likewise, when McCarthy chastises Rorty and remarks on the need for a 'philosophically minded social theory', it is to Habermas's account of the 'unconditionality' of truth claims that he turns (1991: 33). Looked at in this way, to side with those like Habermas who wish to preserve the link between the 'polemics against traditional foundationalist philosophy' and 'social theory' (Fraser 1990b: 317) requires adherence to an account of rationality and truth that is invulnerable to those very (ironist) polemics.

Of course, it must be similarly invulnerable to the avuncular deconstruction of the pragmatist. For Rorty, Habermas's talk of communicative rationality is an unsatisfactory halfway house between subject-centred reason and a fully pragmatized notion of truth (Rorty 2001a; *CIS*: 63–9). He suggests that the insistence that

communicative rationality isn't just about 'increased mutual understanding' (2001a: 43), but incorporates 'the notion of universal validity', leaves open the 'resurrection of pure reason' that Habermas
wants to avoid (Habermas 1987: 301). Like the Realist's disdained
talk of 'correspondence to', 'representation of', or 'matching' reality,
he regards Habermas's invocation of a context-independent validity
as a cog that does no pragmatic work beyond reminding us that
what is justified might not be true$_2$. As such, it cannot be used to
parlay philosophy into a discipline that has an emancipatory function. 'If I had to define "critical theory",' he concludes, 'I should say
that it is the attempt of philosophy professors to make the study of
Kant, Hegel, and various other books intelligible only to philosophy
professors, relevant to the struggle for social justice' (Rorty 2001a:
51). This returns us once more to the question of truth (5.5), which
will be taken up in chapter 6. We'll conclude this chapter by looking
in more detail at Rorty's new exemplar for the intellectual and
asking what the relationship is between her liberalism and her
irony.

7   The last ironist

Notwithstanding the question of truth and allied concepts, most
criticisms of Rorty's view of the relationship between philosophy
and politics focus on two concerns: the public–private distinction,
and the concept of the liberal ironist. Respecting the first, it is held
to denote some metaphysical caesura, a split in our Being that will
render us forever alienated from ourselves;[43] regarding the second,
it is found to be unacceptably 'elitist',[44] *even if* it is conceivable that
the ironist could *be* a liberal.[45] I will argue that these objections
originate in Rorty's ambiguity concerning the scope of the term
'liberal ironist' (5.3) and proceed to speculate on its significance.
    The implication of the contingency of language, self and com-
munity is that our identities can be thought of in terms of the possession of a 'final vocabulary': a vocabulary insofar as it is through
the use of words that we justify our beliefs and actions; 'final' in
the sense that the use of the most important of these words cannot
be justified through recourse to more fundamental terms. In addition, the 'ironist' satisfies three conditions:

(1) She has radical and continuing doubts about the final vocabulary she currently uses, because she has been impressed by other

vocabularies, vocabularies taken as final by people or books she has
encountered; (2) she realizes that argument phrased in her present
vocabulary can neither underwrite nor dissolve these doubts; (3)
insofar as she philosophizes about her situation, she does not think
that her vocabulary is closer to reality than others. (*CIS*: 73)

Assuming that 'argument' in (2) can be taken sufficiently broadly,
(3) marks the difference between the ironist *simpliciter* and what
Rorty calls the 'ironist *theorist*' (p. 97). The former has the generic
task of creating the taste by which she will be judged; the ironist
theorist conceives of the past that needs overcoming in terms of the
'Plato-Kant canon' (ibid.). In this regard, the 'problem of self-
reference' (the 'suicide' of subject-centred reason) is just a name for
the *particular* issue confronted by the theorist who would be a self-
creator, thereby distinguishing Nietzsche and Heidegger from
Proust.[46]

The ironist, then, is the person who takes naturally to the claims
for a pervasive contingency that distinguishes Rorty's nominalism
and historicism. Aware that 'anything can be made to look good
or bad by being redescribed' (p. 73), she recognizes that what
Realists characterize as attempts to dig away at *appearances* in order
to confront the underlying *reality* are in fact attempts at redescription. Having overcome the fable of that controlling distinction, she
embraces the idea that final vocabularies are *made*, not *found*. She
cannot therefore rest easy with the terms in which she presently
describes herself, nor resile from the task of seeking out new texts,[47]
other vocabularies that might provide useful metaphors to experiment with in her ongoing attempt to create the best self for herself.
It is in this respect that cultural critics are the ironist's moral
guides, people who can spin complex syncretic narratives that criss-
cross with ease the disciplinary boundaries that other intellectuals
are too timorous to approach; stories that make happy bedfellows
out of (for example) Freud, Nabokov, Orwell, Derrida, Davidson,
Proust, Wittgenstein, Heidegger and so on. Such stories help
assuage the ironist's doubts about the parochiality of their own
final vocabulary.

The ironist's aestheticization of moral growth goes against the
grain of what most people regard as moral activity. However, it is
because their striving is held up as paradigmatic that Rorty wants
to champion the ironist theorists against, for example, Habermas.
But it is their *ironism* he wants to retain, not their 'theory'; that is to
say, he regards ironist theory as an attempt to achieve through *nar-*

rative[48] what the metaphysician aims at through *system*: the 'single vision' that would overcome the public–private split (*CIS*: 120). Both these attempts are 'hopeless', but the ironist theorist's is potentially *cruel* as well. Defending ironism, then, turns on 'making a firm distinction between the private and the public' (p. 83). This brings us to the first of two possible objections Rorty raises:

P(1)   Ironism is incompatible with the view that cruelty is the worse thing that we do, and 'a simple split between private and public concerns is not enough to overcome the tension' (p. 88).

P(2)   'Recognition of a common susceptibility to humiliation' (p. 91) is insufficient to hold together liberal society. We need the public metaphysical rhetoric of truth, objectivity, and rationality.

Rorty considers P(2) to designate a *public* problem. His speedy response is that Western societies didn't undergo collapse when they became increasingly secularized. Since they are characterized more by social hope than the quest for knowledge,[49] nothing motivates discarding the possibility that the ideal language of the liberal utopia would be 'commonsensically nominalist and historicist' (p. 87). Its citizens would feel no need to have their 'sense of human solidarity' justified and would be 'every bit as self-critical and every bit as devoted to human equality' (p. 87) as their metaphysically or theologically inclined predecessors. Although Rorty indicates that they might be more 'blasé about their own final vocabularies', they wouldn't feel 'any particular doubts about the contingencies they happened to be' (ibid.). In short the nonintellectuals 'would not . . . be ironists' (ibid.). So here we have a division between radically doubting intellectuals and relatively credulous non-intellectuals. However, we have been told previously that nominalism and historicism are more or less synonymous with ironism and that the Freudian decentring of the self democratizes self-creation. This appears to make ironists, and consequently doubters, out of all of us.[50]

While this contradiction cannot be resolved simply, it seems to relate to (1) the specific nature of the ironist's doubt.[51] Although not motivated explicitly by the same consideration, a number of critics[52] have questioned how committed to solidarity the ironist can be if she has 'radical and continuing doubts' about her final vocabulary. What makes this pressing is that it needn't be a Realist who raises it. A *pragmatist* might point out that the ironist can acknowledge that her commitments are authorized by social norms without generating grounds for such radical doubt. After all, Rorty has told us that the contingency of one's beliefs is no impediment to 'stand[ing] for them unflinchingly' (quoting Berlin (1969), quoting Schumpter; *CIS*: 46); and that, after all, is the basis for the claim that ethnocentrism isn't relativism (5.5).[53] How does this imputed epistemic tragedy link up with the 'spirit of playfulness' (p. 39) that is said to characterize the irony of Wittgenstein, Nietzsche, Heidegger et al.?

The oddity of Rorty's invocation of 'radical doubt' is heightened when he elsewhere claims that 'on the public side of our lives, nothing is less dubious than the worth of [democratic freedoms]' (*CIS*: 197). Lest we are tempted to conclude that this part is somehow insulated from such doubt, he adds that on the private side too 'there may be much which is *equally* hard to doubt' (ibid.). Again, this sounds like the sort of fallibilistic account of one's commitments to be expected from a pragmatist. Moreover, it is followed by a discussion of the public–private split in which it is made clear that when it comes to negotiating conflicts amongst commitments 'all we can do is work with the final vocabulary we have, while keeping our ears open for hints about how it might be expanded or revised' (ibid.). The relaxed, 'nominalistic and historicist' fallibilism of this latter 'we', and the attendant understanding of the public–private divide, seems to take in all liberals, and not just 'liberal ironists'. In this respect, the objections that focus on (1) evoke the charge that Rorty is overly preoccupied with the elitist concern to carve out a privileged space in his utopia for those 'special' doubters, the ironists.

Perhaps light can be cast on the nature of this characteristic doubt if we turn to P(1), which Rorty designates a *private* problem. His response is that since the ironist is aware of the fact that redescription humiliates, and liberals want to avoid humiliation, the liberal ironist is motivated to avoid the humiliation of others. In particular, she wants to avoid the humiliation inflicted as a result of her own and kindred attempts to experiment with the *private* parts of their own final vocabularies, aware of the extent to which these interfere with the desire others have to understand themselves in their own terms. The public–private distinction serves as a reminder that with this power of redescription comes the danger of misuse. This divide, then, is one the ironist makes; or, rather, not the ironist but the *liberal* ironist, since she is aware that ironism poses a threat to liberalism if interpreted as having political implications. Privatizing these ironist texts constitutes an *inversion* of the hermeneutics of suspicion: it creates for them a space of interpretation in which any pronouncements they make bearing on her public commitments can be ignored. This means that she distinguishes between the private and public parts of her final vocabulary; that is to say, between 'redescription for private and for public purposes' (p. 91). Where the latter relates to the liberal ironist's sense that, lacking a single vision, the only basis for the social bond is the 'recognition of a common susceptibility to humiliation' (ibid.), the former takes in whatever she needs to create herself. Both aspects have their own fund of texts, those that expand her awareness of such humiliation and those that allow her to experiment with herself. In this sense P(1) is a private problem because irony is a *private* matter.

This suggests that the liberal ironist cannot have 'radical and continuing doubts' about her commitment to social amelioration, nor to the requirement for the public–private divide, because these constitute the content of her *liberalism*. However, there seems to be no reason why she shouldn't have 'radical and continuing doubts' about the public and private *content* of her final vocabulary if that implies only that she is alert to the fact that in regard both to public and private morality something better might arise. Of course, this implies *everyone* should be a liberal ironist. After all, what distinguishes such a figure is their heightened attentiveness to the possible humiliations they and others might inflict. The non-intellectual might not need his sense of human solidarity justifying, but that doesn't mean it can't be rendered subtler. Who is going to attend to the new voices of the formerly (linguistically) dispossessed if not the citizenry of the liberal utopia?

One could simply *stipulate* that in this utopian state there is no further room for such expansions of solidarity; that all the possible 'moral' innovations have been played out, every 'metaphor' that might tip one off to a new humiliation literalized. However, since that runs counter to the Deweyan concern with growth, perhaps we should reverse this line of questioning and ask why *anyone* would be ironic? If a fallibilistic attitude towards one's final vocabulary were pervasive, what would the supplementary content of the ironist's 'radical and continuing doubt' amount to?[54] If it subserves some moral end it should be desirable in all. Since Rorty denies that the liberal can back up their attempt to get the ironist to 'privatize their projects, their attempt at sublimity – to view them as irrelevant to politics and as therefore compatible' with human solidarity (*CIS*: 197), this invites the restatement of P(1).

At this point it should be noted that we are overlooking something; namely, that the figure of the liberal ironist represents the promised new *self*-image for the intellectual. This referential aspect is important, for the image of this figure is one that *we* readers, *we* intellectuals, are being *invited* to adopt. This implies that the ironist's relationship with humiliation is much more existentially charged than appears at first blush. Recall that the 'ironist' features in a narrative of maturation through which she comes to see that her own project of self-creation should not lead her towards nihilistic revilement of the herd because they too are striving to make the best job they can of the bundle of contingencies they happen to be. Although 'the power of redescribing' (p. 39) is the 'generic trait of the intellectual' (p. 90), the ironist is characterized by her *awareness* of the fact. However, the claim that 'redescription often humiliates' (ibid.)[55] implies that the ironist should be aware of this too, and that she therefore has a potentially heightened sense of the fragility of human existence. This seems to put her in a specifically ethical orientation vis-à-vis others.

This suspicion is borne out when we return to Rorty's Nietzschean Freud and observe that the strong poet's project of self-creation comes up against the fact that such attempts are 'marginal and parasitic' (p. 41). And, lest we forget that the idea of 'parasitism' is associated with Rorty's analysis of transcendental arguments, he makes the link explicit: the desire to create oneself *ex nihil*, to be 'pure metaphor', is as impossible as the solipsist's private language (ibid.). On this view, Nietzsche's subtitle for *Zarathustra* ('a book for everyone and for no one') might be read (*contra* Nietzsche) as an acknowledgement that one can neither be entirely self-created nor speak in the voice of the universal subject: to write, to speak and to think is to use public language; without *normal* language, upon which they are parasitic, metaphors wouldn't just be 'unfamiliar noises', they would be 'just babble' (p. 41). Given this 'needed corrective to Nietzsche's attempt to divinize the poet' (ibid.), the ironist comes to realize that what the poet does is just 'a special form of an unconscious need everyone has': to create themselves by redescribing the contingencies of their pasts in ways that 'if only marginally' (p. 43) are their own. To put a familiar slogan to this mélange, it would seem that if the ironist is an existentialist, then her 'existentialism is a humanism'.[56]

In *PMN*, Rorty makes the point that since 'Education has to start from acculturation' public discourse has to be 'normal' not 'abnormal' (p. 365). This claim was to remind us that, like the admonition to the poet, ' "existential" discourse is always parasitic upon normal discourse' (ibid.): it pertains to 'an intrinsically reactive movement of thought that has point only in opposition to the tradition' (ibid.: 366). Likewise, in *CIS* we are told that 'Irony is, if not intrinsically resentful, at least reactive. Ironists have to have something to have doubts about, something from which to be alienated' (p. 88). So the ironist's supplementary doubt is an expression of their *alienation*. The ironist *theorist* incarnates the 'existential' reaction against the philosophical tradition, held in aspic by their adherence to the single vision. Freed from the sense that her identity has to be established in and through a single narrative – philosophy – the (liberal) ironist has 'matured' to the point where her resented dependence on others (through normal discourse) has become emancipatory through her recognition that in some small way, because of the democratization of the mechanism of genius, they share her fate.

CIS is thus an apologia for the resentful, self-absorbed quest of the post-philosophical intellectual to find a role for herself. The quest is redeemed because in describing its own nature it allows it to be privatized while discovering therein a connection with others, a connection that can form the basis of a (public) political commitment. The scope of 'irony' is unstable because while at times it appeals to 'we' questing intellectuals, it also takes in our shared predicament. And herein I think the problem lies. Ultimately, public and private commitments are united in a lived life.[57] Rorty knows this, of course: that's where the relaxed 'inside' view of the general 'we' comes in. But in trying to ward off the temptation of that single vision, he adopts an 'outside' view, aiming to give a narrative of intellectual life that might serve as a model for all.

But why would one think there is such a thing? And, even if we accept that intellectuals incarnate the tension between the 'abnormal' and the 'normal', need we see the citizens of the future do so in this particular, Nietzschean way? Why isn't the ideal liberal the Mill-cum-Rawlsian figure? She will lack the felt obligation to examine her preferences, projects and idiosyncratic ideas with the aim of identifying those that do and those that don't glory in their universal moral significance. That is to say, she won't be one of Nietzsche's 'despisers of the body' and reject all that is near and close to one in favour of what is lofty and noble. As with Mill, she might have come to see that the fulfilment of a 'public ethic of mutual accommodation' (*CIS*: 34; cf. Mill 1971) can leave one feeling desolate and alone, and so refuses to allow herself to diminish and wither because not all her preferences either conduce to the commonweal or are socially acceptable to her community. For her, the public–private split bespeaks not our tragic condition but the pragmatic task incumbent upon each of us to work through these competing demands, drawing the line when and where we have to in search of a 'genuinely stable character'.

Such a figure would not be an ironist because just as the *justification* of solidarity means nothing to them, good ethnocentrists that they are, neither does that talk of a single vision, either to be effected *or* to be avoided. From their historicist perspective, irony is not so much the predicament of the intellectual as a certain sort of intellectual's predicament, one deriving from an ongoing concern with achieving an 'outside view'. Perhaps when the urge for such a view is no longer felt we will have seen the passing of the last ironist.

6

The Whole Truth

1 The authority of norms

For Rorty, the naturalization of normativity both undermines and substitutes for philosophy's traditional sources of authority. Rather than advert to our normative relatedness to the World, or to the logic of our language, he regards our peers as determining the rules to which we are answerable. Programmed with language, linguistic communities interact causally with the world; but their members' sentences stand in no relation to an antecedent order of facts. Whether they constitute the natural or human sciences, aesthetics, morals or folk-psychology, such 'vocabularies' are ways of coping with the world, not of representing or corresponding to it.

This wholesale collapse of 'genre-distinctions' between vocabularies implies a renaissance for discourses like aesthetics and morals, whose 'cognitive' status troubled philosophers confronted with the 'hard facts' of science. But, since all vocabularies now live and die according to the standards of a linguistic economy red in tooth and claw, none can lay claim to being necessary. It may have helped bequeath us the 'precious values' of the Enlightenment, but on this account philosophy, or at least philosophy on the Kantian, legislative model, has exhausted its potential to contribute to further 'moral growth'. Those values are now best served by vocabularies that will extend and embed them, not offer the impossible promise of metaphysical justification.

This Darwinian contrast between Realism and Rorty's nominalistic, anti-represenationalist alternative casts in too sharp relief a philosophical landscape that is more topologically interesting. In particular, it neglects those who share much of Rorty's animus against Realism but regard his eliminativist quick-fix as betraying its underlying motivation. What unites these otherwise sympathetic critics is the conviction that we need an account of truth (and related concepts like objectivity and rationality) that neither inflates it to the status of Realism's supernorm, nor levels it to a mere 'property of linguistic entities'.

It might help here to borrow from Wellmer what he calls the 'antinomy of truth' (1993: 109). This amounts to the ancient sceptical problem concerning our inability, when challenged, to back up the criteria we draw on when making validity claims in a non-question-begging way. In the contemporary setting, it suggests that we are caught between two equally unattractive alternatives: on the one hand, the 'absolutist' view that 'there are . . . correct standards, right criteria . . . an objective truth of the matter' which 'seems to imply metaphysical assumptions'; on the other hand, the 'relativist' view that truth is indexed to 'cultures, languages, communities, or even persons' (ibid.). For Wellmer, this allows us to contrast the approach of Habermas, Apel and Putnam (to which we can add that of Bernstein, Elshtain, McDowell et al.) with that of Rorty. Where the former try 'to show that absolutism need not be metaphysical', the latter aims to demonstrate that 'the critique of absolutism needn't lead to relativism' (ibid.: 110).

The precise details of what this non-Rortian alternative represents or will achieve varies, of course. As we've seen (5.5–5.6), some hold that liberating the normativity of truth from the traditional sources of authority redeems its emancipatory content and makes it available for political theory; others that it allows us to work through philosophical problems in a way that is essentially ethical in nature (or at least more respectful of their source). The details are less important than their collective focus on the normativity of truth, and this topic will take centre-stage in this concluding chapter. Of particular interest will be the extent to which criticisms of Rorty's position on normative authority undermine the moral views outlined in the preceding chapter. I will argue that for the most part they don't, but that they reveal on Rorty's part an attachment to the 'outside' view I associated with the liberal ironist in 5.7.

It will help dramatize the debate between the two sides of Wellmer's 'antinomy of truth' if we take a look at it from the other side of the 'mirror' (so to speak) and consider an example of someone who adopts a Realist (absolutist) position, regarding his opponent as committed necessarily to one or more forms of relativism.[1] In the above terms, proponents of Realism take it that the normativity of our epistemic practices of truth and justification makes sense only on the assumption that our beliefs either do or do not represent the mind-independent facts. That is to say, norms derive their authority from being answerable to the world as it is in itself.

2 The view from nowhere

In *Fear of Knowledge*[2] Boghossian (2006) outlines the 'three objectivisms' that comprise the '*Classical Picture of Knowledge*'. Here are the first two:

> *Objectivism about Facts* [*OF*]: The world which we seek to understand and know about is what it is largely independently of us and our beliefs about it. Even if thinking beings had never existed, the world would still have had many of the properties that it currently has.

> *Objectivism about Justification* [*OJ*]: Facts of the form – information E justifies belief B – are society-independent facts. (2006: 22)

Boghossian's definition of *OJ* continues by informing us what these facts *aren't*, not what they *are*. This reappears in his definitions of '*Constructivism about Knowledge*':

> *Constructivism about Facts* [*CF*]: The world which we seek to understand and know about is not what it is largely independently of us and our social context; rather, all facts are socially constructed in a way that reflects our contingent needs and interests.

> *Constructivism about Justification* [*CJ*]: Facts of the form – information E justifies belief B – are not what they are independently of us and our social context; rather, all facts are constructed in a way that reflects our contingent needs and interests. (ibid.)

Boghossian then goes on to ascribe both these forms of relativism to Rorty. We'll begin by dealing swiftly with the second. One reason for doing so is that the first is regarded as the 'more radical' and the second entirely distinct from it (ibid.: 59, 63). The purpose of his dialectic is clear enough: Boghossian aims to dispense with the radical version first, leaving open the possibility of a more plausible form of relativism, which he then aims to rebut. Since the two are held to be separable, it is unclear what relation Boghossian thinks exists between the two in Rorty's work. The second reason for taking this approach, then, is to show that Rorty's views cannot be pulled apart in this way, and that Boghossian's attempt to do so serves to highlight the metaphilosophical differences between them.

Boghossian characterizes *OJ* – epistemic relativism – in the following way:

> Let us begin by looking at particular unrelativized epistemic judgements, such as:
>
> 1   Copernicanism is justified by Galileo's observations.
>
> The relativist says that all such judgements are doomed to falsehood because there are no absolute facts about justification. (2006: 84)

Let's cast (1) in the form Boghossian uses in his definition:

(CJ_1)   The information provided by Galileo's observations (E) justifies the belief in Copernicanism (B).

Since 'doomed to falsehood' doesn't mean 'fated to be disconfirmed at some point in the future', but simply *false*, Boghossian clearly holds that the epistemic relativist endorses the following:

(OF_1)   (CJ_1) is false.

In other words, the epistemic relativist is committed to *OF*; which is to say, to the falsity of *CF*. The reason Boghossian holds *CJ* to be distinct from *CF*, then, is that the former are committed to the existence of unconstructed facts, amongst which number those of the form of OF_1. Everything would therefore seem to turn on whether *OF* or *CF* can be ascribed to Rorty. Since neither party is interested in seeing Rorty as an *objectivist* about facts, let's turn to *CF*, defined as follows:

> it is a *necessary* truth about any fact that it obtains only because we humans have constructed it in a way that reflects our contingent needs and interests . . . This thesis is clearly a version of the view that all facts are mind-dependent since it is clearly only minds that are capable of describing the world. (Boghossian 2006: 25, 28)

If would be odd if this were the sole basis upon which *CF* is ascribed to Rorty. As we have seen, Rorty follows Quine in rejecting the idea that there's *anything* philosophically useful about talk of necessity: a necessary truth is simply one that we can't presently imagine doing without. More importantly, Rorty would disdain both this talk of facts and the idea that such things might be 'constructed by humans'. A house might be built to reflect our need for shelter and our interest in keeping dry; but no sense can be given to constructing something as impalpable as a *fact*. Finally, in the light of earlier chapters, it is unwarranted to ascribe to Rorty the view that something could – or indeed *could* not – be *mind*-dependent[3] since he supplants the ontological category of the mind with the linguist category of mind-talk. In that mode, it is people – and perhaps dolphins and Martians – that describe the world, not minds. 'Mind' just relates to a particular, potentially eliminable, aspect of that descriptive repertoire.

Boghossian does have another attempt at ascribing *CF* to Rorty, however. The main problem *CF* has, he says, is avoiding the conclusion that, since facts are constructed, one community might construct the fact that P and another the fact that not-P. But how, he says, 'could one and the same world be such that, in it, it is possibly the case that both P and that not-P' (p. 40). Of course, it follows trivially from the way *OF* understands the world *to be* that it can't be the case that both P and not-P. That is to say, since 'fact' for *OF* means something different from 'fact' for *CF* – on the hypothesis of the *OF* – then the objectivist can't even *state* the contradiction the constructivist is accused of making.

Boghossian regards Rorty's as the most sophisticated form of *CF*, then, because he is taken to be proposing a view that would back up something like this sort of response. In other words, since he assumes that *CF* and *OF* *exhaust the range of possibilities*, the relativism imputed to Rorty is seen as a necessary condition for making sense of *CF*. Rorty, then, is held to maintain the following:

It's true according to C1's theory T1, that there are X's,

in no way contradicts

It's true according to C2's theory T2, that there are no X's. (2006: 46)

Although Boghossian gives no reference in the text, this evokes Rorty's early work on eliminativism. Indeed, it was the rejection of this reliance on theory, associated with Quine's limited range of scientifically relevant purposes, which I associated with Rorty's 'turn'. We've discussed this in detail, but it's worth noting parenthetically that the only time we've encountered Rorty stating *anything* like this is in the context of conceptual change *through time*, redescribed as:

'There are X's' is true$_1$ (but it might not be true$_2$).

Pressing on, what does Boghossian think his formulation of relativism commits Rorty to? Although he talks of *theories* here, on previous pages it is to 'ways of talking' (p. 44) that truth claims are held to be relative. What then does he mean by a 'way of talking'? As we saw in 3.3, the usual way to generate relativism is to talk of conceptual schemes; and indeed that's what Boghossian seems to think Rorty means:

> As [Rorty] puts it, there are many alternative schemes for describing the world, none of which can be more faithful to the way things are in and of themselves. (2006: 51)

In the final analysis, then, Rorty's 'sophisticated' form of *CF* is taken to depend on a dualism of 'descriptive scheme' and 'things in themselves', a version of the scheme–content distinction.

Confronted with Rorty's oft-stated rejection of the 'very idea' of this distinction, this is an odd attribution to make; indeed, it would clearly have been poison to Rorty to 'put it' this way. One might of course endeavour to show that he unwittingly presupposes such a commitment, but Boghossian offers no further support for his claim (and makes no mention of Davidson's work in this respect). On Boghossian's behalf, then, note that Rorty's repeated juxtaposition of metaphors of *finding* with those of *making* doesn't always help matters.[4] If one begins with the traditional view that the (found) *world* is contrasted with the (passive) *mind* that mirrors or represents it, talk of making as opposed to finding suggests that the world has gone from being wholly mind-*independent* to wholly mind-*dependent*. Adding in the associations clustering around 'making', it's not surprising that Rorty ends up saddled with the view that facts are constructed (*CF*) *as opposed to* being mind-independent (*OF*), or that there are different ways of 'describing the world'. Of course, Rorty wants to opt out of the discourse that is structured around oppositions like mind–world, subjective–objective, absolute–relative, and – most importantly – scheme–content. Given the view he held until at least the end of the 1990s that the only non-discursive significance the 'world' has is in terms of 'its' causal impacts on us, there are no grounds for claiming that what is out there is *made* not *found* because the conceptual space occupied by the 'found' has disappeared. To recall Nietzsche's aphorism, it has become a fable.

Ultimately, Boghossian's response to Rorty demonstrates the extent to which the former's thinking is structured around the exclusive opposition between a 'commitment to absolute truth' (p. 57) and a relativism so 'bizarre . . . that it is hard to believe that anyone actually endorses it' (p. 25).[5] For Rorty, of course, what Bernard Williams (1978) calls 'the absolute conception of reality' is just an uncashable metaphor that has come to impede the progress it was intended to inspire. The absolute–relativist see-saw is what you get when you start off with the idea that the mind represents the (mind-independent) world and then try to avoid the scepticism that it ushers in. In a sense, Realists like Boghossian, Nagel et al. are right to associate relativism with 'idealism' and 'subjectivism' because the Realist and the Idealist, unlike the farmer and the cowman, never will be friends. But this is not box social Rorty wished to attend.

3   Relativism redux

Although Boghossian takes Rorty to propound the most cogent form of relativism, his other primary target is Putnam. Putnam observes repeatedly that we are beings 'who cannot have a view of the world that does not reflect our interests and values' (Putnam 1990: 178). This echoes William James's oft-quoted gnome that 'the trail of the human serpent is over all' and reflects the convergence between Putnam's attack on Realism and the pragmatist tradition of Peirce, James and Dewey. Indeed, this parallel has become increasingly self-conscious in Putnam's work. With Rorty, he denounces 'the whole programme of providing a metaphysical foundation for ethics and society' (2001: 31), holding that the genuine political reforms of the Enlightenment have been held back by a scientistic faith in metaphysical projects. He likewise contends that Dewey's 'fallibilistic and antimetaphysical' (ibid.: 31) alternative to this

Kantian (ibid.: 22) rationalist programme promises a new participatory and deliberative model for democracy, pointing the way towards a renewal of the Enlightenment project.

Despite the evident similarities, however, Putnam is a staunch critic of Rorty's so-called 'cultural relativism' (cf. 1981, 1990, 1992, 2001). As a fellow pragmatist who has rejected metaphysical thinking and, presumably, shares Rorty's politics, this is a more telling charge than that levelled by Boghossian and others. Unfortunately, when it comes to isolating its precise nature Putnam isn't always helpful. He will characteristically remark that 'since Rorty is too hard to interpret, let us simply imagine a typical relativist' (1992: 69),[6] and proceeds to ascribe to such a figure the theses that Rorty disdains. For example, Putnam notes that 'Relativism, just as much as Realism, assumes that one can stand within one's language and outside it at the same time' (1990: 25), evoking Davidson's thought that it is the correspondence theory of truth that engenders 'intimations of relativism' (2001b: 46). But, as we have seen, Rorty will have no truck with such views.

One way into this is to examine Putnam's response to Bernard Williams. Williams contrasts the absolute conception of reality that a perfected science would converge on (cf. 1985: 136) with two 'lower levels' of cognition: that relating to judgements whose generality derives from our common human constitution (judgements involving secondary properties), and moral judgements, whose 'truth' is indexed to the relevant community. The 'truth in relativism' (B. Williams 1982) amounts to recognition that, since moral judgements in particular fall short of the standards demanded of an absolute conception, with respect to cultures that differ radically from our own 'the question of appraisal does not genuinely arise' (B. Williams 1985: 141).[7] Although science *can* be said to progress because it can *vindicate* concept change – offer genuinely rational justifications – such vindications are not available in ethical discourse (cf. B. Williams 2000).

Putnam's response is to argue that the 'absolute conception', like the associated idea of 'the world as it is in itself', is not one we can make any sense of (1992: 91–103) and that 'claims concerning evaluations of problematical situations can be more or less warranted without being absolute' (2001: 48). Although aware that Rorty has no time for Williams's 'absolute conception',[8] he argues that Rorty is committed similarly to denying that 'our norms and standards of anything – including warranted assertibility – are capable of reform' (1990: 21). To take the usual inflammatory example, Putnam contends that for Rorty one cannot *vindicate* a liberal egalitarian over a Nazi racist 'vocabulary' (cf. *TP*: 51).

Rather than answer this directly, note that what Putnam *might* have claimed is that it is Williams's absolute-true dualism (objective–subjective) that leads to the evacuation of critical normativity from the moral realm. If science weren't put on a cognitive pedestal one wouldn't conclude that life-world doings had a diminished status. Recalling Wellmer's 'antinomy', Putnam implies that having rejected a metaphysical absolutism (like Williams's), Rorty is left with the other ('subjectivist') half of the original dualism and unable to show how we can reflect critically on 'problematical situations'. Rorty's view is rather that, having eliminated the genre distinction between science and the rest of culture, a new standpoint emerges that has no space for relativism and entitles us to the distinction between the more or less warranted.

This brings us to the crux of the matter. What Putnam dismisses as *relativism*, Rorty embraces as *ethnocentrism*. Following the Davidsonian injunction that 'only a belief can justify another belief', justifications are always to some *specific* historico-cultural community sharing the relevant range of beliefs. 'We' can denounce the paradigmatic Nazis as our moral inferiors because we judge their loathsome racism from the perspective of our shared liberal values. But there is no neutral standpoint from which a set of facts or order of reasons acceptable to Nazis and democrats alike could be used to demonstrate that a rejection of the latter in favour of the former would constitute moral progress. Choices are made by people, in concrete situations and with particular ranges of values that more or less fix what counts *as* progress. When Putnam says he is an 'unreconstructed believer in progress' (1990: 27), Rorty would have doubtless rejoined that he was an equally unreconstructed believer in *hope*; combined with the *fear* that the progress we have made so far might be reversed, and that no invocation of truth or reason – only power and effort – will keep the barbarians from the door.

The underlying issue, then, is whether or not we can make sense of the view that S's belief that P might be subject to a norm even if (*ex hypothesi*) everyone else believes not-P. Since that norm can't be introduced by shifting the context of evaluation, we cannot assert

(I)   S's belief that Nazism is morally wrong is unwarranted (in Nazi-world),

just because *we* can assert

(II)   *S*'s belief that Nazism is morally wrong is warranted (in democrat-world).

Or, rather, that new norm can't be invoked *unless* there is a context of evaluation that encompasses *our* liberalism and *their* racism, facilitating the assertion of

(III)   *S*'s belief that Nazism is morally wrong is warranted (*simpliciter*).

Since Rorty regards 'warrant as a sociological matter, to be ascertained by observing the reception of *S*'s statements amongst his peers' (*TP*: 50), he supposes that a notion of warrant *simpliciter* must be devoid of any sociological context and therefore meaningless. A critic is therefore presented with two options: either (i) deny that warrant must be rooted in a sociological context; or (ii) argue that we can make sense of a sociological context sufficiently broad to warrant an assertion of (III). To adopt (i) is to revert to some form of Realism (recall *OJ*), and a universalist, subject-centred conception of reason. Since the critics we're presently considering are post-metaphysically inclined, their preferred option is (ii), answering to Putnam's invocation of a non-absolutist, context-transcending norm. Putnam changed his mind about the solution, but here's an early statement of the problem:

> The whole purpose of relativism is . . . to deny the existence of any intelligible notion of objective 'fit'. Thus the relativist cannot understand talk about truth in terms of objective justification-conditions . . . The relativist must end by denying that any thought is about anything either in a realist or a non-realist sense; for he cannot distinguish between thinking one's thought is about something and actually thinking about that thing. In short, what the relativist fails to see is that it is a presupposition of thought itself that some kind of objective 'rightness' exists. (1981: 123–4)

Until recently, the pragmatically inclined philosopher's solution was to invoke some version of Peirce's (1877) idea that since a belief is – following Bain (1859) – a habit of action, a true belief would be stable insofar as it didn't give rise to doubt in the form of a felt need for further inquiry: something achieved at the end of *ideal* inquiry.[9] Although Putnam and Habermas reject the notion of a promissory terminus, Peirce nevertheless suggests a way of cashing out the 'ideal' idea in a way that rescues reason from the decentring attacks of the ironists: reformulating it in inter-subjective terms by defining truth as 'idealized rational acceptability'. This is one of Habermas's formulations:

(IV) [P] is true *iff* it can be justified in an ideal epistemic situation. (2003: 37)

The aim, remember, is to show that we can distinguish between 'practices that are regulated merely by social convention' – Rorty's 'sociological matter' – and 'practices of justification orientated to truth claims' (Habermas 1996: 15), while rejecting conjointly the subject-centred conception of reason and the Realist idea that what grounds the truth of a belief is its confirmation by the mind-independent facts. The 'moment of unconditionality' that under-writes this distinction is taken to be 'built into *factual processes* of mutual understanding' (Habermas 1987: 322–3). We thus have the idea that confirmation takes place 'under the normatively rigorous conditions of the practice of argumentation':

> This practice is based on the idealizing presuppositions (a) of public debate and complete inclusion of all those affected; (b) of equal distribution of the right to communicate; (c) of a nonviolent context in which only the unforced force of the better argument holds sway; and (d) of the sincerity of how all those affected express themselves. (ibid.)

On this response to (ii), the relevant meaning of 'sociological context' is that which fulfils these idealizing presuppositions. We can assert (III) because *truth* provides the required norm for inquiry, and truth transcends what is merely the subject of (localized) consensus; namely, the Nazis agreeing with one another against S. Of course, talk of 'sociological context' here is misleading because these conditions are not *strictly* empirical. As Wellmer notes, the idealizations must be 'supposed to operate already as "necessary presuppositions" on the level of ordinary communication and discourse' (1993: 111). They are (at least *quasi*) transcendental conditions of the possibility of communication and discourse; and it is on this basis that the connection between truth and democratic politics can be claimed. R's assertion that Nazism is morally acceptable is taken to involve a 'performative contradiction' insofar as the norms governing assertion ((a)–(d)) rule out the moral position (Nazism) he is purporting to advance. In terms of the transcendental arguments we've already discussed, scepticism about democratic principles is self-defeating because it requires a rejection of the conditions of *possibility* of doubt.

Recalling Rorty's account of transcendental arguments, it should be evident how his response to this might go: Nazi morality is 'parasitic' on the practices of democracy. In his politically orientated idiom this just affirms the central tenet of ethnocentrism; namely, that when Habermas convicts Nazis of a 'performative contradiction' he is simply giving expression to the fact that *we* judge Nazi morality from *our* democratic perspective. Before filling out Rorty's response in more detail, it should be noted that despite its promise both Habermas and Putnam abandoned the idea that truth can be analysed in terms of assertibility under ideal conditions. To see why, recall that the intuition is that, while justification and truth are linked at the level of ordinary discourse, the truth of an assertion somehow transcends the context of utterance. Although asserting (truly) that P requires being in a good position to justify the claim if challenged,[10] justification is not equivalent to the truth. Rational acceptability under *ideal* conditions is meant to do the work of contrasting this *local* justification with truth. However, *defining* truth in this way asserts a *conceptual* connection with rational acceptability under ideal conditions, equivalent to claiming that X is a triangle *just in case* X is three-sided. However, just as this implies one cannot conceive of X being n-sided (where n is other than 3), Habermas and Putnam's definitions of truth imply one cannot conceive of any change to what constitutes the 'ideal epistemic situation' for asserting P. But if the 'processes of mutual understanding' are in any way to be regarded as *factual*, one can imagine such changes and it seems unwarranted (indeed, *false*) to stipulate that there couldn't be any. As Davidson remarks of Putnam's formulation, 'if the conditions under which someone is ideally justified in asserting something were spelled out, it would be apparent either that those conditions allow the possibility of error or that they are so ideal as to make no use of the intended connection with human abilities' (1990: 307).

Recognition of this problem by Habermas and Putnam is a tardy acknowledgement that the criticism levelled against the Peircean notion of the ideal end of inquiry applies to all 'idealizations' (cf. *TP*: 50; Rorty 2000a: 5–8). One can no more identify having arrived *at* the end of inquiry than one can know *when* the epistemic situation is 'ideal', as opposed to having invited all the people one can think of to the debate. But how, then, is one to explain that intuition about the non-identification of truth and justification? Rorty's view is familiar: the 'only indispensable function of the word "true", or any other indefinable normative such as "good" or "right", is to caution' (2000a: 12). If one embraces the Bainian notion of belief, the 'transcendence' of truth over justification just registers the warning that one's present 'habits of action' might not pass muster in the future. Just as many of the beliefs held by our ancestors are no longer well received, so too might some of ours come to be seen as provincial by a future, better-informed audience. Indeed, such a view is essential to Rorty's notion of how solidarity might be strengthened. The lesson he takes from critics of the Enlightenment such as Foucault is that we have a history of *excluding* voices from the conversation, of not welcoming everyone to the debate. As we saw in 5.5, Rorty's concern is that there are people who might not even have anything to contribute to the debate if invited because they have yet to acquire a language in which to articulate their sense of exclusion. In this respect, talk of 'idealization' (like that of the transcendental) risks reifying what are just the platitudes of normal discourse, excluding the potential of the abnormal. Finally, even this fallibilism about our beliefs cannot be 'idealized' to construct a platform from which we might criticize the Nazis who disdain such contingency: *it too* is a feature of our democratic communities[11] and might succumb if the fundamentalists get their way. In short, the only idea of transcendence Rorty will sanction is that of some more inclusive, better-informed audience; but there is no 'ideally' informed audience that might authorize our present norms; and there are no 'idealizing' norms standing as conditions of possibility of our everyday discourse.

Although Putnam and Habermas have rejected the 'ideal' idea, they haven't embraced Rorty's naturalization of warrant. Putnam continues to designate the function of philosophy as 'reflective transcendence' – 'the act of standing back from conventional beliefs, received opinions, and even received practices, and asking a penetrating "Why should we accept this as right?"' (2001: 31) – an attitude he associates with what Habermas (1971) calls 'the emancipatory interest'. In order to redeem the Realist intuition and restore respect for terms like 'objectivity', 'reality' and 'reason', he has embraced the recent renaissance of interest in perception, and with what McDowell calls our 'answerability to the world' (1994: *passim*). Similarly, Habermas continues to develop his 'Kantian pragmatism' (2003: 30) by showing how 'by orienting themselves to unconditional validity claims and presupposing each other's accountability, interlocutors aim beyond contingent and merely local contexts'

(p. 17).[12] Unconditionality, as that towards which justification strives but falls short, is now cashed out in terms of the (necessary) presupposition of an objective world of things, which 'provides a justification-transcendent point of reference for discursively thematized truth claims' (p. 39).

Once one steps back from a 'strong', constitutive idea of idealizations, however, the *direct* link between 'the practice of argumentation' and 'the universalist idea of democracy and human rights' (Wellmer 1993: 115) disappears. The fact that the 'unconditional' nature of discursive claims now turns on the 'supposition . . . of a single objective world' (Habermas 2000: 48) seems to weaken that link to breaking point. There may, however, be a way of thinking about this that lends support to this new Habermasian view. First off, this talk of Nazis and democrats constituting independent, norm-authorizing communities sounds rather artificial. After all, the National Socialist movement arose not so very long ago in the middle of the continent that came up with most of the ideas we associate with modern democracies. Nazism didn't spring into being as a fully fledged belief-system, and it didn't disappear overnight. If things had gone differently, those earnest readers of *Mein Kampf* might have been talked out of their foolishness and won over to an egalitarian world-view. Talk of Nazi-world versus democracy-land seems to imply two incommensurable, rationally closed systems, but such an idea is clearly absurd. As Wellmer observes '[1] rationality . . . cannot end at the borderline of closed language games (since there is no such thing); but then [2] the ethnocentric contextuality of all argumentation proves quite compatible with the raising of truth claims which transcend the local or cultural context in which they are raised and in which they can be justified' (1993: 120).

The inference from [1] to [2] betokens Wellmer's 'weak' (by a 'series of links' (p. 15)) attempt to link truth to the ethnocentric context of democracy. Rorty, of course, rejects it. Like all attempts to milk something out of the concept of 'unconditionality', he regards it as a mere flourish, marking a willingness to embrace the abnormal in its myriad forms and keep the conversation going (2000a: 12–13). However, since he later associates [2] with a commitment to 'a single community of justification . . . created by the ability to communicate' (p. 14), one might be able to secure a critical toe-hold here. To that end, recall that Rorty's rejection of the assimilation of ethnocentrism to relativism turns on an acknowledgement of Davidson's argument against the coherence of alternative conceptual schemes. As we noted in 3.3, when first articulated the conclusion drawn is that Davidson shows us that we can dispatch the Realist's conception of the world as something that we *either* are (if the Realist is right) *or* are not (if the sceptic is right) in touch with because 'The fact that the vast majority of our beliefs must be true will . . . guarantee the existence of the vast majority of the things we now think we are talking about' (*CP*: 14). In the sense that these things comprise the world we *keep*, 'it is the world that determines truth. All that "determination" comes to is that our belief that snow is white is true because snow is white, that our beliefs about the stars are true because of the way the stars are laid out, and so on' (ibid.).

Now a question that arises is what use of 'truth' is being deployed here? It is clear from the context what *isn't* required; namely, 'a controversial and nontrivial doctrine of truth as correspondence' (ibid.: 15). The argument, he tells us:

> makes us remember . . . what a very small proportion of our beliefs are changed when our paradigms of physics, or poetry or morals, change – and makes us realize how few of [our beliefs] *could* change . . . that the number of beliefs that changed among the educated classes of Europe between the thirteenth and nineteenth centuries is ridiculously small compared to the number that survived intact. (p. 13)[13]

This piece was written before Rorty came to distinguish, in particular, the normative/justificatory from the cautionary use of truth, but it is evident that he takes the argument to proceed by showing that we can only recognize someone *as* a language user if we ascribe to them beliefs that are mostly the same as our own (p. 9[14]); which is to say, beliefs that are justified. But now one might suppose that if all language users necessarily share vast tracts of justified beliefs then they share a 'rational' structure. After all, what on Rorty's pragmatist account would a rational structure *be* other than this holistic web of inferentially connected beliefs? And, since most of one's beliefs are not at any one time accessible to reflection, one might conclude that, in this sense at least, rational structure 'transcends' any local context.

Rorty's response to this takes us back to the preceding quotation. Although the proportion of beliefs that differ synchronically and diachronically is small, it is these beliefs that are all important when it comes to a community's moral identity. The massive overlap between the fundamentalist and the democrat ensures that they are not 'mutually unintelligible' (2000a: 15). But to get from [1] mutual intelligibility to [2] is, for Rorty, to infer from the bare *possibility* that some *S* might be able to justify a belief to some *R* to a readiness on the part of each and all to justify their beliefs to anyone. As one might expect, given our prior discussion of solidarity, it is the local sense of the 'we' that's important here, the range of those to whom we're willing to justify ourselves. Although I can *comprehend* what the racist says, I feel no need to *justify* my egalitarianism to them; though I may try to argue them out of their sentiment if the conditions are propitious. However, I did feel a need to justify my opposition to the invasion of Iraq to fellow liberals who took the converse view, and part of the reason for that was to test the coherence of my own moral views.

For Rorty, then, to infer [2] from [1] requires belief in a prior order of reasons that will be revealed when communication is made distortion-free. Since he thinks that 'any community of justification will do to make you a language-user and a believer, . . . philosophy of language runs out before we reach the moral imperatives' that claims like [1] express (2000a: 16). Ultimately, of course, he regards a concern with the 'unconditionality' of truth as a part of philosophy's attempt to retain a privileged place for itself. By presupposing that the human essence is to *know*, to transcend context in the direction of truth, it sets itself the task of standing *above* politics, pursuing the task of identifying principles that ultimately no subject can fail to acknowledge because their truth 'bursts every provinciality asunder' (Habermas 1987: 322). What Rorty takes to be the underlying commitment to a 'planet-wide inclusivist community' (2000a: 1) is best served not by associating it with a goal called 'truth', but by acknowledging that the political ambition it constitutes, like the countries which imperfectly embody it, is the dream[15] of a contingent community. His redescriptions of concepts like 'truth', 'objectivity' and 'rationality' are intended to help realize that dream by putting them at the service of 'democratic politics' (ibid.: 25).

4   Triangulation

Misgivings related to the foregoing are expressed from many directions. A potentially serious one comes from Davidson, whose views Rorty strongly associates with his own. In 'Truth Rehabilitated', Davidson echoes Rorty's contention that the epistemological tradition encouraged the 'confused idea' that 'philosophy was the place to look for the final and most basic truths on which all other truths . . . must rest' (2000: 65). He likewise disparages the idea that understanding 'the *concept of truth*' will either lead one to discover 'important general *truths* about justice or the foundations of physics', or provide the key to how to go about discovering such truths (ibid.). Given such views, it is clear that Davidson offers no succour to those, such as Habermas and Putnam, who take the philosophical concern with truth to express an 'emancipatory interest'. Davidson's agreement with Rorty extends to the following:

1   We are never in a position to tell which of our beliefs are true.
2   Truth is not a goal of inquiry (Davidson 2000: 67; cf. Rorty 2000b: 262).

However, Davidson rejects the idea that accepting (1) and (2) involves abandoning the idea that there is an 'ordinary, but philosophically interesting concept of truth' (2000: 66). That concept amounts to the claim that:

3   Truth is objective: 'the truth of a belief or sentence is independent of whether it is justified by all our evidence, believed by our neighbors . . .' (ibid.)

On the face of it we have here a 'merely philosophical' difference that might make a difference. The upshot of Davidson's view is that we cannot distinguish between the uses made of 'truth' in the way that Rorty does. Recall that in his original attempt to conscript Davidson into the pragmatist camp, Rorty distinguishes the field-linguist's 'outside' view from that of the 'earnest seeker after truth' (*ORT*: 141). The former constitutes Rorty's metaphilosophical response to the diagnosis that it is only if one can 'picture' stepping outside of language or of our minds, and contemplating whether or not our beliefs 'represent' the world, that *either* the Realist's aspiration *or* the sceptic's threat can be made to appear compelling. The standpoint of the field-linguist is regarded as the 'naturalistic' alternative to this metaphysical (or transcendental) god's-eye view. From the perspective of the philosopher-as-field-linguist, the standpoint is *descriptive*, not *normative* (p. 132). When adopted, a subject's beliefs are viewed as 'causal interactions with the environment' (p. 139), not as standing in *normative* relations with extra-linguistic items like facts. From the 'outside', then, 'true' is used disquotationally to compile the T-sentences of a theory of truth. So we have descriptive sentences of the form:

(T₃) 'Snow is white' is true₃ just in case snow is white,

which contrasts with the use of normative use of truth made from the 'inside' of a social practice

(T₁) 'Snow is white' is true₁,

where warrant is of course a 'sociological matter'. Crucially, then, Rorty aims to undermine the inside (mind)–outside (world) dichotomy while retaining a detached standpoint for the philosopher (as field-linguist) acknowledging the contingency of beliefs. Moreover, he associates the desire to run the normative and descriptive stories together with the philosophical picture that would make conceptual space for the philosopher's 'view from nowhere', and for which a Realist account of truth – as normative for inquiry – is required to close the gap between beliefs and the World.

The gist of Davidson's response is to deny that one can distinguish between these uses of truth; or, rather, that since truth is 'primitive' different *uses* do not connote differences of *meaning* (Davidson 2000: 74, fn. 4). Although Davidson doesn't align his 'uses' of true with Rorty's, he makes two relevant claims. This first is that it's 'easy to explain why we use the same word' to nominate the property preserved in valid inferences and 'to talk about what we have to know to understand a sentence' (ibid.). Consider the fact that, from the truth of 'Rachel is happy' and 'Rachel is at home', you can determine that Rachel is at home; or that the truth of 'If Rachel is happy and Rachel is at home then Rachel is at home' can be determined, even though you don't know Rachel, her whereabouts or her mental state. *What* you have to know to understand a sentence is its truth-conditions, and it is to the truth-conditions of sentences that we appeal when we explain the rules of inference employed in these examples. Both cases exemplify (3), the objectivity of truth. His second point is that he doubts whether we can explain 'in a philosophically interesting way' why we use the same word to 'caution' people as we do to talk about validity.

We'll return to this latter point below. Taking up the first, Rorty holds that what you might be said to 'know' when you understand a sentence is *know-how*; specifically, the know-how that is involved in having internalized the norms that warrant one saying that, for example, 'Snow is white' and it 'passing muster amongst one's peers'. Accordingly, what is preserved by valid inference is truth under its normative guise. However, there is cause for confusion here. As we observed in 6.3, Rorty takes it that the supposition that most of someone's beliefs must be true by our lights, if we are to count them as believers, goes with the *normative* use of truth; and we've just added that he contrasts this with the 'disquotational' use of truth associated with the *descriptive* travails of the field-linguist. But Davidson employs his argument as part of a demonstration of the rational constraints placed on interpreters aiming to derive the theorems of a Tarski-style theory of truth. That is to say, it is precisely because the concept of truth comes as part of the same conceptual apparatus as 'language, belief, thought and intentional action' (Davidson 2000: 73) that the 'meaning' of truth doesn't change in the way Rorty – talking of 'uses' – suggests. Needless to say, this is not a conclusion that would faze Rorty. His interest is in *redescribing* Davidson to support a picture wherein we can ignore problems arising from the mind's seemingly fraught relationship to the world (response: it's not problematic (namely, normative); it's just causal). He doesn't dispute the revisionary nature of the suggestions relating to, for example, the 'uses' of truth and the rejection of objectivity-talk in favour of solidarity-talk. On the contrary, the gamble is that these will help with the task of democratic growth.

The question this raises is on what terms might one engage *critically* with Rorty's work; especially with regard to abstract concepts like truth and objectivity, which Rorty regards as 'up for grabs' (2000a: 25). With this in mind, let's turn to one of the more edifying responses to Rorty's views. In his preface to *Mind and World*, McDowell reports that the goad to his own version of 'Kantian pragmatism'[16] was 'my usual excited reaction to a reading . . . of . . . *Philosophy and the Mirror of Nature*' (1994: ix). Like Rorty, McDowell rejects Realism, or what he calls 'bald naturalism', on this usage of the view that 'reality has an intrinsic character . . . captured by . . . the language of the natural sciences' (1998b: 420). He likewise wants to dispose 'therapeutically' of the 'intellectual obligations of traditional philosophy' (1994: 146) that arise from regarding the relationship between mind and world as somehow problematic: 'to exorcize the feeling of distance rather than trying to bridge the felt gap' (ibid.: 147). Finally, he concurs with Rorty that if there is no such gap to bridge, there is no sense in which philosophy maintains a privilege with respect to other areas of inquiry: there is no 'need for philosophy as priestcraft' (2000: 110). Despite the overlap of metaphilosophical ends, Rorty and McDowell differ dramatically on how to go about achieving them. For present purposes, this focuses on their respective appropriations of Davidson's work, which relates to the observed discord about 'uses'. What Rorty dismisses as the unfortunate side of Davidson's thinking, McDowell regards as acknowledgement of an all-important insight. Moreover, their respective accounts of how to understand truth turn on their reactions to this. The significance of this particular metaphilosophical disagreement will be better appreciated after a quick look at McDowell's project.

McDowell's aim is to elucidate a *philosophical* thought to the effect that there *ought* to be no mystery in the idea that our thinking has objective purport;[17] that in an oft-repeated phrase, 'our thinking is answerable to the world'. For McDowell, this thought has been 'deformed' (1998a: 366) by association with another; namely, that what the world delivers up to us in the way of experience ('the receptivity of sensibility') is independent of the concepts we use to arrive at a world-view ('the spontaneity of the understanding'). On this dualistic account, however, it seems as if nothing rationally constrains our thinking. This gives rise to 'an intolerable oscillation' (1994: 23) between two positions. On the one hand, there are appeals to something 'given' in experience, which offers an ultimate ground for empirical judgements; on the other hand, we reject the need for rational constraint on thought 'from the outside' and embrace a fully fledged coherentism. For McDowell, these are equally unacceptable, the first for Sellarsian reasons, and the second because it 'cannot make sense of the bearing of thought on objective reality' (ibid.). McDowell's aim, then, is to give us an account of experience wherein it is not held absolutely distinct from conceptual thinking, 'a notion of experience as an actualization of conceptual capacities in sensory consciousness itself' (1998a: 366).

Since Rorty dismisses as distractingly metaphysical any concern with 'objective purport' and 'answerability to the world', one might ask where he fits into this? Note that for McDowell the aforementioned 'deformation' arises from an improper contextualization of 'the distinctive intuition . . . that the conceptual apparatus that centers on the idea of objective purport belongs in a logical space of reasons that is *sui generis*, by comparison with the logical space in which the natural sciences function' (1998b: 421). While those caught up in the oscillation are guided by this intuition, their responses are 'controlled' by the view that modern science offers a form of understanding that circumscribes what counts *as* 'natural'. On this 'disenchanted' view, exercises of conceptual capacities are excluded from 'our' nature and sensibility ('a natural capacity' (1998a: 367)) falls on the wrong side of the divide opened up between the mind's 'space of reasons' and the 'logical space' of its (natural) world. One reaction to this is to level the genre distinction between all forms of discourse and thus deny that there are distinct logical spaces here at all. This expression of 'bald naturalism' *can* take the form of a Realist claim that a natural-scientific view of nature can provide all the concepts required to 'reconstruct the structure of the space of reasons' (1994: 73). Insofar as it refers to Rorty, however, it amounts to his rejection of McDowell's 'distinctive intuition' that the idea of objective purport belongs in that 'logical space of reasons'. McDowell's diagnosis, then, is that Rorty seeks to avoid the 'intellectual obligations of traditional philosophy' that arise from the 'distinctive intuition' by embracing a picture that simply *eliminates* it.

At first blush, then, it is on the significance of the 'distinctive intuition' for Davidson that Rorty and McDowell disagree. Where McDowell takes it to be of paramount importance, and ascribes a similar conviction to Sellars[18] (1994: *passim*; 1998b: 422), Rorty regards it as nothing more than a 'dubious' throwback to Quine (1998: 390). And, again, on the face of it Rorty seems under no obligation to take it seriously. The reason McDowell thinks he should is that the intuition is regarded as philosophically interesting insofar as it helps to 'diagnose and dissolve' (1998b: 424) the very problems that Rorty wants to simply dismiss. McDowell's thought that there *oughtn't* to be any mystery about objective purport is a (non-constructive but nevertheless) *philosophical* thought because he acknowledges the force of that normative requirement. It's a *philosophical* task to inculcate the 'frame of mind within which those apparent intellectual obligations [of traditional philosophy] are seen as illusory' (ibid.: 421), not by rejecting the 'distinctive intuition' but by 'seeing it aright'.[19] At this level, then, the charge against Rorty is twofold. He cannot 'give philosophy peace' (Wittgenstein 1953: §133) because his 'external approach can easily leave the philosophical questions looking as if they *ought* to be good ones', thus resulting in 'continuing philosophical discomfort, not an exorcism of philosophy' (McDowell 1994: 142); and his revisionist proposals concerning truth and objectivity cannot be made intelligible because they turn on an account of inquiry that denies itself one of the resources required to be viewed *as* such an account.

McDowell's contention, then, is that we can preserve a pre-lapsarian sense that our thinking is answerable to the world *without* implying that philosophy stands in a normatively privileged relation with respect to how things are: 'the resources of ordinary investigative activity can suffice to put us in touch with the subject matter of investigation' (2000: 110–11). Epistemology needn't be conceived of as complicit in the 'frame of mind' that leads to traditional philosophical problems by seeing it as an activity *internal* to the dissolution of those problems. In this respect, McDowell is placing himself in the position Rorty associated with Wittgenstein et al. at the end of his introduction to *TLT*: that of those who are seeking to 'end' philosophy through practising it; the position, that is to say, 'beyond' which Rorty has tried to define a discursive space since *PMN*. From that perspective, the implication is that Rorty has failed in at least one respect to elucidate that space. In 'Towards Rehabilitating Truth', McDowell suggests this in two ways. In the first part he offers an alternative history of the epistemological tradition, one that usefully questions Rorty's rather cavalier tendency to run together 'philosophy since Plato' with the modern tradition that reaches its apotheosis with Kant. Given the role that narrative plays in Rorty's work, alternative stories are propaedeutic; but I want to focus on the more substantive features of McDowell's criticism.

One might redescribe McDowell's objection as follows. There is an 'inside' way of seeing ourselves and an 'outside' way. Rorty and Putnam associate the latter with the metaphysician's longing for a 'god's-eye view'; McDowell prefers the phrase 'sideways on'. Recall Rorty's treatment of truth (and reference): where the Realist (or 'representationalist') sees the truth$_3$ of our beliefs (from the 'outside') as signifying a normative relatedness or conformity to things as they are in themselves, Rorty sees it (from the 'inside') as signifying possession of a sociological warrant (truth$_1$). The intimation, then, is that Rorty's thinking is structured around the opposition between the Realist's outside view and the pragmatist's inside view, and involves a rejection of the 'outside' view *in favour of* the 'inside' view. In other words, rather than reconceptualize the 'singular' view, he accepts what was the 'inside' view *as* the singular view. In this sense, Rorty's conception of the singular view is still caught up in the logic of its original opposition to the 'outside' view. From McDowell's perspective, then, Rorty's rejection of talk of objective purport goes with his idea that the only significance that can be given to it is from the (rejected) outside view, and that an innocent, and as it were pre-epistemological understanding of objectivity is lost thereby. And we can extend this to include the thought that, having rejected the idea that philosophy finds its identity in the coherence of that 'outside' standpoint, the only one left to it is the 'field-linguist's' descriptive, detached view, from which reference$_3$ has no meaning, non-normative (non-cautionary) truth is reduced to truth$_3$, and there is no place for a reformed, singular view of normative philosophical reflection.

It is in the light of this sort of diagnosis that McDowell criticizes Rorty's fragmentation of the uses of truth. Normativity (truth$_1$) is restricted to what was formerly the inside view on the assumption that any other invocation of norms would presuppose that the world being appealed to was the World (well lost). Accordingly, the cautionary use must be regarded as non-normative, its meaning exhausted through the implied reference to the authority of some future community. For McDowell, however, Davidson's application of Tarski's theory of truth to the interpretation of persons embodies *all* Rorty's uses of truth. In

(T$_1$) 'Cold-fusion hasn't been achieved' is true *iff* cold-fusion hasn't been achieved,

the (disquoted) right-hand side of the bi-conditional specifies the norm governing the correct usage of the quoted sentence (2000: 116). When you claim that cold-fusion hasn't been achieved then, if what you say is true, you get the world right; or, to put it another way, if you get the world right what you say is disquotable: 'Norms of inquiry are normative for inquiry precisely because disquotability is the norm for its results' (1994: 150). As we've seen, this is not far from Davidson's criticism of Rorty. But we also noted that Davidson does not think that a philosophical story can be told about how the cautionary use relates to the other use (relating to validity/what we understand). Given his view that truth is not a norm, this is perhaps not surprising. One of the things that distinguishes McDowell from Davidson as well as Rorty, then, is that he thinks that the cautionary use is also captured by disquotation. So where Rorty, for example, aims to isolate the justification-transcending use of 'true' by distinguishing the cautionary from the normative by writing (say):

(R) 'Cold-fusion hasn't been achieved' is true$_1$, but it might not be true$_2$,

McDowell thinks that disquotability can do the same job without relinquishing the univocality of truth. So instead we have something like:

(Mc)   It might not be true that ' "cold-fusion hasn't been achieved" is true'.

To see how this works, note that the clause forms part of the theorem:

(T$_2$)   ' "Cold-fusion hasn't been achieved" is true' is true *iff* 'cold-fusion hasn't been achieved' is true

and since the disquoted right-hand side of the biconditional can be written as:

(T$_3$)   'Cold-fusion hasn't been achieved' is true *iff* cold-fusion hasn't been achieved,

by substitution, (Mc) gives:

(Mc')   It might not be true that cold-fusion hasn't been achieved.

To defend the view that one is justified in claiming that cold-fusion hasn't been achieved, not in the light of what one's peers will let one get away with (the old, inside view) but in the light of how things are, McDowell then goes on to offer something like the following (transcendental) argument:[20]

1'.   One *conceives* of oneself as claiming that cold-fusion hasn't been achieved – as making a claim with a specific content, rather than as 'vocaliz[ing] in step with one another'. (2000: 119)

only if

2'.   One can discern the difference between whether or not it's the case that cold-fusion hasn't been achieved and whether or not saying 'cold-fusion hasn't been achieved' will pass muster in one's linguistic community.

only if

   3′. 'cold-fusion hasn't been achieved' is justified 'in the light of
        how things stand with its subject-matter'. (ibid.: 118)

(1′) is the shared claim that we have a world-view; (2′) is another
expression of the being right (norms of inquiry)/seeming right
(discourse-governing norms) distinction; and (3′) expresses the
disputed claim that truth (as disquotability) is normative for
inquiry.

Now it should be noted that the normativity of truth here is
'innocuous' (ibid.: 119). It tells us nothing about how we would go
about finding out how things are with the world, and we understand what the norm of disquotability comes to sentence by sentence. There are as many norms as there are true sentences, the
content of the norm being the disquoted right-hand side *of* those
sentences. If this conclusion appears less than incendiary, that is of
course the point. It is only if, with the Realist, one thinks that the
mind requires tethering to the World that one will regard truth as
some sort of encowled *super*-norm. And, by implication, it is only if
one's notion of the singular view is caught up in the logic of an
opposition to Realism that one will think that regarding truth as a
norm for inquiry is problematic.

The latter is McDowell's diagnosis of Rorty's position, and maps
on to our earlier discussion of standpoints. If one denies that the
(inside) normative standpoint is to be contrasted with the (outside)
descriptive standpoint of the philosopher as field-linguist, on the
grounds that the 'inside view' is caught in the logic of the old
dichotomy, then it leaves open the possibility that the philosophical
standpoint is the standpoint one takes from *amidst* one's practices.
And for McDowell those practices, like the practice of claim-making,
involve the innocuous use of truth as a norm – 'as a mode of justi-
fiedness' (ibid.) transcending consensus. It is the possibility of such
a standpoint that allows McDowell to claim that one can bring about
a negotiated philosophical peace, rather than accept a *Pax Rortiana*.
For McDowell, Rorty's restriction on the nature of the 'internal'
makes it impossible for us to regard as anything other than a
mystery 'how we manage to direct our thoughts and speech . . . past
the endorsements of our fellows and to the facts themselves' (ibid.),
in part because it denies that there's a way to interpret this aspiration that doesn't presuppose that the claim invites a god's-eye view.

On this account, Rorty's conceptual restriction on what constitutes a practice, and the consequent rejection of the vocabulary of objectivity, leads to the very 'philosophical trouble' (ibid. 121) he seeks to avoid. By ruling out the innocuous notions of truth and of objective purport, he leaves Realism looking like the only plausible option remaining. *Incipit* Boghossian!

Rorty does not, of course, accept this argument. Unfortunately, his responses tend to reinforce rather than undermine McDowell's criticisms. Amongst these, two are of note. First, he rejects (2') on the basis that it involves the introduction of a pragmatically useless distinction between *two* norms, one relating to inquiry and the other relating to truth (2000b: 125). But, of course, one would only ascribe this position to McDowell if one thought he was aiming to *supplement* the norm relating to sociological warrant with a context-busting supernorm. And one would only do that if one conceived of the first sort of norm on the image of the 'old' inside view, one whose authority was undermined by adverting to the world. As McDowell makes clear elsewhere – and this is the point of 'deducing' (3'), of course – 'answerability to the world and answerability to each other have to be understood together . . . we cannot make sense of discourse-governing norms prior to and independently of objective purport' (2002: 275).

Rorty later confesses that 'it was a mistake to locate the norms . . . where my peers are' (2000b: 376), though he does so in the context of repeating the 'two norm' accusation against McDowell. We'll turn to this change of heart momentarily. On the way, consider the second response; namely, the rejection of (1'). Rorty (ibid.: 126) notes that he sees nothing wrong with the description of claim-making as 'achieving vocal unison' and adds that one might be terribly upset if, for example, one staked one's reputation on the likelihood of utterances of 'cold-fusion hasn't been achieved' being vocalized in unison by one's peers and that turning out not to be the case. Of course, characterizing this social practice in terms of 'vocal unison' sounds like the outside descriptive standpoint (of Rorty's field-linguist). But from that perspective one cannot talk about 'staking reputations' and 'bitter disappointments'. As both Davidson and McDowell remind us, when we take up the standpoint of the field-linguist in order to attribute beliefs and desires to biological entities qua persons, we do so from the midst of our practices. From the (external; descriptive) standpoint of the field-linguist, as Rorty conceives of it, one is not entitled to regard beliefs as 'causal interactions with the environment' because one is not entitled to the concept of belief. One might offer a neurological story linking brain-states or 'vocalizations' to their distal causes, but there's no reason to think that what one is talking of here are *beliefs*. And, indeed, insofar as one accepts the architectonic of Davidson's account of interpretation, one accepts that the attribution to a subject of mostly true beliefs goes along with talk of 'language, belief, thought and intentional action'.

What this amounts to is recognition of McDowell's 'distinctive intuition'; in Davidson's terms, the irreducibility of talk about persons to talk about (inanimate) things. In one of his reactions to *Mind and World*, Rorty (1998) notes that after correspondence with McDowell he'd come to see that what the latter 'prized most' in Davidson's essay 'Mental Events' were the pages relating to this and 'about which I had always had qualms' (p. 390). This is an issue we looked at in 4.4, and again in 4.5, where it was associated with Rorty's attack on the *Geistes-/Naturwissenschaften* distinction; and, indeed, in his reply to Rorty, McDowell associates the thought he takes 'to be common to Davidson and Sellars' with 'the distinction between *Verstehen* and *Erklären*, which is familiar from the way it has been exploited in separating' the sciences (1998b: 423).

To summarize (Rorty 1998), the matter turns on what Rorty regards as Davidson's recidivistic (namely, Quinean) distinction between 'indeterminacy' and 'under-determination'. That is to say, Rorty cannot see how what distinguishes the sort of nomological exactitude one aspires to in certain vocabularies (say, particle physics) from the lesser ambitions of others (say, the special sciences like biochemistry, neurology, etc.) differs from what distinguishes the former from the vocabulary of intentionality, in which beliefs, desires and so on are assigned. In what way, he asks, is the relative *under-determination* marking the first contrast different from the purported *indeterminacy* that marks the latter? It is not that Rorty is arguing for reduction here: rather – to repeat the metaphilosopical point made in 4.4 – his claim is that there is *nothing philosophically interesting* about the difference.

Now, even in this piece, Davidson is ambivalent about the basis for irreducibility; in any event, within a few years he has come to reject openly the idea that indeterminacy per se has anything to do with the irreducibility of the intentional (cf. 2001a: chs. 9 and 10). It is with this work in mind that we've already touched on his response to Rorty's question: the irreducibility that derives from the indeterminacy of interpretation comes down to the fact that the process of interpretation is guided by 'the constitutive ideal of rationality' (Davidson 1980: 222), the idea that the attitudes attributed are 'placed' in the normative space (the 'space of reason') in which they provide an understanding of why people do the things they do. In a later, more explicitly Wittgensteinian piece, Davidson restates his view. He was mistaken, he says, to rest the case for the irreducibility of the mental on the question of indeterminacy: 'that turns up in both domains' (2001b: 215). It is the *specific source* of the indeterminacy that distinguishes mental concepts from physics and the special sciences that's important:

> We depend on our linguistic interactions with others to yield agreement on the . . . structures in nature . . . We cannot in the same way agree on the structure of sentences or thoughts we use to chart the thoughts and meanings of others, for the attempt to reach such an agreement simply sends us back to the process of interpretation on which all agreement depends. It is here . . . that we come to the ultimate springs of the difference between understanding minds and understanding the world as physical. A community of minds is the basis of knowledge; it provides the measure of all things. It makes no sense to question the adequacy of this measure, or to seek a more ultimate standard. (p. 218)

For Davidson, this is part of an integrated view of self-knowledge, knowledge of the minds of others, and knowledge of the world in which the 'I', the 'we' and the 'world' form the vertices of a triangle: 'until the triangle is completed connecting two creatures, and each creature with common features of the world . . . thought and speech would have no content at all' (p. 212). As he concludes, 'when we look at the natural world we share with others we . . . acknowledge membership in a society of minds' (p. 219).

Rorty's response to this piece is to restate the conviction that talk of normativity and rationality adds nothing to the fact that all vocabularies are alike under-determined: that since the irreducibility of one vocabulary to another applies across the board – 'no two ways of describing anything can ever do precisely the same job' (2000b: 393) – irreducibility does not make a distinction between vocabularies philosophically interesting. Of course, this is Rorty in by now familiar 'external', descriptive mode, and McDowell remarks that these considerations 'are irrelevant to the point' as he has explained it (1998b: 423). This, to repeat, is just the view that with respect to persons the appropriate way of finding them intelligible is in terms of 'the pattern of a life led by an agent who can shape her action and thought in the light of an ideal of rationality' (ibid.).

Now it's interesting to note that shortly after this exchange, Rorty appears to concede something like this point, along with the earlier one about truth. In short, he notes that one has to be part of a community of persons (not minds[21]) – a community that imposes checks and balances on one another's utterances – in order to deploy any descriptive vocabulary: 'the describing counts *as* describing only if rule-governed, only if conducted by people who talk about each other in the vocabulary of agency' (Rorty 2000b: 372). So what privileges the *normative* vocabulary of agency is not the fact that it's irreducible (since all vocabularies are) but that it's 'inescapable' (p. 371). Whereas Rorty implied previously that the 'outside' descriptive view – beliefs as causal links – was not only distinct from but *unrelated to* the 'inside' normative vocabulary, he comes to see that the deployment of any descriptive vocabulary, *including* that of the philosopher as field-linguist, presupposes a normative vocabulary.

Referring back to McDowell's transcendental argument, it looks as though Rorty comes close to conceding the inference from (1') to (2'), since claim-making requires membership of a norm-governed community. The being right/being wrong distinction is not yet the right one, however. Now it should be noted in passing that Rorty regards the relationship between the normative and descriptive vocabularies as pragmatic, not inferential (2000b: 372). Likewise, he continued to reject the idea that there are constitutive principles of rationality guiding the attribution of beliefs. However, even that pragmatic link leads to the already flagged concession on truth. Recall that, hitherto, Rorty had taken Davidson's claim to the effect that most of someone's beliefs must be true as meaning 'true by our lights'; which is to say, justified (true₁). We've already noted that as an interpretation of Davidson this is odd, since Rorty takes the field-linguist's standpoint – from which, for Davidson, this 'mostly true' assumption is deduced – to be *descriptive*, involving the non-normative 'use' of true. The problem is that if 'justified by our lights' means justified by *my* lights, then we lose any sense of what justified might mean – that, after all, is Wittgenstein's point. But then, if we take 'our' here to denote some normative community of fellow-believers, we seem to have begged the question, since it's membership of such a community we're (as it were) auditioning for. It is for this reason that we must take people to have mostly *true* beliefs:

'most of what anybody says about whatever they are talking about *gets that thing right*' (p. 374). And it is on this assumption that we get Rorty's concession to McDowell's (2'): 'you can only get right what you can get wrong' (p. 375). If we can only get right what we can get wrong, and what it is to be right is to have true beliefs about the things talked about, then it would seem we have an acknowledgement of (3'). Given the apparent centrality of Rorty's revisionary account of truth and objectivity, it therefore behoves us to conclude by examining what implications this has for Rorty's bigger project.

Conclusion: The Ends
of Philosophy

Gradually it has become clear to me what every great philosophy so
far has been: namely, the personal confession of its author and a kind
of involuntary and unconscious memoir; also that the moral (or
immoral) intentions in every philosophy constituted the real germ
of life from which the whole plant had grown.

Nietzsche, *Beyond Good and Evil*

-

1 Double vision

As we saw in the Introduction, Rorty came to characterize his
project in terms of a requirement to avoid what is deemed common
to 'leftist' Realists and 'rightist' Radicals; namely, the presupposition that philosophy possesses normative authority with respect to
political discourse. From the position of retrospection accorded the
author of 'Trotsky . . .', that presupposition turns out to be based on
a 'controlling' desire for a 'single vision' that would unify theoretically goods *public* and *private*. The ensuing task takes shape around
this contrast. The public undertaking is to free the discourse of
liberalism from its cathectic relationship to traditional sources of
authority; to revivify the precious values of the Enlightenment by
demonstrating that norms operate 'horizontally' within the *com-
munis*, not 'vertically' through some relation to the Real. To acknowledge that we move forward under the banner of a solidarity *to be
achieved*, not an objectivity *awaiting discovery*, is to help release man
from his 'self-incurred tutelage'. But that tutelage also comes under

a private aspect: the philosopher's acknowledgement of the authority of the tradition *over his own thinking*. Rorty's 'voluntary and conscious memoir' therefore presents its narrator restaging in his own career the trajectory of Western thought from Platonic realism, through Hegelian historicism to an existential awareness that philosophy as a mode of self-deception can be bid farewell only through the identification *of* that controlling urge for a single vision. Having been brought to consciousness, its 'immoral intention' is redeemed as a valuer's *private* striving for revaluation with no implication for the public project. The intellectual is emboldened to *live* the unity that must not be theorized.

The trajectory to this conception of his project takes Rorty from eliminativism to redescription; or, to be more precise, this transition is the corollary of rejecting the notion that there are philosophically significant differences between contrasting stretches of discourse. This generalized levelling of genre-distinctions implies that there is no 'natural' order of reasons or values dictating the ontological commitments in terms of which proposed changes to our concepts are to be evaluated. Indeed, I suggested that Rorty's rejection of such a natural order was driven by the suspicion that his own thinking had been controlled by an unacknowledged Realist assumption; one that led him to conclude that the elimination of the referring use of mental terms lent philosophical support to materialism. From this 'turn', there ensued a sustained attack on the concepts deemed central to an articulation of Realism, beginning with a redescription of the use of 'reference' itself and extending therefrom to revisionary accounts of the uses of 'truth', 'rationality' and 'objectivity'. These formed the basis of the articulation of that Bergmannian 'ideal' language in terms of which, conjointly, traditional philosophical problems can no longer be articulated and there is a wholesale migration of normative authority into the realm of social practices.

The elaboration of what is known variously as 'methodological nominalism', 'epistemological behaviourism' and 'anti-representationalism' is meant to facilitate the *pragmatic* justification of liberalism by opening up the space for a post-philosophical culture (the post-Bergmannian 'ideal' language). However, where for Rorty this offers us the possibility of expanding the horizon of our ethnos to embrace all, for such as Putnam and Habermas (and Searle) it threatens a nihilistic relativism that will leave insecure the very culture we wish to promulgate. Rorty's non-

Realist accounts of truth, rationality and objectivity seem required to renew the Enlightenment project and yet are for many the likely agents of its destruction. We've explored in sufficient depth how Rorty aims to rebut this charge of relativism. However, considerations arising from the previous chapter seem to cast doubt on his persisting adherence to the revisionary accounts of truth and objectivity. Given the connection between these and the project articulated in *CIS*, it seems natural to inquire what the implications of Rorty's seeming change of heart are for the bigger project.

2   Nothing but the truth

At the end of 6.4 we arrived at the conclusion that, although Rorty rejected McDowell's transcendental argument against the intelligibility of his account of inquiry, concessions made elsewhere appear equivalent. When evaluating the broader significance of this, it must first be noted that 'recognizing some beings as fellow-obeyers of norms, acknowledging them as members of a community' (Rorty 2000b: 373), does not relate to the morally relevant 'we'. It just represents an entry condition to Davidson's process of triangulation. Colin and Angie might be sufficient to constitute such a community, and thus gain access to the world; but their shared core of (mostly true) beliefs will not mean they won't fight over how to organize their world.[1] Likewise, getting things right doesn't give much succour when it comes to the bigger issues. Granted, Colin might be right and Angie wrong about the moral superiority of liberal democracy over the divine right of kings, but the relevant norm here is not going to be much use in guiding inquiry. 'Mycroft Holmes is Sherlock's brother' is true *iff* . . . , just as 'Nazism is morally wrong' is true *iff* . . . ; but the commonality of truth doesn't seem of much use if there's no Reality *as it is in itself* to answer to. And, of course, for Rorty there continued to be *nothing* to answer to: if one accepts Davidson's metaphor of triangulation then the world is but one vertex, and cannot be regarded in isolation: 'the norms . . . hover [. . .] over the whole process of triangulation' (Rorty 2000b: 376). There is, he writes, no 'superthing' to which a super-norm might herald our answerability (2003: 14, fn. 28).

Of course, McDowell does not conceive of answerability in this way; but in any event Rorty retained the conviction that one needn't invoke talk of 'answerability to the world', or 'objective purport', to sustain the latter's 'distinctive intuition'.[2] In this respect, the debate passes on to the next generation, Rorty having favoured Brandom's account of how 'the notion of "talking about the same thing" comes into the language' (ibid.).[3] Whomever one finds plausible on this topic, it is evident that neither involve a notion of truth or objectivity likely to serve the interests of those who wish to milk these concepts for their 'emancipatory content'.

We cannot dwell on this here, but I want to draw attention to a noteworthy feature of Rorty's apparent concession; namely, that it appears not dissimilar to the kinds of things he was saying about truth thirty years earlier. As we noted in 6.3, in his original appropriation of Davidson's attack on the conceptual scheme idea Rorty is happy to conclude that 'it is the world that determines truth . . . that our beliefs about the stars are true because of the way the stars are laid out, and so on' (*CP*: 14). Although I went on to interpret this in the light of Rorty's subsequent work on the uses of 'true', it is clear from the context that what is being opposed is the Realist's view of truth, and that nothing stands in the way of interpreting it in the light of how Davidson intended it and Rorty came to view it.

The question this raises is why Rorty didn't adopt the (ancient) sceptical attitude towards truth, deploying the work of Davidson, Heidegger, Wittgenstein and others to oppose Realist attempts to inflate the concept, but otherwise remaining loftily above the fray and refusing to offer any 'analysis' of his own. Indeed, the appropriateness of this question is confirmed when one recalls Rorty's 'parasitism' account of transcendental arguments. In 3.3 we determined that if one refuses the epistemological sceptic the *right* to assume a gap between mind and world, the contrast between *modest* (necessities of thought) and *immodest* (necessities of existence) interpretations of transcendental arguments disappears. What remains is the view that such arguments demonstrate that revisionary suggestions are parasitic on the norms that presently shape discourse. Without the sceptic's dualism there is no requirement to situate the norms 'where our peers are' *as opposed to* in the world. Like other norms, then, the norm for the use of 'true' 'hovers over the whole process of triangulation'.

On this basis, one might interpret McDowell's transcendental argument against Rorty's revisionary account of truth in a thoroughgoing *pragmatic* way, which returns us to the question why Rorty didn't remain sceptical or quietist on the issue of truth.

Picking up that hint about the norm for the use of 'true', we've already noted (3.2) that Rorty's revisionary account was motivated in part by awareness that deflating epistemically truth to warrant falls foul of the naturalistic fallacy. For the pragmatist, however, there is a perhaps more fundamental reason for *not* desiring to do so. In other words, not only is the case that one *could not* now warrantedly assert that:

S's belief that P is true *iff* S's belief that P is warrantedly asserted.

In addition, one *would not* want such a situation to arise, because such an eventuality would indicate that the 'growth' that constitutes the basis of moral hope had come to an end. We would have arrived at a point at which we simply could not imagine ourselves doing or believing something different. On this account, the cautionary use of 'true' is required to contrast the *now* with an imagined (and perhaps hoped for) *future*.

There are four obvious ways in which content might be given to that cautionary use: the Realist's correspondence to how things are; the pragmatist's 'ideal' end of inquiry; the relativist's radical caesura between the present and the future; and some projection from where we are now. Hostility to the first is clearly documented, and the second threatens to be indistinguishable from the condition outlined above (the simple loss of hope that the future might be better). Regarding the remaining options, if the future is not to be a projection of the present it must be one that is not *in principle* imaginable from where we are now: in a phrase, the radical incommensurability would amount to a different (untranslatable) conceptual scheme; another 'world'. So Rorty requires sufficient continuity between the present and the future to rule out the possibility of radical otherness, but enough of a contrast to warrant the cautionary use: a projection from where we are now.[4]

Since the purpose of redescription is to ramify (justify *pragmatically*) the values we have *now*, perhaps we have an answer to our question. But in response to the foregoing it seems natural to remind ourselves that, although some beliefs undergo radical change, the vast majority don't (*CP*: 13; cf. 6.3); and the reason they don't is because they get the world right and (thought collectively, though not individually) don't require the cautionary use. Disagreement requires large-scale agreement, and agreement merely at the level of justification leaves open the possibility that at some point in the future there might have been sufficient 'drift' to allow relativism to creep back in. So it turns out that the contrast with what is warranted that is required by the pragmatist – what gives the cautionary use its content – constitutes a fifth possibility: what is *true* (that 'hovering' norm). And this conclusion is supported by the fact that the radical interpreter requires the distinction between warrant and truth in order to see agents *as* agents, as purposive creatures responding differentially to their environment and adjusting their actions when (from the field-linguist's point of view) warrant *doesn't* issue in success: when truth and warrant come apart.

The conclusion to which we appear to have been led is that Rorty needn't have offered a *positive* account of truth and objectivity to achieve the contrast required by the pragmatist. We began with a question concerning the implications for Rorty's project of the change of heart on the topic of truth and objectivity. To that we might therefore add another: why did he feel compelled to offer his revisionary accounts? A crudely speculative response to this might diagnose a combination of the following: a lingering suspicion that anything less than a radical revision of the central concepts of Realism would leave the thinker still controlled by the 'picture' that had once held him captive; and a narrowed sense of the philosophical possibilities on offer, partly dictated by the conjoint desire to champion a (revisionary) pragmatic notion of concept change and avoid the humility of (descriptive) Wittgensteinian therapy. It is, however, more usefully addressed indirectly, through a brief consideration of the original question. As we'll now see, this is related insofar as the most significant implication concerns philosophy itself.

3   The ends of philosophy

When Rorty introduces his concessions on truth he does so in a response to Ramberg's contribution to *Rorty and His Critics* (2000). In this, Ramberg argues that Rorty's critical evaluation of Davidson's anti-reductivist account of propositional-attitude talk is distorted by an overly restrictive notion of what it would *be* for something to be of philosophical interest (Ramberg 2000: 353). The implication is that Rorty interprets Davidson's opposition to reduction as being 'controlled' by the notion that its bare *possibility* has ontological significance, a possibility that must therefore be robustly opposed. Ramberg's thought is that if one doesn't presuppose such a restrictive understanding of philosophical interest one should be open to the fact that such distinctions between vocabularies can be of interest (ibid.: 364–8). Indeed, the suggestion is that Rorty is being 'insufficiently Rortyan' (p. 353) in disallowing that the distinction Davidson is keen to preserve is expressive of what one could call a post-ontological philosophical interest.

Ramberg doesn't say very much about this notion of 'philosophical interest', and in his otherwise accommodating 'redescription' of Ramberg's criticisms Rorty makes no mention of the metaphilosophical device used to frame them. However, one can readily see what he has in mind. To take the case in point, our interest in preserving – protecting, ramifying, *pragmatically* justifying – the distinctness of our self-understanding as agents might be exactly what is required if we are to promote the sort of liberal enlightenment that Rorty is committed to. The crushing weight of outside, descriptive, scientistic accounts of what 'we' are – accounts that, for example, the Sortians try to press on us – might be linked up in all sorts of inferentially relevant and important ways with the sorts of goods we, albeit contingently, favour. Perhaps the pragmatic value of Putnam and Habermas's invocations of context-transcendence and universality is that the normative person–thing distinction is crucial if we are to pursue the project of realizing the liberal utopia – of seeing others not as 'things' but as persons. Of course, in response one might add that the very idea of a 'philosophical interest' conflates the pragmatically respectable concept of the ends and needs that one might think of a vocabulary as allowing us to pursue and satisfy, with what a small section of the population – philosophers – find of interest. From this perspective, it might be argued that there is no reason to think that the desire to talk up the vocabulary of agency in order to resist the overweening ambitions of instrumental rationality expresses a peculiarly *philosophical* interest; or that the vocabulary of philosophy, post-ontological or otherwise, is best suited to serve it.

I'm inclined to think that part of the reason Rorty neglected the vocabulary of agency is that in the 1960s – as we have seen – the 'problem of the mental' devolved to the treatment of mental-states like 'raw feels' and images, and not to mental features which Rorty thought could be dealt with in Rylean-cum-Dennettian terms. Even in *PMN*, these dominate the narrative of how epistemology came to take centre-stage. Nevertheless, although Ramberg's suggestion about an order of philosophical interests is problematic, the point about a controlling concern with ontology is evocative. Indeed, it helped shape the suggestion (2.1) that Rorty's *Kehre* was driven by the suspicion that such a concern vitiated his account of eliminative materialism. I have tried to show that Rorty's increasing hostility to philosophy was driven in part by the desire to avoid such a controlling influence.

In this light, a more useful way to describe what Ramberg is getting at is that Rorty was somehow held captive by a 'picture', according to which philosophy's interests are exhausted in the traditional activity of attempting to disambiguate what is *found* from what is merely *made*. To see what I have in mind here, recall that the starting point for Rorty's call for metaphilosophical reform is his conclusion that the struggle for the future of philosophy is between those who regarded it as an activity of making and those who regarded it as an activity of finding (5.3). From this perspective, Rorty's growing pessimism about philosophy can be diagnosed as arising from the conviction that as a 'maker' it no longer had much to offer culturally. As we went on to discover (6.2), however, Rorty comes to regard this finding–making opposition as infelicitous, since it can imply that what were once regarded as having been *found* – bits of the World – were in fact *made*.[5] It suggests, in other words, that the logical space previously occupied by 'finding-talk' has been replaced by 'making-talk'; that we have erased one half of the dichotomy, but left the other unaltered.

It was Kant's metaphilosophy that provided for the possibility of a legislative standpoint on our practices. As we've seen, with the naturalistic turn towards language this gave rise to two competing philosophical traditions: the revisionary (embodied by Quine) and the descriptive (Wittgenstein; Strawson; Austin). What I am suggesting, then, is that the opposition between these two traditions is an expression of the metaphilosophical distinction between finding and making, and that the latter constitutes the factor 'controlling' Rorty's thinking. This echoes the comments made in chapter 6 regarding the descriptive/inside–normative/outside dichotomy; but it also picks up the concluding point made in 5.7 to the effect that Rorty's account of the figure of the liberal ironist seems haunted by the appeal of some 'outside' view. Once one abandons the finding–making distinction as applicable to philosophy, one abandons the final basis for an 'outside' view. Indeed, if we interpret the transcendental method in the pragmatic-verificationist way outlined in chapter 3 (and recalled above), we deflate the distinction between revision and description. On this account, we are still answerable to each other; but since we are in and of the world, to be answerable to each other is to be answerable to the world (and vice versa). Moreover, in this respect, a fully pragmatized philosophy takes its place amidst other 'vocabularies', in the service of our precious values and interests and able to contribute to their modification. It is perhaps the view Rorty himself arrived at when he observed that 'The more philosophy interacts with other human activities . . . the more relevant to cultural politics it becomes, and thus the more useful' (*PCP*: x). As his younger self might have reminded him, had he been given a voice in 'Trotsky . . .': '*No philosopher can bear [to] . . . be left out of the conversation . . . and this is why philosophy makes progress*' (*TLT*: 2).

Notes

Introduction: No Single Vision

1 Rorty's model here is Dewey (1930), but there are interesting connections with Mill (1971).
2 The sort associated with Nietzsche, Foucault, Heidegger et al.
3 See *TP*: ch. 3 for a reply.
4 Searle's warning resonates with that given by theists in the nineteenth century concerning the dangers to public morals of denying the existence of God.
5 This would be the view of the ancient sceptics, who suspended belief about all contentious matters in order to attain tranquillity. See Gascoigne (2003: ch. 2).
6 Rorty was at Princeton from 1961 until 1982; the University of Virginia until 1997; and at Stanford until his death in June 2007.
7 Cf. Feuerbach, Freud, Marx, Nietzsche and Heidegger; and, of course, Dewey.
8 Cf. Conant (2000: 268–9).

Chapter 1   Out of Mind

1 MBIPC, section 3 ('The Analogy between Demons and Sensations').
2 Rorty calls them the 'Antipodeans', named by Terran philosophers 'in reference to an almost forgotten school of philosophers, centring in Australia and New Zealand' (*PMN*: 72).
3 At the time Hempel assumed that 'all statements of empirical science are *translatable*, without loss of theoretical content, into the language

of physics', a position he revises to '*reducible* to the language of physics' in a footnote added in 1947 (1935, fn. 1).

4 Cf. Wittgenstein: 'We must do away with all *explanation*, and description alone must take its place' (1953: §109).

5 As Hempel says, 'one cannot expect the question as to the scientific status of psychology to be settled by empirical research in psychology itself. To achieve this is rather an undertaking in epistemology' (1935: 373).

6 There will of course be other 'physical tests sentences' relating to the description of alcohol thermometers, galvanic thermometers, etc.

7 Insofar as any translation will involve intentional/mentalist terms the process of translation will be endless, revealing more and more of the complex relations between mental and non–mental terms.

8 Cf. Hume's closing remarks at the end of his first *Enquiry* (1975).

9 Cf. the different senses of 'rising' in 'the tide is rising' and 'hopes are rising' (Ryle 1966: 24).

10 See the concluding section of Ryle (1966) for reflections on behaviourism.

11 In philosophy, Place (1956) is usually regarded as the originator of the position, though it had been suggested in psychology in the 1930s.

12 This is simplified since it neglects the difference between intensional/intentional and extensional properties, which needn't be shared in the case of contingent identities. See Routley and Macrae (1966: 90–8) and Cornman (1971: 45–6).

13 'By "non–inferential report" I mean a statement in response to which questions like "How did you know?" "On what evidence do you say . . . ?" and "What leads you to think . . . ?" are normally considered misplaced and unanswerable, but which is nonetheless capable of empirical confirmation' (MBIPC: 183).

14 See Cornman (1962: 76–9, 1971: 43–6).

15 See Carnap (1947: 47–9) where the relationship between meaning, verification and confirmation through experiment is elucidated.

16 Cf. Grice and Strawson (1957); and Putnam (1975).

17 Brodbeck's comments are framed by reflections on the 'the growing prestige of the scientist, the increasing rôle of the scientific expert in social affairs' (1953: 3). In this sense, normative philosophy of science hopes to preserve for itself something of the priestly mystique attaching to the scientist.

18 This will be discussed in more detail in 4.4.

19 Just how to interpret Kuhn on this talk of 'worlds' is contentious. See Hoyningen–Huene (1993).

20 A. Bird (2000: 156–9) misrepresents Kuhn's reflections on Quine.

21 Cf. Strawson (1966) and (for criticism) Bird (1962) and Allison (2004).

Chapter 2   What is Eliminative Materialism?

1   Category talk was intended to allow for linguistic distinctions without tempting ontological distinctions.
2   'Mental Events' (in Davidson 1980) is an alternative response to this 'crisis'.
3   This appellation was originally coined by Cornman to contrast Quine's position with the reductive materialism of Smart et al. (1968a), but he extends it to include Rorty's position (1968a: 48, fn. 3), and Rorty himself adopts it (1970a; *PMN*).
4   Cf. Strawson: The descriptive metaphysician 'describe[s] the actual structure of our thought about the world' whereas the 'revisionary metaphysician' is concerned 'to produce a better structure' (1959: 9).
5   Thus emerges the philosopher-as-therapist, to assemble his 'reminders for' the 'particular purpose' in which concepts find correct application and thereby 'bring back words from their metaphysical to their everyday use' (Wittgenstein 1953: §127, §116).
6   Cf. Quine (1960: §53–§55).
7   Cf. Quine (1980: ch. 1).
8   Cf. Cornman (1968a: 46).
9   Since one can make sense of 'correct' naming only where there is a possibility of misnaming, and the idea of a 'direct awareness' seems to rule that out.
10 See Sellars (1997: section I).
11 This is a presupposition of some consequence, and we will return to it.
12 See Ayer (1963).
13 Rorty adds that this is an example where Quine's thesis 'is directly relevant to philosophical issues' (1970a: 416).
14 Sellars: '[The philosopher] construes as data the particulars and arrays of particulars which he has come to be able to observe and believes them to be antecedent objects of knowledge which have somehow been in the framework from the beginning. It is in the very act of taking that he speaks of the given' (Sellars 1997: 116–17).
15 Cf. Shaffer: 'our language and conceptual scheme does not allow us to locate mental events in the brain. So an Identity Theory in any of its variants cannot be accepted' (1965: 98).
16 Adapted from Lycan and Pappas, as presented in Hiley (1978).
17 Cf. *PMN*: 80–1 for the acknowledgement of this problem.
18 Championing Davidson to a Chinese audience, Rorty writes: 'American philosophy has now reached a position which, though still plausibly described as "materialist" or "physicalist" . . . [is free] from the familiar charge of "reductionism"' (*PSH*: 113).

19 Cf. *PMN*: 84–5, fn. 5.
20 The use of this term sometimes seems more of a provocation than a statement of substance. Cf. Rorty's characterization of his position as (in McDowell's phrase) 'bald naturalism' (1998: 389) and McDowell's demurral (1998b: 419–20).

Chapter 3   Rorty's *Kehre*

1   This is the sort of diagnosis that M. Williams (1991) will come to develop in considerable detail.
2   Tilting against the view of Bernstein (1991), Habermas (2000) and M. Williams (2003), Hall (1994) disdains this talk of a *Kehre* in Rorty's thinking. In deploying this term I invoke not the authority of friends and former students, however; rather, I hope that, just as the debate about whether or not Heidegger underwent such a 'turn' helps bring into focus what is important about his work, its use will yield some similar pragmatic benefit.
3   This also avoids the need for topic-neutral translations, as brain-processes don't have the same properties sensations have.
4   Cf. Donnellan (1972); Kripke (1980); Putnam (1975).
5   The extent to which Rorty is diagnosing a commitment of his own earlier view on sensations should be apparent here.
6   There are of course other (more ancient) forms of scepticism that aim to show that our beliefs aren't even justified. See, for example, Pritchard (2005).
7   Cf. Putnam (1978: 108).
8   Cf. *TP*: ch. 1.
9   In *PMN*, Rorty distinguishes between the 'homely and shopworn', 'commending' sense and the 'special philosophical sense' (p. 308).
10 To do so is to engage in 'impure' as opposed to 'pure' philosophy of language (*PMN*: 257–66).
11 Or even, 'there's no such thing as the truth$_3$ and that's the truth$_2$ (and might become the truth$_1$)'.
12 Cf. McGinn (1986).
13 The identification of scepticism with revisionary metaphysics is Strawson's.
14 Note the similarity to the reference argument: 'There are Xs' is true just in case 'X' is a referring term.
15 For the modest/immodest distinction, see McDowell (2006).
16 Rorty offers a similarly back-handed defence of Malcolm's (1954) reading of the private-language argument against Thomson (1966).
17 Associated usage of this term goes back to Strawson (1956) and Sellars (1962). For early Rortian thoughts on the subject, see *TLT*: 38.

18 At the risk of abusing the trope, it is an *elimination* of the referring use of 'Transcendental Argument$_r$': 'what people call 'Transcendental Arguments$_r$' are nothing but Transcendental Arguments$_p$.

19 In simplified form.

20 This is what Kant's transcendental philosophy aims to do. See Gascoigne (2003: ch. 4).

21 Cf. Sellars (1968); Rorty (1979: 85–6, *PMN*: 296–8).

Chapter 4 Overcoming Philosophy

1 Cf. Rorty (1961a, 1961b, and 1962). New introductions added to subsequent editions provide an interesting overview of Rorty's increasing disenchantment with traditional philosophy.

2 Cf. Sextus Empiricus (1994); Popkin (1979).

3 One might argue that vaguely 'existential' questions provide no clear criteria for satisfactory answers, and the criteria for answering many abstract questions only start to become evident through the process of inquiry itself.

4 The assumption here is that since the non-philosophical uses are the shared fund of experience, philosophers can distinguish between ordinary and philosophical uses right from the outset. But 'philosopher' does not designate a natural kind, and if philosophical thinking pervades common-sense thinking then no clear distinction can be presupposed.

5 Cf. Austin (1962) on Ayer. For Wittgenstein's satire on silliness, see *CP*: 33–5.

6 The presupposed 'truth' of methodological nominalism is what Rorty will later formalize in terms of truth$_{1/2}$: that which a concrete audience of the philosophically literate will (come to) think of as justified.

7 On specific occasions. It is not, however, a 'philosophically important' distinction, since it cannot be drawn globally.

8 See *CP* (ch. 2) for more on the difference between philosophy as 'the study of certain definite and permanent problems' (p. 31) and philosophy as 'the attempt to sketch new ways in which parts of our life can be seen' (p. 35).

9 Although Rorty quotes Sellars's phrase frequently, the understanding in question is of a prospective nature. *EHO*: 27–49 shows how the later Heidegger can be 'read . . . in this way' (ibid.: 49), and thereby inducted into the pragmatist pantheon. For further 'uses' of Heidegger, see in particular *EHO*: 50–65 and *CIS*: ch. 5.

10 Cf. Carnap (1931).

11 The philosopher as field-linguist, who operates with non-dogmatic verificationist requirements for evidence, is an attempt to realize the ambition behind Quine's 'philosophical behaviorism'.

12 The link between truth and this 'relaxed' view of ontology is reflected in Rorty's approval (cf. *TP*: 117, *ORT*: 8, fn. 14, 49) of Fine's (1986a) 'natural ontological attitude' (NOA): 'NOA does not think that truth is an explanatory concept, or that there is some general thing that makes truths true' (Fine 1986b: 175).

13 Hookway (1988: 136–7) claims that Rorty (and Chomsky 1968) 'misread' Quine here, but then goes on to make precisely this point.

14 Cf. Dennett (1987).

15 Cf. Dreyfus (1980); Taylor (1980); and Rorty's (1980) response. Okrent (1984) is a defence (with reservations) of Rorty's view of hermeneutics.

16 See Dilthey (1883) for the original distinction. For present purposes, the *locus classicus* is Gadamer (1975).

17 Cf. Taylor (1971).

18 See Taylor (1980) for an account of this antagonism.

19 For more on Sellars and picturing, see Bonjour (1973).

20 Warnke (1985, 1987) accuses Rorty of having misinterpreted Gadamer's hermeneutics. But if hermeneutic inquiry involves the fusing of horizons of interpretation, Rorty is consistent in 'fusing' the horizon of Gadamer's hermeneutics with his own (post-positivistic) concerns.

21 As he later observes: 'What I am calling "pragmatism" might also be called "left-wing" Kuhnianism' (*ORT*: 38). 'Left' here is to be understood as the area of culture where 'criteria are constantly changing' (*PSH*: 180).

22 The distinctness of science is developed in *ORT*: 35–45, 46–62.

23 The classic example here is Sartre's waiter, who wishes to make himself an object, an *en-soir* (1957a: ch. 2. pt. 1).

24 For explicit discussion of Darwin's importance in helping formulate the naturalistic vocabulary of pragmatism, see Rorty *TP*: 290–306.

25 Polanyi, whom Rorty mentions favourably on several occasions, held that 'the very nature of knowledge is in the Third *Critique* not in the First *Critique*', and that 'all comprehension is informal and personal: this is the real theme of the Third *Critique*', Letter from Polanyi to Marjorie Grene (dated 13 October 1959), quoted in Ujlaki (1992–3: 127).

26 Cf. Gibbons: 'reflective judgment, and the broader coherence of sensible intuition provided by imagination, underlie determinant judgement' (1994: 191). For the link between Kant's concerns and hermeneutics, see Makkreel (1990). See also Gasché (2003); Bowie (2003); and Pluhar's introduction to Kant (1987).

27 It's the sort of problematic wherein each subsequent philosopher insists on identifying 'metaphysical' commitments in the texts of their predecessor. See, for example, Heidegger's work on Nietzsche; Derrida (1982) on Heidegger. Rorty cites Heidegger's (1938) discussion of the problem with approval.

Chapter 5   New Selves for Old

1   Bernstein (1980: 775) agrees; Guignon and Hiley (1990) demur.
2   Cf. Rorty *TP*: 290–306. See Hegel (1977: chapter 1) for the attack on sense-certainty.
3   Cf. Dewey's Sellarsian conclusion that sensations are 'challenges to an act of inquiry which is to *terminate* in knowledge' (Dewey 1988: 131), not 'gateways of knowing' (p. 129).
4   Cf. Goodman's (1983) attack on the induction–deduction distinction as well as Quine's on the dogmas of empiricism.
5   For modern variants of ethical particularism, see Dancy (1993, 2004) and (in particular) McDowell (1979).
6   It is the purpose of Dewey's final lecture (1988: ch. 8) to contest the Platonic, traditional liberal, and Hegelian conceptions of the relationship between these two concepts.
7   Unless noted, all references are to this text.
8   Sometimes Rorty associates this with the whole philosophical tradition, sometimes with Kant (cf. *CIS*: 30). The implication is that Kant pulls together the two great strands of this story of the West. For objections to Rorty's historico-metaphysical–epistemological epic, see Farrell (1994); McDowell (2000); and M. Williams (2000).
9   Rorty (*CIS*: 45–7) associates this claim with Berlin's (1969) defence of pluralism.
10   I owe this point to a discussion with Richard Raatzsch.
11   Respectively, Proust, Heidegger, Nietzsche and Derrida in Part II, and Nabokov and Orwell in Part III.
12   The title of the final collection of Rorty's essays (*PCP*).
13   Black (1962), quoted by Davidson (2001a: 260). I take the gasses example from Hesse's (1980: 112–13) discussion of Black.
14   Familiar metaphors have already accreted levels of literal meaning: have begun to 'die'.
15   Cf. Davidson (2001b: ch. 3).
16   In the context of 4.6, the 'metaphor' metaphor substitutes for the 'reflexive judgement' metaphor.
17   For more on Rorty's style, see Hall (1994).
18   Shusterman's (1988) criticism that Rorty is left with the classically metaphysical problem of the persistence of the self through time rather misses the point.
19   Freud develops more fully this 'three blows to mankind's self-esteem' material in a short text 'A Difficulty in the Path of Psychoanalysis' (SE 17: 137–44). I'm grateful to Julia Borossa for bringing this material to my attention.
20   For Rorty, this decentring of the self supports the approach to consciousness one finds in (for example) Dennett (1991). Cf. Rorty (1982b, *TP*: 98–121).

21　Nietzsche (1977): 'How the "True World" Finally Became A Fable. The History Of An Error'.

22　'How To Become What You Are' is the subtitle to Nietzsche (1968) and appears as an aphorism in *Zarathustra* (Nietzsche 1974: §61). The 'History of an Error' section ends with the words 'INCIPIT ZARATHUSTRA'.

23　See Breton (1924).

24　See Geertz (1986) for a contrasting view and *ORT*: 203–10 for a response.

25　For a discussion of Bentham on rights, see Edmundson (2004: 51–9).

26　Cf. Dworkin's (1978b) claim that 'rights are trumps' and Gewirth's (1982) even stronger conception.

27　Freeman (2002) argues that basing human rights on sympathy 'confuses *motivation* and *justification*' (p. 56). Since Rorty does not 'base' human rights 'on' anything and aims to undercut the motivation–justification distinction this criticism has little bite.

28　For feminist responses to Rorty's neo-pragmatism, see Bickford (1993); Fraser (1990a, 1990b); Leland (1988); Lovibond (1992); Schultz (1999); and Wilson (1992).

29　Some critics (Conant 2000) have assumed mistakenly that Rorty is suggesting an *analysis* or *reduction* of objectivity to solidarity.

30　Cf. *TP*: 186–201 for a treatment of (three again . . .) uses of 'rationality'.

31　Elshtain (2003: 142). Lovibond (1992) uses the same strategy as do most of Rorty's 'Realist' critics.

32　Taylor's work oftentimes appears on this side of the debate, though, as Mulhall and Swift (1996: 102) point out, it escapes easy classification.

33　'Morality, then, is the relation of actions to the autonomy of the will, that is, to the potential universal legislation by its maxims.' (Kant 2005: 97).

34　Cf. Sandel (1996, 1997, 2005); Taylor (1985a, 1985b, 1990b, 1995); and MacIntyre (1981, 1988, 1990). See Mulhall and Swift (1996) for an overview.

35　See Sandel (1997).

36　The option of what Rorty (following Henry Gates) calls the 'cultural left': those who 'believe that we have recently acquired a radically new understanding of the nature of language and of literature' (*EHO*: 129) which reveals that 'contemporary democratic states' are 'either imperialist powers of disciplinary societies or both' (ibid.: 133). For more on the (mostly) insidious influence of the cultural left, see *AOC*: 75–107.

37　For Foucault's appropriation of Nietzsche's methodology, see his 'Nietzsche, Genealogy, History' (1984). For that methodology at work, see Foucault (1991, 1998). *EHO*: 193–8 suggests that Foucault can also be read as a liberal.

38 Rorty expresses doubt about the need for such theorizing (*TP*: 209, fn. 15) in reply to a similar *cri de coeur* from Fraser and Nicholson (1988: 90).

39 For example Haber (1994: 68). Seaton (1996) has a useful discussion.

40 For not unsympathetic accounts of the ethical function of literature, see, for example, Parker (1994) and Adamson et al. (1998).

41 As Rorty blithely remarks, the cold war was 'a good war' (1991: 6).

42 See *CIS*: 67 for a similar comment about Habermas.

43 For a contrasting view, see Arcilla (1995).

44 See Bhaskar (1991: 134–5).

45 For doubts about the ironist's public commitments, see Blackburn (1998); MacIntyre (1999); Haack (1995); Foelber (1994); Gander (1999); Horton (2001).

46 See *CIS*: 96–137 for Rorty's discussion of ironists and ironist theorists. Rorty suggests that what distinguishes the ironist from the ironist theorist is that the latter is not yet 'a fully-fledged nominalist' (p. 100).

47 One can only assume that the failure of ironist theorists qua ironists is that by restricting themselves to the 'Plato-Kant canon' they have limited their possibilities for 'growth' and become stuck with the 'problem of self-reference'.

48 As, for example, in the genealogies offered by Nietzsche and Foucault.

49 Cf. *PSH*: 23–90.

50 Fish (1994: 20) claims that an awareness of contingency has no effect on our arguments, and later makes a pragmatically useless distinction between 'normative rightness' and 'context-bound rightness' (2003: 416).

51 Owen (2001: 83) takes it that Rorty's 'radical and continuing doubt' implies taking up a detached standpoint on all one's beliefs, though this is clearly anathema to Rorty's official position.

52 Cf. Bernstein (1991: 280). Making the same point, Michael Williams concludes that this 'echo . . . of ancient Pyrrhonian scepticism' (2003: 76) marks an unfortunate 'Humean Turn' in Rorty's thought. This attribution seems to hinge on confusing the ironist with the ironist theorist; not entirely unforgivable given that Rorty at times treats the terms as synonymous.

53 Relativism in this context would be the obverse of Berlin's 'deep and incurable need' which if allowed to dictate one's politics 'is a symptom of an equally deep, and more dangerous, moral and political immaturity' (1969: 172). Blackburn (1998: 288) sees the ironist's attitude lending support to relativism.

54 Bacon tries to resolve this problem by associating irony with a 'tendency to doubt' (2005: 411) which intellectuals just happen to do more than others. Since this turns on an understanding of doubt deriving

from our inability to 'compare one's final vocabulary with something that would guarantee its being "closer to reality"'(ibid.), it is a view the ironist has only 'insofar as she philosophises about her situation'. This fallibilistic levelling of irony simply *writes over* (cf. p. 412) the problem, neglecting the fact that what is being presented is a mode of self-understanding for intellectuals.

55 Rorty's example is O'Brien's attempt to get Smith to describe himself in O'Brien's terms (*CIS*: 169–88).
56 Cf. Sartre (1957b).
57 In responses to critics (2000b, 2001b) Rorty has acknowledged 'friendly amendments' to the way the public–private distinction is made. Cf. Brandom (2000b: 172 ff.), who offers a more 'revisionary' reading.

Chapter 6   The Whole Truth

1 For an exhaustive account of the varieties of relativism, see Baghramian (2004), especially chs 4–8.
2 According to Siegel (2007), 'the book does a fine job of assessing in brief compass the sort of relativism/constructivism advocated by Rorty and his fellow travellers, and Boghossian's sophisticated and careful arguments against that Rortian view are often ingenious and invariably telling'.
3 Lynch (2004: 24–5) makes a similar claim, much to Rorty's (2005: 234) consternation.
4 For Rorty's acknowledgement of this problem, see *PSH*: xvi–xxxii.
5 For criticisms ranging from the equally incredulous to morally outraged, see Nagel (1997: 5, 6, 29); Lynch (2004: 5); Geras (1995: 107); Conant (2000: 269, 303, *passim*); Diamond (1993: 210); and even Bernstein remarks that 'O'Brien is the true "disciple" of Rorty' (1991: 290).
6 Cf. Putnam (1990: 22–3).
7 Cf. Nagel (1986) for an attempt to deal with a similarly conceived problematic.
8 For Rorty's criticisms of Williams on this and kindred points, see *ORT*: 4–9, 55–61.
9 Rorty notes that he flirted with such an idea and that Putnam talked him out of it (*CP*: xlv, fn. 25).
10 The inspiration here is Austin (1946).
11 This is part of Rorty's response to Wellmer (1993). Cf. Rorty (2000a: 9–14).
12 See Habermas's 'Realism after the Linguistic Turn' (2003: 1–49) for a pithy account of the obstacles to this. His solution combines a '*nonclassical* form of epistemological realism' with '"weak" naturalism' (ibid.: 22).

13 Since he later describes the vast majority that don't change as 'not currently in question' (*CP*: 14), charity suggests that only a few could *change* at a time.

14 Rorty acknowledges he had been 'tempted to construe' Davidson's argument in this way (2000b: 376).

15 'I should like to make it sound attractive by dubbing it "American"' (Rorty 2000a: 3). For more on Rorty's hopes and fears for this American Dream, see *AOC*.

16 'What I recommend . . . could be represented as a pragmatism . . . even though . . . I borrow from thinkers such as Kant' (McDowell 1994: 155).

17 McDowell calls this thought 'transcendental' (McDowell 1998a: 365, fn. 2). This deviates from his usage in *Mind and World* where his thinking appears to be 'held captive' by Strawson's (1966) misguided 'two-world' reading of Kant. See Bird (1962) and Allison (1969) for 'the' alternative reading, and Bird (1996) for the criticism of McDowell.

18 See McDowell (1998e) for his fullest account of Sellars. Disagreement over the lessons to be learned from Sellars are brought to the fore in McDowell's exchanges with Brandom. Rorty took Brandom for his champion in confronting McDowell's attempt to revive philosophical interest in the concept of experience: Brandom's 'writings provide the best weapons for defending my version of James' pragmatism' (*PCP*: 7). Cf. *TP*: 122–52, 2003: 16.

19 A good example of McDowell's Wittgensteinian therapy in action is his contribution to the post-Kripkean debate about rule-following (1998c: 221–62).

20 McDowell (2000: 117–20).

21 He makes a distinction between the *normative* category of persons ('one of us') and the descriptive vocabulary of minds (bearers of attitudes) (Rorty 2000b: 371).

Conclusion: The Ends of Philosophy

1 Pragmatically, of course, more cooperation might be required. But the further one gets from the 'origin' of the minimal norm-constituting community the more difficult it is to see how the conditions of the possibility of communication might have an emancipatory import.

2 Neither did he take it to allow the reintroduction of the Natural/ Human science distinction. See *PCP*: 134–41 where he revisits his fondness for Fine's 'Natural Ontological Attitude' and rolls it in with Brandom's inferentialist semantics. In one of his last papers he comments: 'Pragmatism puts natural science on all fours with politics and art. It is one more source of suggestions about what to do with our lives' (Rorty 2006).

3 One might, for example, regard McDowell's revival of talk of 'spontaneity' and 'receptivity' as revivifying precisely the sort of philosophical problems he aims to dissolve.
4 This view coincides at points with Okrent (1993).
5 When Rorty acknowledges the finding–making problem (cf. *PSH*:
   xvi–xxxii), he notes that this means he rejects the idea that philosophical problems are made *as opposed to* found (*PSH*: xxii). But he does
   not reject the philosophy-as-making versus philosophy-as-finding
   distinction.

Bibliography

Works by Rorty

Books
(1979; *PMN*). *Philosophy and the Mirror of Nature*. Princeton: Princeton University Press.
(1984). (ed. with J. B. Schneewind and Q. Skinner). *Philosophy in History*. Cambridge: Cambridge University Press.
(1989; *CIS*). *Contingency, Irony, and Solidarity*. Cambridge: Cambridge University Press.
(1992; *TLT*). (ed.). *The Linguistic Turn*. With two Retrospective Essays. Chicago, IL: Chicago University Press.
(1998; *AOC*). *Achieving Our Country*. Cambridge, MA: Harvard University Press.

Collections of essays
(1982; *CP*). *Consequences of Pragmatism*. Minneapolis: University of Minnesota Press.
(1991a; *ORT*). *Objectivity, Relativism, and Truth*. Philosophical Papers, vol. 1. Cambridge: Cambridge University Press.
(1991b; *EHO*). *Essays on Heidegger and Others*. Philosophical Papers, vol. 2. Cambridge: Cambridge University Press.
(1998; *TP*). *Truth and Progress*. Philosophical Papers, vol. 3. Cambridge: Cambridge University Press.
(1999; *PSH*). *Philosophy and Social Hope*. London: Penguin.
(2007; *PCP*). *Philosophy as Cultural Politics*. Philosophical Papers, vol. 4. Cambridge: Cambridge University Press.

Other works

(1961a). 'Pragmatism, Categories, and Language', *Philosophical Review* 70: 197–223.

(1961b). 'Recent Metaphilosophy', *Review of Metaphysics* xv: 299–318.

(1962). 'Realism, Categories, and the "Linguistic Turn" ', *International Philosophical Quarterly* 2: 307–22.

(1965; MBIPC). 'Mind–Body Identity, Privacy, and Categories', *Review of Metaphysics* 19: 24–54.

(1970a). 'Incorrigibility as the Mark of the Mental', *Journal of Philosophy* 67: 399–424.

(1970b). 'In Defense of Eliminative Materialism', in D. M. Rosenthal (ed.), 2000, pp. 223–31.

(1971). 'Verificationism and Transcendental Arguments', *Noûs* 5: 3–14.

(1972a). 'Dennett on Awareness', *Philosophical Studies* 23: 153–62.

(1972b). 'Functionalism, Machines, and Incorrigibility', *Journal of Philosophy* 69: 203–20.

(1972c). 'Indeterminacy of Translation and of Truth', *Synthese* 23: 443–62.

(1976). 'Realism and Reference', *The Monist* 59: 321–40.

(1979). 'Transcendental Arguments, Self-Reference, and Pragmatism', in P. Bieri et al. (eds), 1979, pp. 77–103.

(1980). 'Reply to Dreyfus and Taylor', *Review of Metaphysics* 34/1: 39–46.

(1982a). 'Comments on Dennett', *Synthese* 53: 181–7.

(1982b). 'Contemporary Philosophy of Mind', *Synthese* 53: 323–48.

(1988). 'The Priority of Democracy to Philosophy', in M. Peterson and R. Vaughan (eds), *The Virginia Statute of Religious Freedom*. Cambridge: Cambridge University Press; in *ORT*, pp. 257–88.

(1990). 'Pragmatism as Anti-representationalism', in J. P. Murphy, 1990, pp. 1–6.

(1991). 'Just One More Species Doing Its Best', *London Review of Books* (25 July): 3–7.

(1993). 'Feminism, Ideology, and Deconstruction: A Pragmatist View', *Hypatia* 8/2: 96–103.

(1997). 'Comments on Michael Williams: *Unnatural Doubts*', *Journal of Philosophical Research* 22: 1–10.

(1998). 'McDowell, Davidson, and Spontaneity', *Philosophy and Phenomenological Research* 53/2: 389–94.

(2000a). 'Universality and Truth', in R. Brandom (ed.), 2000a, pp. 1–30.

(2000b). 'Response to . . .', in R. Brandom (ed.), 2000a, *passim*.

(2001a). 'The Ambiguity of "Rationality"', in W. Rehg and J. Bohman (eds), *Pluralism and the Pragmatic Turn*. Cambridge, MA: MIT Press, pp. 41–52.

(2001b). 'Responses to . . .', in M. Festenstein and S. Thompson (eds), 2001, *passim*.

(2002). 'Fighting Terrorism with Democracy', *The Nation*, 21 October: 11–14.

(2003). 'Putnam, Pragmatism, and Parmenides', downloaded from <http://www.hf.uio.no/ifikk/forskning/internordic/Putnam,%2 0Pragmatism,%20and%20Parmenides.doc>.

(2004). 'Philosophy as a Transitional Genre', in S. Benhabib and N. Fraser (eds), *Pragmatism, Critique, Judgement*. Cambridge, MA: MIT Press, pp. 3–28.

(2005). 'True to Life: Why Truth Matters', *Philosophy and Phenomenological Research* 71/1: 231–9.

(2006). 'Dewey and Posner on Pragmatism and Moral Progress', *The University of Chicago Law Review* 74/3: 915–27.

Collections of Essays on Rorty

Brandom, R. (ed.) (2000a). *Rorty and His Critics*. Oxford: Blackwell.

Festenstein, M. and Thompson, S. (eds) (2001). *Richard Rorty: Critical Dialogues*. Cambridge: Polity.

Guignon, C. B. and Hiley, D. R. (eds) (2003). *Richard Rorty*. Cambridge: Cambridge University Press.

Malachowski, A. (ed.) (1990). *Reading Rorty*. Oxford: Blackwell.

Malachowski, A. (ed.) (2002). *Richard Rorty*. 4 vols. London: Sage.

Peters, M. and Ghiraldelli, P. (eds) (2002). *Richard Rorty: Philosophy, Culture and Education*. Boulder, CO: Rowman & Littlefield.

Saatkamp, H. J. (ed.) (1995). *Rorty and Pragmatism*. London: Vanderbilt.

Other Works

Adamson, J., Freadman, R. and Parker, D. (eds) (1998). *Renegotiating Ethics in Literature, Philosophy, and Theory*. Cambridge: Cambridge University Press.

Adorno, T. and Horkheimer, M. (1997). *Dialectic of Enlightenment*. London: Verso.

Allison, H. E. (1969). 'Transcendental Idealism and Descriptive Metaphysics', *Kantstudien* 60: 216–33.

——(2004). *Kant's Transcendental Idealism*, revised and enlarged edn. New Haven, CT: Yale University Press.

Apel, K.-O. (1984). *Understanding and Explanation*, trans. G. Warnke. Cambridge, MA: MIT Press.

Aquinas, T. (1947). *Summa Theologica*, trans. Fathers of the English Dominican Province. New York: Benziger Bros.

Arcilla, R. V. (1995). *For the Love of Perfection: Richard Rorty and Liberal Education*. London: Routledge.

Armstrong, D. M. (1968). *A Materialist Theory of Mind*. London: Routledge.

Austin, J. L. (1946). 'Other Minds', in J. L. Austin (1961), *Philosophical Papers*. Oxford: Oxford University Press.

——(1962). *Sense and Sensibilia*. Oxford: Clarendon Press.

Ayer, A. J. (1936). *Language, Truth and Logic*. London: Victor Gollancz Ltd.

——(ed.) (1959). *Logical Positivism*. Glencoe, IL.: The Free Press.

——(1963). *The Concept of a Person*. New York: St Martin's Press.

Bacon, M. (2005). 'A Defence of Liberal Ironism', *Res Publica* 11: 403–23.

Baghramian, M. (2004). *Relativism*. Abingdon: Routledge.

Baier, A. (1991). *A Progress of Sentiments: Reflections on Hume's Treatise*. Cambridge, MA: Harvard University Press.

Bain, A. (1859). *Emotion and the Will*. New York: Longmans Green.

Beck, L. W. (ed.) (1988). *Kant: Selections*. London: Collier Macmillan.

Beiser, F. C. (ed.) (1993). *The Cambridge Companion to Hegel*. Cambridge: Cambridge University Press.

Bentham, J. (1830). *The Rationale of Reward*. London: Robert Heward.

——(1843). 'Critique of the Doctrine of Inalienable, Natural Rights', in *Anarchical Fallacies*, vol. II of J. Bowring (ed.), *Works*. Edinburgh: W. Tait, pp. 489–534.

——(1945). *The Limits of Jurisprudence Defined.* New York: Columbia University Press.

Bergmann, G. (1960). *Meaning and Existence*. Madison, WI: University of Wisconsin Press.

——(1964). *Logic and Reality*. Madison, WI: University of Wisconsin Press.

Berlin, I. (1969). *Four Essays on Liberty*. Oxford: Oxford University Press.

Bernstein, R. J. (1968). 'The Challenge of Scientific Materialism', in D. M. Rosenthal (ed.), 2000, pp. 200–22.

—— (1980). 'Philosophy in the Conversation of Mankind', *The Review of Metaphysics* 33/1: 766–75.

—— (1991). *The New Constellation*. Cambridge, MA: MIT Press.

—— (2003). 'Rorty's Inspirational Liberalism', in C. B. Guignon and D. R. Hiley (eds), 2003, pp. 124–38.

Bhaskar, R. (1991). *Philosophy and the Idea of Freedom*. Oxford: Blackwell.

Bickford, S. (1993). 'Why We Listen to Lunatics: Antifoundational Theories and Feminist Politics', *Hypatia* 8/2: 104–23.

Bieri, P., Horstmann, R.-P. and Krüger, L. (eds). (1979). *Transcendental Arguments and Science*. Dordrecht: Reidel.

Bird, A. (2000). *Thomas Kuhn*. Chesham: Acumen Publishing Limited.

Bird, G. (1962). *Kant's Theory of Knowledge*. London: Routledge.

—— (1996). 'McDowell's Kant: *Mind and World*', *Philosophy* 71: 219–43.

Black, M. (1962). *Models and Metaphors*. Ithaca, NY: Cornell University Press.

—— (1979). 'How Metaphors Work: A Reply to Donald Davidson', in S. Sacks (ed.), *On Metaphor*. Chicago, IL: University of Chicago Press, pp. 181–92.

Blackburn, S. (1998). *Ruling Passions*. Oxford: Clarendon Press.

Bloom, H. (1975). *The Anxiety of Influence*. Oxford: Oxford University Press.

Boghossian, P. (2006). *Fear of Knowledge: Against Relativism and Constructivism*. Oxford: Oxford University Press.

Bonjour, L. (1973). 'Sellars on Truth and Picturing', *International Philosophical Quarterly* 13: 243–65.

Boorst, C. V. (ed.) (1970). *The Mind–Brain Identity Theory*. London: Macmillan.

Bowie, A. (2003). *Introduction to German Philosophy*. Cambridge: Polity.

Brandom, R. (1994). *Making It Explicit*. Cambridge, MA: Harvard University Press.

—— (2000a). *Rorty and His Critics*. Oxford: Blackwell.

—— (2000b). 'Vocabularies of Pragmatism', in R. Brandom (ed.) 2000, pp. 156–83.

—— (2000c). *Articulating Reasons*. Cambridge, MA: Harvard University Press.

Breton, A. (1924). 'Manifesto of Surrealism', in *Manifestoes of Surrealism* (1969), trans. R. Seaver and H. Lane. Ann Arbor, MI: University of Michigan Press.

Brodbeck, M. (1953). 'The Nature and Function of the Philosophy of Science', in H. Feigl and M. Brodbeck (eds), 1953, pp. 3–7.

Burke, E. (1986). *Reflections on the Revolution in France*. Harmondsworth: Penguin.

Bush, E. (1974). 'Rorty Revisited', *Philosophical Studies* 25: 33–42.

Calder, G. (2003). *Rorty*. London: Weidenfeld & Nicolson.

Carnap, R. (1931). 'The Elimination of Metaphysics through Logical Analysis of Language', in A. J. Ayer (ed.), 1959, pp. 60–81.

——(1936–7). 'Testability and Meaning', in H. Feigl and M. Brodbeck (eds), 1953, pp. 47–92.

——(1947). *Meaning and Necessity*, 2nd edn. Chicago, IL: University of Chicago Press.

——(1967). *The Logical Structure of the World and Pseudoproblems in Philosophy*, trans. R. A. George. London: Routledge.

Cavell, M. (1986). 'Metaphor, Dreamwork and Irrationality', in E. LePore (ed.), 1986, pp. 495–507.

Chomsky, N. (1968), 'Quine's Empirical Assumptions', *Synthese* 19: 53–68.

Churchland, P. M. (1979). *Scientific Realism and the Plasticity of Mind*. Cambridge: Cambridge University Press.

——(1984). *Matter and Consciousness*. Cambridge, MA: MIT Press.

Collingwood, R. G. (1940). *An Essay on Metaphysics*. Oxford: Oxford University Press.

Conant, J. (2000) 'Freedom, Cruelty, and Truth', in R. Brandom (ed.), 2000a, pp. 268–342.

Cooke, V. M. (1988). 'Kant's Godlike Self', *International Philosophical Quarterly* 28: 313–23.

Cornman, J. (1962). 'The Identity of Mind and Body', in D. M. Rosenthal (ed.), 2000, pp. 73–9.

——(1968a). 'Mental Terms, Theoretical Terms, and Materialism', *Philosophy of Science* 35/1: 45–63.

——(1968b). 'On the Elimination of "Sensations" and Sensations', *The Review of Metaphysics* 22: 15–35.

——(1971). *Materialism and Sensations*. New Haven, CT and London: Yale University Press.

Dancy, J. (1993). *Moral Reasons*. Oxford: Blackwell.

——(2004). *Ethics without Principles*. Oxford: Clarendon Press.

Davidson, D. (1980). *Essays on Actions and Events*. Oxford: Oxford University Press.

——(1982). 'Paradoxes of Irrationality', in R. Wollheim and J. Hopkins (eds), *Philosophical Essays on Freud*. Cambridge: Cambridge University Press, 1982, pp. 289–305.

——(1986). 'A Nice Derrangement of Epitaphs', in E. LePore (ed.), 1986, pp. 459–76.

——(1987). 'Afterthoughts, 1987', in A. Malachowski (ed.), 1990, pp. 134–8.

——(1990). 'The Structure and Content of Truth', *The Journal of Philosophy* 87/6: 279–328.

——(2000). 'Truth Rehabilitated', in R. Brandom (ed.), 2000a: 65–74.

——(2001a). *Inquiries into Truth and Interpretation*, 2nd edn. Oxford: Oxford University Press.

——(2001b). *Subjective, Intersubjective, Objective*. Oxford: Oxford University Press.

Dennett, D. (1981). *Brainstorms*. Cambridge, MA: MIT Press.

——(1982a). 'How to Study Human Consciousness Empirically or Nothing Comes to Mind', *Synthese* 53: 159–80.

——(1982b). 'Comments on Rorty', *Synthese* 53: 349–56.

——(1987). *The Intentional Stance*. Cambridge, MA: MIT Press.

——(1991). *Consciousness Explained*. London: Allen Lane/Penguin Press.

Derrida, J. (1978). *Writing and Difference*, trans. A. Bass. Chicago, IL: University of Chicago Press.

——(1982). *Margins of Philosophy*, trans. A. Bass. Chicago, IL: University of Chicago Press.

Descartes R. (1986). *Meditations on First Philosophy*, trans. J. Cottingham. Cambridge: Cambridge University Press.

Dewey, J. (1927). 'Philosophy and Civilisation', *The Later Works*, 1925–1953, vol. 3. Carbondale and Edwardsville: Southern Illinois University Press, 1984, pp. 3–10.

——(1929). 'The Quest for Certainty', *The Later Works*, 1925–1953, vol. 4. Carbondale and Edwardsville: Southern Illinois University Press, 1984, pp. 1–250.

——(1930). 'From Absolutism to Experimentalism', *The Later Works*, 1925–1953, vol. 5. Carbondale and Edwardsville: Southern Illinois University Press, 1984, pp. 147–60.

——(1958). *Experience and Nature*, 2nd edn. New York: Dover Publications.

——(1988). *Reconstruction in Philosophy. The Middle Works*, 1899–1924, vol. 12. Carbondale and Edwardsville: Southern Illinois University Press, 1984, pp. 77–201.

Diamond, C. (1993). 'Truth: Defenders, Debunkers, Despisers', in L. Toker (ed.), *Commitment in Reflection*. Hamden, CT: Garland Press, pp. 195–221.

Dilthey, W. (1883). *Introduction to the Human Sciences: An Attempt to Lay a Foundation for the Study of Society and History*, ed. R. A. Makkreel and F. Rodi, trans. R. A. Makkreel. Princeton, NJ: Princeton University Press (1989).

Donnellan, K. (1972). 'Proper Names and Identifying Descriptions', in *Semantics of Natural Language*, eds D. Davidson and G. Harman. Dordrecht: Reidel, pp. 356–79.

Dreyfus, H. L. (1980). 'Holism and Hermeneutics', *Review of Metaphysics* 34/1: 3–23.

Dummett, M. (1975). 'What is a Theory of Meaning?', in S. D. Guttenplan (ed.), *Mind and Language*. Oxford: Clarendon Press, 1975, pp. 97–138.

——(1976). 'What is a Theory of Meaning? (II)', in G. Evans and J. McDowell (eds), *Truth and Meaning*. Oxford: Oxford University Press, pp. 67–137.

——(1978). *Truth and Other Enigmas*. London: Duckworth.

——(1986). 'A Nice Derangement of Epitaphs; Some Comments on Davidson and Hacking', in E. LePore (ed.) (1986), pp. 459–76.

Dworkin, R. (1978a). 'Liberalism', in S. Hampshire (ed.), 1978, pp. 113–43.

——(1978b). *Taking Rights Seriously*. London: Duckworth.

Edmundson, W. A. (2004). *An Introduction to Rights*. Cambridge: Cambridge University Press.

Elshtain, J. B. (2003). 'Don't Be Cruel: Reflections on Rortyan Liberalism', in C. B. Guignon and D. R. Hiley (eds), 2003, pp. 139–57.

Evnine, S. (1991). *Donald Davidson*. Stanford, CA: Stanford University Press.

Farrell, F. B. (1994). *Subjectivity, Realism and Postmodernism*. Cambridge: Cambridge University Press.

Feigl, H. (1943). 'Logical Empiricism', in H. Feigl and W. Sellars (eds), 1949, pp. 3–26.

——(1949). 'The Scientific Outlook: Naturalism and Humanism', in H. Feigl and M. Brodbeck (eds), 1953, pp. 8–18.

——(1967). *The 'Mental' and the 'Physical'*. Minneapolis, MN: University of Minnesota Press.

Feigl, H. and Brodbeck, M. (eds) (1953). *Readings in the Philosophy of Science*. New York: Appleton-Century-Crofts.

Feigl, H. and Sellars, W. (eds) (1949). *Readings in Philosophical Analysis*. New York: Appleton-Century-Crofts.

Feyerabend, P. (1963). 'Mental Events and the Brain', in D. M. Rosenthal (ed.), 2000, pp. 172–3.

Fine, A. (1986a). *The Shaky Game: Einstein Realism and the Quantum Theory*. Chicago, IL: University of Chicago Press.

——(1986b). 'Unnatural Attitudes: Realist and Instrumentalist Attachments to Science', *Mind* 95: 149–79.

Fish, S. (1985). 'Pragmatism and Literary Theory', *Critical Inquiry* 11: 433–58.

——(1989). *Doing What Comes Naturally*. Durham, NC: Duke University Press.

——(1994). *There's No Such Thing as Free Speech, and It's a Good Thing*. Oxford: Oxford University Press.

——(2003). 'Truth but No Consequences', *Critical Inquiry* 29: 389–417.

Foelber, R. E. (1994). 'Can an Historicist Sustain a Diehard Commitment to Liberal Democracy?', *The Southern Journal of Philosophy* 32: 19–48.

Foucault, M. (1984). 'Nietzsche, Genealogy, History', in P. Rabinow (ed.), 1984, pp. 76–100.

——(1991). *Discipline and Punish*, trans. A. Sheridan. London: Penguin.

——(1998). *The History of Sexuality*, vol. 1, trans. R. Hurley. London: Penguin.

Fraser, N. (1990a). 'From Irony to Prophecy to Politics: A Response to Richard Rorty', in R. B. Goodman (ed.), 1995, *Pragmatism*. London: Routledge, pp. 53–75.

——(1990b). 'Solidarity or Singularity? Richard Rorty between Romanticism and Technocracy', in A. Malachowski (ed.), 1990, pp. 303–21.

Fraser, N. and Nicholson, L (1988). 'Social Criticism Without Philosophy: An Encounter Between Feminism and Postmodernism', in A. Ross (ed.), 1988, *Universal Abandon?* Minneapolis, MN: University of Minnesota Press, pp. 83–104.

Freeman, M. (2002). *Human Rights*. Cambridge: Polity.

Freud, S. (1953–74). *The Standard Edition of the Complete Works of Sigmund Freud* (SE), 24 vols, ed. James Strachey et al. London: The Hogart Press and the Institute of Psychoanalysis.

Friedman, M. (2000). *A Parting of the Ways: Carnap, Cassirer, and Heidegger*. Chicago, IL: Open Court.

Gadamer, H.-G. (1975). *Truth and Method*. New York: Seabury Press.

Gander, E. M. (1999). *The Last Conceptual Revolution: A Critique of Richard Rorty's Political Philosophy*. Albany, NY: SUNY Press.

Garlan, E. N. (1945). 'Review of *The Limits of Jurisprudence Defined*', *The Journal of Philosophy* 42/22: 607–15.

Gasché, R. (2003). *The Idea of Form*. Stanford, CA: Stanford University Press.

Gascoigne, N. (2003). *Scepticism*. Montreal and Ontario: McGill-Queen's University Press.

——(2007). 'Richard Rorty: No Single Vision', *Radical Philosophy* 146: 62–5.

Geertz, C. (1986). 'The Uses of Diversity', *Michigan Quarterly Review* 25/1: 105–23.

Geras, N. (1995). *Solidarity in the Conversation of Mankind*. London: Verso.

Gettier, E. (1963). 'Is Justified True Belief Knowledge?', *Analysis* 23: 121–3.

Gewirth, A. (1982). *Human Rights: Essays on Justification and Applications*. Chicago, IL: University of Chicago Press.

Gibbons, S. L. (1994). *Kant's Theory of Imagination*. Oxford: Clarendon Press.

Godwin, W. (1842). *Enquiry Concerning Political Justice*, 4th edn. London: J. Watson.

Goodman, N. (1983). *Fact, Fiction, and Forecast*. Cambridge, MA: Harvard University Press.

Grice, H. P. and Strawson, P. F. (1957). 'In Defense of a Dogma', *The Philosophical Review* 65/2: 141–58.

Guignon, C. B., and Hiley, D. R. (1990). 'Biting the Bullet: Rorty on Private and Public Morality', in A. Malachowski (ed.), 1990, pp. 339–64.

Gutting, G. (1999). *Pragmatic Liberalism and the Critique of Modernity*. Cambridge: Cambridge University Press.

Haack, S. (1995). 'Vulgar Pragmatism: An Unedifying Prospect', in H. J. Saatkamp (ed.), 1995, pp. 126–47.

Haber, H. F. (1994). *Beyond Postmodern Politics*. Routledge: London.

Habermas, J. (1971). *Knowledge and Human Interests*, trans. J. J. Shapiro. Boston, MA: Beacon Press.

——(1987). *The Philosophical Discourse of Modernity*. Cambridge, MA: MIT Press.

——(1988). 'Philosophy as Stand-In and Interpreter', in K. Baynes et al. (eds), *After Philosophy: End or Transformation*. Cambridge, MA: MIT Press, pp. 296–318.

——(1996). *Between Facts and Norms*. Cambridge, MA: MIT Press.

——(2000). 'Richard Rorty's Pragmatic Turn', in R. Brandom (ed.) 2000a, pp. 31–55.

——(2003). *Truth and Justification*. Cambridge, MA: MIT Press.

Haliburton, R. (1997). 'Richard Rorty and the Problem of Cruelty', *Philosophy and Social Criticism* 23/1: 49–69.

Hall, D. L. (1994). *Richard Rorty.* Albany, NY: SUNY Press.

Hampshire, S. (ed.) (1978). *Public and Private Morality.* Cambridge: Cambridge University Press.

Hegel, G. W. F. (1977). *Phenomenology of Spirit,* trans. A. V. Miller. Oxford: Oxford University Press.

Heidegger, M. (1938). 'The Age of the World View', trans. M. Grene, in W. V. Spanos (ed.) (1979), *Martin Heidegger and the Question of Literature.* Bloomington, IN: Indiana University Press, pp. 1–15.

——(1962). *Being and Time,* trans. J. Macquarrie and E. Robinson. New York: Harper and Row.

——(1977). *Basic Writings,* ed. D. Krell. New York: Harper and Row.

Hempel, C. G. (1935). 'The Logical Analysis of Psychology', in H. Feigl and W. Sellars (eds), 1949, pp. 373–84.

Hesse, M. (1980). *Revolutions and Reconstructions in the Philosophy of Science.* Brighton: Harvester Press.

——(1984). *Metaphor and Religion (Theolinguistics II),* ed. J.-P. van Noppen, new series no. 12. Brussels: V.U.B. (Studiereeks T.U.B.), pp. 27–45.

Hiley, D. R. (1978). 'Is Eliminative Materialism Materialistic?', *Philosophy and Phenomenological Research* 38: 325–37.

——(1988). *Philosophy in Question.* Chicago, IL: Chicago University Press.

——, Bohman, J. F. and Shusterman, R. (eds) (1991). *The Interpretive Turn: Philosophy, Science, Culture.* Ithaca, NY: Cornell University Press.

Hookway, C. (1988). *Quine: Language, Experience and Reality.* Cambridge: Polity.

Horton, J. (2001). 'Irony and Commitment: An Irreconcilable Dualism of Modernity', in M. Festenstein and S. Thompson (eds), 2001, pp. 15–28.

Hoy, D. C. and McCarthy, T. (eds) (1994). *Critical Theory.* New York: Blackwell.

Hoyningen-Huene, P. (1993). *Reconstructing Scientific Revolutions: Thomas S. Kuhn's Philosophy of Science,* trans. A. T. Levine. Chicago, IL: Chicago University Press.

Hume, D. (1975). *Enquiries Concerning Human Understanding and Concerning the Principles of Morals,* ed. L. A. Selby-Bigge, 3rd edn. Oxford: Clarendon Press.

——(1978). *A Treatise of Human Nature,* ed. L. A. Selby-Bigge, 2nd edn. Oxford: Oxford University Press.

——(1987). *Essays: Moral, Political, and Literary*, ed. E. F. Miller. Indianapolis, IN: Liberty Classics.

Kant, I. (1784). 'What is Enlightenment?', in L. W. Beck (ed.), 1988, pp. 462–7.

——(1987). *Critique of Judgement*, trans. W. S. Pluhar. Indianapolis, IN: Hackett.

——(1993). *Critique of Pure Reason*, trans. J. M. D. Meiklejohn and V. Politis. London: Everyman.

——(2005). *Groundwork for the Metaphysic of Morals*, ed. L. Denis. Peterborough, Ontario: Broadview Press.

Kripke, S. (1980). *Naming and Necessity*. Oxford: Blackwell.

Kuhn, T. (1970a). *The Structure of Scientific Revolutions*, 2nd edn. Chicago, IL and London: University of Chicago Press.

——(1970b). 'Reflections on My Critics', in I. Lakatos and A. Musgrave (eds) (1970), *Criticism and the Growth of Knowledge*. London: Cambridge University Press, pp. 231–78.

——(1977). *The Essential Tension*. Chicago, IL and London: University of Chicago Press.

Lear, J. (1982). 'Leaving the World Alone', *Journal of Philosophy* 79: 382–403.

——(1984). 'The Disappearing "We" ', *Aristotelian Society Supplementary Volume* 58: 219–42.

Leland, D. (1988). 'Rorty on the Moral Concern of Philosophy: A Critique from a Feminist Point of View', *Praxis International* 8/3: 273–83.

LePore, E. (ed.) (1986). *Truth and Interpretation*. Oxford: Blackwell.

Lovibond, S. (1989). 'Feminism and Postmodernism', *New Left Review* 178: 5–28.

——(1992). 'Feminism and Pragmatism', *New Left Review* 193: 56–74.

Lynch, M. (2004). *True to Life: Why Truth Matters*. Cambridge, MA: MIT Press.

Lyotard, J-.F. (1979). *The Postmodern Condition*, trans. B. Masumi and G. Bennington. Manchester: Manchester University Press.

McCarthy, T. (1991). *Ideals and Illusions*. Cambridge, MA: MIT Press.

McDowell, J. (1979). 'Virtue and Reason', *The Monist* 62: 331–50.

——(1994). *Mind and World*. Cambridge, MA: Harvard University Press.

——(1998a). 'Précis of *Mind and World*', *Philosophy and Phenomenological Research* 53/2: 365–8.

—— (1998b). 'Reply to Commentators', *Philosophy and Phenomenological Research* 53/2: 403–32.

—— (1998c). *Mind, Value, and Reality*. Cambridge, MA: Harvard University Press.

—— (1998d). *Meaning, Knowledge, and Reality*. Cambridge, MA: Harvard University Press.

—— (1998e). 'Having the World in View: Sellars, Kant, and Intentionality', *Journal of Philosophy* 95: 431–91.

—— (2000). 'Towards Rehabilitating Objectivity', in R. Brandom (ed.) 2000a, pp. 109–23.

—— (2002). 'Responses', in N. H. Smith (ed.), *Reading McDowell. On Mind and World*. London: Routledge, pp. 269–305.

—— (2006). 'The Disjunctive Conception of Experience as Material for a Transcendental Argument', *Teorema* 25/1: 19–34.

McGinn, C. (1986). 'Radical Interpretation and Epistemology', in E. LePore (ed.), 1986, pp. 356–68.

McGinn, M. (1989). *Sense and Certainty*. Oxford: Blackwell.

MacIntyre, A. (1981). *After Virtue*. London: Duckworth.

—— (1988). *Whose Justice? Which Rationality?* London: Duckworth.

—— (1990). *Three Rival Versions of Moral Inquiry*. London: Duckworth.

—— (1999). *Dependent Rational Animals*. London: Duckworth.

MacKinnon, C. (1987). *Feminism Unmodified*. Cambridge, MA: Harvard University Press.

Makkreel, R. (1990). *Imagination and Interpretation in Kant*. Chicago, IL: Chicago University Press.

Malcolm, N. (1954). 'Wittgenstein's Philosophical Investigations', *The Philosophical Review* 63: 530–59.

Mill, J. S. (1838). 'Bentham', reprinted in J. M. Robson (ed.). (1969), *Essays on Ethics, Religion, and Society*. Toronto: University of Toronto Press, pp. 77–115.

—— (1971). *Autobiography*. Oxford: Oxford University Press.

—— (1974). *On Liberty*. Harmondsworth: Penguin.

Moufe, C. (ed.) (1996). *Deconstruction and Pragmatism*. London: Routledge.

Mulhall, S. and A. Swift (1996). *Liberals and Communitarians*, 2nd edn. Oxford: Blackwell.

Murphy, J. P. (1990). *Pragmatism: From Peirce to Davidson*. Boulder, CO: Westview Press.

Nagel, T. (1979). *Mortal Questions*. Cambridge: Cambridge University Press.

——(1986). *The View from Nowhere*. Oxford: Oxford University Press.

——(1997). *The Last Word*. Oxford: Oxford University Press.

Nehamas, A. (1985). *Nietzsche: Life as Literature*. Cambridge, MA: Harvard University Press.

——(1990). 'A Touch of the Poet', *Raritan Quarterly* 10: 104–25.

Nietzsche, F. (1968). *Ecce Homo*, in W. Kaufmann (ed. and trans.), *Basic Writings of Nietzsche*. New York: Random House.

——(1973). *Beyond Good and Evil*, trans. R. J. Hollingdale. Harmondsworth: Penguin.

——(1974). *Thus Spoke Zarathustra*, trans. R. J. Hollingdale. Harmondsworth: Penguin.

——(1977). *Twilight of the Idols*, in W. Kaufmann (ed. and trans.), *The Portable Nietzsche*. Harmondsworth: Penguin.

——(1988). *The Birth of Tragedy*, ed. and trans. W. Kaufmann. New York: Vintage Books.

——(1989). *On the Genealogy of Morals*, trans. W. Kaufmann and R. J. Hollingdale. New York: Vintage.

Okrent, M. (1984). 'Hermeneutics, Transcendental Philosophy, and Social Science', *Inquiry* 27: 23–49.

——(1988). 'The Metaphilosophical Consequences of Pragmatism', in A. Cohen and M. Dascal (eds), *The Institution of Philosophy: An Institution in Crisis?* Totowa, NJ: Rowman and Littlefield, pp. 177–98.

——(1993). 'The Truth, the Whole Truth, and Nothing but the Truth', *Inquiry* 36: 381–404.

Owen, J. J. (2001). *Religion and the Demise of Liberal Rationalism*. Chicago, IL: University of Chicago Press.

Parker, D. (1994). *Ethics, Theory and the Novel*. Cambridge: Cambridge University Press.

Peirce, C. S. (1877). 'The Fixation of Belief', *Popular Science Monthly* 12 (November), at: <http://www.peirce.org/writings/p107.html>.

Place, U. T. (1956). 'Is Consciousness a Brain Process?', *British Journal of Psychology* 47: 44–50.

Polanyi, M. (1974). *Personal Knowledge*. Chicago, IL: Chicago University Press.

Popkin, R. H. (1979). *The History of Scepticism from Erasmus to Spinoza*. Berkeley and Los Angeles, CA: University of California Press.

Popper, K. (1986). *The Logic of Scientific Discovery*. New York: Basic Books.

Pritchard, D. (2005). *Epistemic Luck*. Oxford: Oxford University Press.

Putnam, H. (1963). 'Brains and Behaviour', in R. J. Butler (ed.), 1963, *Analytical Philosophy: Second Series*. New York: Barnes and Noble, pp. 211–35.

——(1965). 'The Analytic and the Synthetic', in H. Putnam, 1975, pp. 33–69.

——(1975). *Mind, Language and Reality*. Cambridge: Cambridge University Press.

——(1978). *Meaning and the Moral Sciences*. London: Routledge & Kegan Paul.

——(1981). *Reason, Truth, and History*. Cambridge: Cambridge University Press.

——(1987). *The Many Faces of Realism*. La Salle, IL: Open Court.

——(1988). *Representation and Reality*. Cambridge, MA: MIT Press.

——(1990). *Realism with a Human Face*. Cambridge, MA: Harvard University Press.

——(1992). *Renewing Philosophy*. Cambridge, MA: Harvard University Press.

——(1995). *Pragmatism*. Oxford: Blackwell.

——(2001). *Enlightenment and Pragmatism*. Amsterdam: Koninklijke Van Gorcum.

Quine, W. V. (1951). 'Two Dogmas of Empiricism', in *From a Logical Point of View* (1980), pp. 20–46.

——(1960). *Word and Object*. Cambridge, MA: MIT Press.

——(1970). 'On the Reasons for Indeterminacy of Translation', *Journal of Philosophy* 67/6: 178–83.

——(1980). *From a Logical Point of View*, 2nd edn, revised. Cambridge, MA: Harvard University Press.

Rabinow, P. (ed.) (1984). *The Foucault Reader*. Harmondsworth: Penguin.

Ramberg, B. (1989). *Donald Davidson's Philosophy of Language: An Introduction*. Oxford: Blackwell.

——(2000). 'Post-ontological Philosophy of Mind: Rorty versus Davidson', in R. Brandom (ed.) 2000a, pp. 351–70.

——(2002). 'Rorty and the Instruments of Philosophy', in M. Peters and P. Ghiraldelli (eds), 2002, pp. 15–46.

Rawls, J. (1971). *A Theory of Justice*. Cambridge, MA: Harvard University Press.

——(1980). 'Kantian Constructivism in Moral Theory', *Journal of Philosophy* 77/9: 515–72.

——(1982). 'Social Unity and Primary Goods', in A. Sen and B. Williams (eds), *Utilitarianism and Beyond*. Cambridge: Cambridge University Press, pp. 159–85.

——(1985). 'Justice as Fairness: Political not Metaphysical', *Philosophy and Public Affairs* 44/3: 223–51.

——(1993). *Political Liberalism*. New York: Columbia University Press.

Raz, J. (1986). *The Morality of Freedom*. Oxford: Clarendon Press.

Rieff, P. (1959). *Freud: The Mind of the Moralist*. New York: Viking Press.

——(1966). *The Triumph of the Therapeutic*. New York: Harper and Row.

Rosenthal, D. M. (ed.). (2000). *Materialism and the Mind–Body Problem*, 2nd edn. Indianapolis, IN: Hackett Publishing Company.

Routley, R. and Macrae, V. (1966). 'On the Identity of Sensations and Physiological Occurrences', *American Philosophical Quarterly* 3: 88–103.

Ryle, G. (1966). *The Concept of Mind*. Harmondsworth: Penguin Books.

Sandel, M. (1996). *Democracy's Discontent: America in Search of a Public Philosophy*. Cambridge, MA: Harvard University Press.

——(1997). *Liberalism and the Limits of Justice*, 2nd edn. Cambridge: Cambridge University Press.

——(2005). *Public Philosophy: Essays on Morality in Politics*. Cambridge, MA: Harvard University Press.

Sartre, J. P. (1957a). *Being and Nothingness*, trans. H. E. Barnes. London: Methuen.

——(1957b). *Existentialism and Humanism*, trans. P. Mairet. London: Methuen.

Scanlon, T. M. (1978). 'Rights, Goals, and Fairness', in S. Hampshire (ed.), 1978, pp. 93–111.

Schaper, E. and Vossenkuhl, W. (eds) (1989). *Reading Kant: New Perspectives on Transcendental Arguments and Critical Philosophy*. Oxford: Blackwell.

Schlick, M. (1932). 'The Future of Philosophy', in Rorty (ed.), *TLT*, pp. 43–53.

——(1936). 'Meaning and Verification', in H. Feigl and W. Sellars (eds), 1949, pp. 146–70.

Schultz, B. (1999). 'Comment: The Private and Its Problems – Pragmatism, Pragmatist Feminism, and Homophobia', *Philosophy of the Social Sciences* 29/2: 281–305.

Searle, J. (1992a). 'Rationalism and Realism: What is at Stake?', *Daedelus* 122/4: 55–84.

——(1992b). 'The Storm over the University', in Paul Berman (ed.), 1992, *Debating P.C.* New York: Dell, pp. 85–123.

Seaton, J. (1996). *Cultural Conservatism, Political Liberalism.* Ann Arbor, MI: University of Michigan Press.

Sellars, W. (1962). 'Time and the World Order', in H. Feigl and G. Maxwell (eds), *Minnesota Studies in the Philosophy of Science,* vol. III. Minneapolis, MN: University of Minnesota Press, pp. 527–616.

——(1963). *Science, Perception and Reality.* London: Routledge.

——(1968). *Science and Metaphysics.* London: Routledge.

——(1997). *Empiricism and the Philosophy of Mind,* intro. by R. Rorty and study guide by R. Brandom. Cambridge, MA: Harvard University Press.

Sextus Empiricus (1994). *Outlines of Scepticism,* ed. J. Annas and J. Barnes. Cambridge: Cambridge University Press.

Shaffer, J. A. (1965). 'Recent Work on the Mind–Body Problem', *American Philosophical Quarterly* 2: 81–104.

Shusterman, R. (1988). 'Postmodernist Aestheticism: A New Moral Philosophy?', *Theory, Culture and Society* 5: 337–55.

Siegel, H. (2007). 'Review of *Fear of Knowledge*', *Notre Dame Philosophical Reviews* (1 January), <http://ndpr.nd.edu/review.cfm?id= 8364>.

Smart, J. J. C. (1962). 'Sensations and Brain Processes', in Rosenthal (ed.) (2000), pp. 53–66.

Strawson, P. F. (1956). 'Construction and Analysis', in A. J. Ayer et al., *The Revolution in Philosophy.* London: Macmillan, 1956.

——(1959). *Individuals.* London: Methuen.

——(1961). 'Analysis, Science, and Metaphysics', in Rorty (ed.), 1992, pp. 312–20.

——(1966). *The Bounds of Sense.* London: Methuen.

——(1982). 'Review of Transcendental Arguments and Science', *Journal of Philosophy* 79: 45–50.

Stroud, B. (1968). 'Transcendental Arguments', in Walker (ed.), 1982, pp. 117–31.

——(1984). *The Significance of Philosophical Scepticism.* Oxford: Clarendon Press.

Taylor, C. (1971). 'Interpretation and the Sciences of Man', *Review of Metaphysics* 25: 3–51.

——(1980). 'Understanding in Human Science', *Review of Metaphysics* 34/1: 25–38.

——(1985a). *Human Agency and Language: Philosophical Papers 1.* Cambridge: Cambridge University Press.

——(1985b). *Philosophy and the Human Sciences: Philosophical Papers 2.* Cambridge: Cambridge University Press.

——(1990a). 'Rorty in the Epistemological Tradition', in A. Malachowski (ed.), 1990, pp. 257–75.

——(1990b). *Sources of the Self.* Cambridge: Cambridge University Press.

——(1995). *Philosophical Arguments.* Cambridge, MA: Harvard University Press.

Thomson, J. J. (1966). 'Private Languages', in S. Hampshire (ed.), *Philosophy of Mind.* New York: Harper and Row, pp. 116–43.

Travis, C. (2001). *Unshadowed Thought.* Cambridge, MA: Harvard University Press.

Ujlaki, G. (1992–3). 'Polanyi's Theory of Meaning', *Polanyiana* 2/4: 7–42.

Walker, R. C. S. (ed.) (1982). *Kant on Pure Reason.* Oxford: Oxford University Press.

——(1989). 'Transcendental Arguments and Scepticism', in E. Schaper and W. Vossenkuhl (eds) (1989), *Reading Kant: New Perspectives on Transcendental Arguments and Critical Philosophy.* Oxford: Blackwell, pp. 55–76.

Warnke, G. (1985). 'Hermeneutics and Social Sciences: A Gadamerian Critique of Rorty', *Inquiry* 28: 339–57.

——(1987). *Gadamer: Hermeneutics, Tradition and Reason.* Stanford, CA: Stanford University Press.

Wellmer, A. (1993). 'Truth, Contingency, and Modernity', *Modern Philology* 90, Supplement: 109–24.

——(2003). 'The Debate about Truth: Pragmatism without Regulative Ideas', trans. W. Egginton, *Critical Horizons* 4/1: 29–54.

Williams, B. (1978). *Descartes: The Project of Pure Inquiry.* Harmondsworth: Penguin.

——(1982). *Moral Luck.* Cambridge: Cambridge University Press.

——(1985). *Ethics and the Limits of Philosophy.* Cambridge, MA: Harvard University Press.

——(2000). 'Philosophy as a Humanistic Discipline', *Philosophy* 75: 477–96.

——(2002). *Truth and Truthfulness.* Princeton, NJ: Princeton University Press.

Williams, M. (1971). *Groundless Belief.* Oxford: Blackwell.

——(1991). *Unnatural Doubts.* Oxford: Blackwell.

——(2000). 'Epistemology and the Mirror of Nature', in R. Brandom (ed.) 2000a, pp. 191–213.

——(2001). *Problems of Knowledge: A Critical Introduction to Epistemology*. Oxford: Oxford University Press.

——(2003). 'Rorty on Knowledge and Truth,' in C. B. Guignon and D. R. Hiley (eds), 2003, pp. 61–80.

Wilson, C. (1992). 'How Did the Dinosaurs Die Out? How Did the Poets Survive?', *Radical Philosophy* 62: 20–6.

Wittgenstein, L. (1953). *Philosophical Investigations*. Oxford: Blackwell.

——(1969). *On Certainty*. Oxford: Blackwell.

Index